BICYCLE RIDES
Orange County

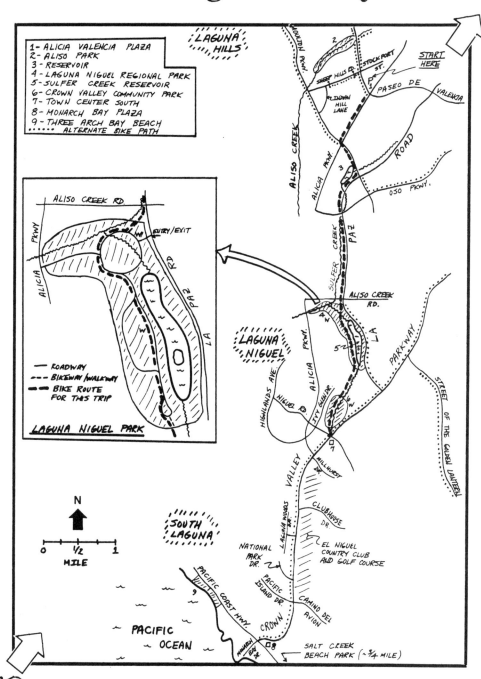

1- ALICIA VALENCIA PLAZA
2- ALISO PARK
3- RESERVOIR
4- LAGUNA NIGUEL REGIONAL PARK
5- SULFER CREEK RESERVOIR
6- CROWN VALLEY COMMUNITY PARK
7- TOWN CENTER SOUTH
8- MONARCH BAY PLAZA
9- THREE ARCH BAY BEACH
..... ALTERNATE BIKE PATH

LAGUNA HILLS

START HERE

— ROADWAY
--- BIKEWAY /WALKWAY
▪▪▪ BIKE ROUTE FOR THIS TRIP

LAGUNA NIGUEL PARK

ENTRY/EXIT

ALISO CREEK RD.

LAGUNA NIGUEL

N

0   ½   1
MILE

SOUTH LAGUNA

PACIFIC OCEAN

SALT CREEK BEACH PARK (~¾ MILE)

BY DON AND SHARRON BRUNDIGE

Other Books by Don and Sharron Brundige:
Bicycle Rides: Los Angeles and Orange Counties (Out of Print)
Bicycle Rides: San Fernando Valley and Ventura County (Out of Print)
Bicycle Rides: Los Angeles County
Bicycle Rides: Inland Empire
Bicycle Rides: San Diego and Imperial Counties
Bicycle Rides: Santa Barbara & Ventura Counties
Mountain Biking L.A. County (Southern Section)

Printed by Griffin Printing & Lithograph Co., Inc.
Glendale, California

First Printing - September 1988
Second Printing (revised) - April 1990
Third Printing (revised) - August 1993
Fourth Printing - November 1996

Published by B-D Enterprises
122 Mirabeau Ave.
San Pedro, California 90732-3117

Photography by Don and Sharron Brundige

We want to hear from you!

Corrections and updates will make this a better book and are gratefully appreciated. Publisher will reply to all such letters. Where information is used, submitter will be acknowledged in subsequent printing and given a free book (see above) of their choice.

TABLE OF CONTENTS

DEDICATION

To our family
....Who we love very much

George, Bernice, Don, Pat, Kathy, Jim, Stevie, Rich, Pon,
Eric, Greta, Greg, Mark, Pete, and Michelle

ACKNOWLEDGEMENTS

We offer our thanks to family, friends, and bicycling acquaintances who gave us ideas, advice, and plenty of encouragement while developing this biking book. This includes a "thank you" to the state, county and city agencies and individuals who offered their services and publications. We show particular gratitude to the folks that were kind enough to review and comment to our manuscript: Al Hook, Jill Morales, and Walt Bond. We also thank Bernice Palmquist for her updates to our previously published bike tours and to Eileen Olson of Wheel Land Bicycle Shop and Barbara and Mike Sentovich of the Orange County Wheelmen for their encouragement of our efforts.

We specifically wish to acknowledge the following individuals and/or organizations who provided some excellent ideas for bicycle trips: Donald K. Jensen and Toshio Kuba of the City of Buena Park, the Community Services Departments of the Cities of Huntington Beach and Tustin, the Citizen's Advisory Committee of Newport Beach, the City of Costa Mesa, CALTRANS District 07: Public Transportation and Ridesharing Branch, Sherri Miller and Richard Sherry of the Orange County Environmental Management Agency: Transportation Planning, and Mary Shimono of the City of Rancho Santa Marguerita.

We also acknowledge getting some nifty ride ideas from the following sources: the *Existing Bikeways* Map provided by the Orange County Environmental Management Agency; *Gousha Weekend Guide to California Bike Tours* published by the H. M. Gousha Company; and *Southern California Bicycling* published by the Automobile Club of Southern California.

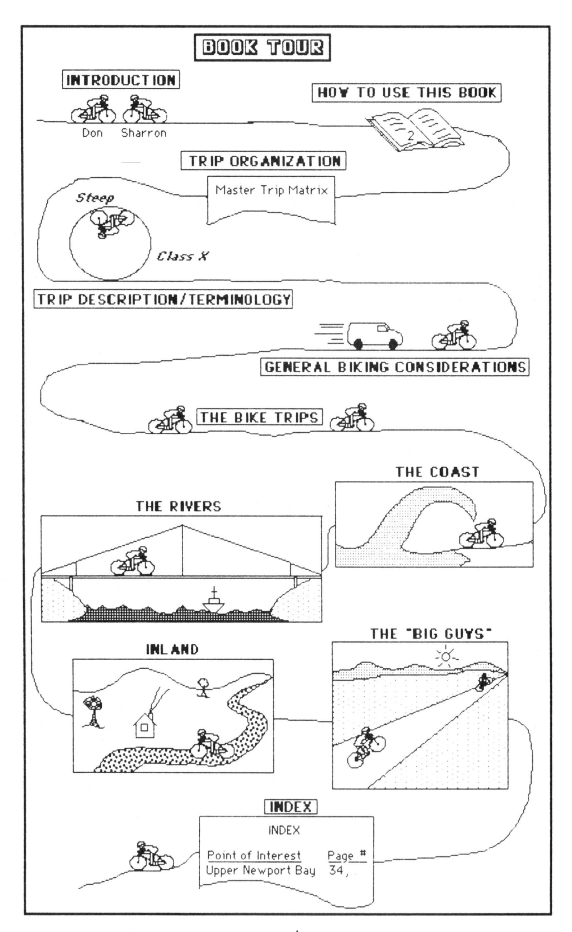

INTRODUCTION

Orange County is one of the finer areas for cycling. It is criss-crossed with routes varying from paved off-road (Class I) trails to a myraid of on-road separated bike lanes (Class II) and on-road signed (but not separated) bikeways (Class III). **The county has plans to add to and improve its bikeway system, including development of major Class I trails as noted in the "Odds N' Ends" section of this book.** With some imagination, the bicyclist can link up various routes described herein and greatly expand the trip options.

Again, we wanted to provide a trip guide that concentrates on trip navigation, contains a large number of well-documented trips, provides the necessary trip maps, and is reasonably priced. Hopefully we have succeeded!

This guide has been developed based on biking trips taken in 1987-1988. Updates on several trips that have changed significantly are based on tours taken in 1990-1993. There are over 600 one-way bike miles described. The document identifies 35 biking trips in Orange County. Trips of exceptional length are broken down into segments or "rides." There are a total of 42 individual bike rides described. Each ride is written to be as complete and self-standing as possible. The authors used eighteen-speed bicycles (a touring bike and a mountain bike fitted with racing tires), although a vast majority of the trips can be easily ridden with ten-speeds.

A cross section of trips is provided. There are some short length family trips on separated bike paths, many longer exploratory and workout trips for more experienced bikers on various quality bike routes, and a few "gut-buster" trips on open roadway for the most physically fit and motivated bikers. The trip domains include parks, beaches, harbors, rivers, lakes, canyons, hills, basins and mountains. The trips vary from extremely scenic to somewhat monotonous (e.g., certain stretches of the concrete "wastelands" along the rivers). There's a little something for everybody!

The strong emphasis in this book is the "getting from here to there." This navigation is provided using detailed route descriptions in terms of landmarks, mileage, and a quality set of trip maps. Scenery, vistas, scenic or historic landmarks, and sightseeing attractions are regularly noted for each trip, although detailed information about these features must be sought out in other publications. Public restrooms and sources of water are identified on trips where these facilities are scarce. Pleasant rest spots are also pointed out. Finally, "wine and dine" spots are noted for two specific circumstances: 1) where places to eat along the trip are scarce; and 2) where the establishment is too unique or exceptional not to mention.

HOW TO USE THIS BOOK

There are two ways to use this book, one way for the person who wants to enjoy the research along with enjoying the bike ride and another way for the biker who is just anxious to get out there "amongst em" on a bike ride.

For the "anxious biker" , follow Steps 1 through 5 below and split!

1. Use the "Master Trip Map" in the "TRIP ORGANIZATION" section to select areas of interest for the bike ride. Note the candidate trip numbers. (Another option is to select a trip based on landmarks and sightseeing attractions referenced in the "INDEX.")

2. Go to the "Master Trip Matrices" in the "TRIP ORGANIZATION" section and narrow down the number of candidate trips by reviewing their general features.

3. Read about the individual trips and select one.

4. Read and understand the safety rules described in the "GENERAL BIKING CONSIDERATIONS" section.

5. See you later. Enjoy the ride!

For the more methodical folks, continue reading the next chapter. By the time you're through, you'll understand the trip description and maps much better than the "anxious biker."

TRIP ORGANIZATION

This bike book is organized by trip number. Extended length trips are broken down into trip segments by ride number, which is the trip number plus a letter. Thus, Trip #17 is the Santa Ana River Trail, while Ride #17A is the Green River Road to Yorba Regional Park segment of the trip. Trip numbers are in a general sequence governed by whether the tours are coastal, river, or inland. Refer back to the "TABLE OF CONTENTS" for the entire trip list.

The "Master Trip Map" shows the general location of trips and rides by a circled reference number (i.e., ⑦ refers to Trip #7). Extended length trips are identified by circled numbers at both beginning and terminal points.

The "Master Trip Matrices" provide a quick reference for selecting candidate trips for more detailed reading evaluation. The matrices are organized by trip/ride number. The key trip descriptors provided in those matrices are briefly explained in the footnotes at the bottom of the last matrix. A more detailed explanation of those descriptors is provided in the "TRIP DESCRIPTION/TERMINOLOGY" section which follows.

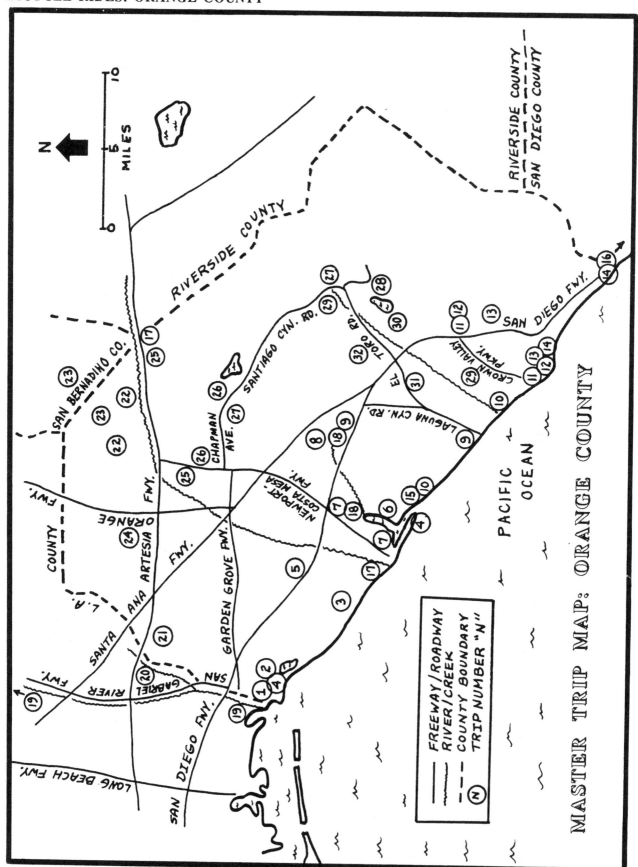

MASTER TRIP MAP: ORANGE COUNTY

FREEWAY/ROADWAY	
RIVER/CREEK	
COUNTY BOUNDARY	
TRIP NUMBER "N"	

MASTER TRIP MATRIX

TRIP NO.	GENERAL LOCATION	LEVEL OF DIFFICULTY			ROUTE QUALITY			TRIP CHARACT.[2]	COMMENTS
		L.O.D.[1]	MILES	ELEV.	BIKE TRAIL (%)	BIKE LANE (%)	OTHER (%)		
1	Seal Beach-Sunset Beach	E (r/t)	4.3	Flat (1-w)	-	60	40	S, L	Seal Beach to Sunset Beach Tour
2	Huntington Beach	E (1-w) M (r/t)	12.0 (r/t)	Flat	-	30	70	S, L	Sunset Aquatic Park/Huntington Harbor Tour
3	Huntington Beach	E	4.7	Flat	100	-	-	S, N, L	Huntington Central Park Loop
4	Sunset Beach-Newport Beach	E (1-w) M (r/t)	13.8 (1-w)	Flat	90	10	-	S, L, S/A	Sunset - Newport Beach Strand
5	Fountain Valley	E	7.6	Flat	100	-	-	S	Mile Square Park Loop
6	Newport Beach	M	6.2	Mod	-	90	10	S	Upper Newport Bay Loop
7	Newport Beach	M	25.3	Mod	15	80	5	S, N, L, S/A	Newport Beach City Loop
8	Irvine	E (1-w) M (r/t)	11.4 (1-w)	Flat	10	90	-	S, N	Irvine Bikeway, Hick's Canyon Wash
9	Laguna Canyon	M (1-w) M-S (r/t)	10.4 (1-w)	Mod	-	80	20	S, L, S/A	Laguna Canyon Road
10	Laguna Beach	M (1-w) M-S (r/t)	9.1 (1-w)	Mod	-	100	-	S, L, E	Laguna Beach Shoreline Tour

1,2 See footnotes on page 9

5

MASTER TRIP MATRIX

TRIP NO.	GENERAL LOCATION	LEVEL OF DIFFICULTY			ROUTE QUALITY			TRIP CHARACT.[2]	COMMENTS
		L.O.D.[1]	MILES	ELEV.	BIKE TRAIL (%)	BIKE LANE (%)	OTHER (%)		
11	Mission Viejo-Laguna Niguel	M (1-w) M-S (r/t)	6.5 (1-w)	Mod	-	100	-	S, E	Laguna Niguel Bikeway
12	Mission Viejo, San Juan Capistrano	E (1-w) E-M (r/t)	6.9 (1-w)	Flat	50	50	-	S, L, S/A	Doheny Bikeway
13	San Juan Capistrano-Dana Point	M (r/t)	17.2 (r/t)	Flat	60	40	10	S, N, L S/A	Del Obispo Bikeway, San Juan Creek
14	San Clemente	M (r/t)	17.1 (r/t)	Mod	20	70	10	S, L, S/A	Doheny/San Clemente Bike Route
15	Newport Beach	M	10.1	Mod	-	40	60	S, L	Newport - Corona Del Mar Beach Loop
16	San Clemente-San Diego	S (1-w)	67.2 (1-w)	Mod-Sheer	20	80	-	S, N, L, S/A,E, M	San Clemente - San Diego Bicentennial Bike Route
17	Santa Ana Canyon-Huntington Beach	M (1-w) S (r/t)	30.6 (1-w)	Flat	90	5	5	S, N, M	Santa Ana River Trail (Santa Ana Cyn to Ocean)
17A	Santa Ana Canyon-Yorba Linda	M (1-w) M (r/t)	7.2 (1-w)	Mod	50	30	20	S, N, M	Green River Road to Yorba Regional Park
17B	Yorba Linda - Orange	E (1-w) M (r/t)	10.0 (1-w)	Flat	100	-	-	S, L, M	Yorba Regional Park to El Camino Park
17C	Orange-Huntington Beach	E (1-w) M (r/t)	13.4 (1-w)	Flat	100	-	-	S, N, M	El Camino Park to Huntington Beach

1,2 See footnotes on page 9

MASTER TRIP MATRIX

TRIP NO.	GENERAL LOCATION	LEVEL OF DIFFICULTY			ROUTE QUALITY			TRIP CHARACT.[2]	COMMENTS
		L.O.D.[1]	MILES	ELEV.	BIKE TRAIL (%)	BIKE LANE (%)	OTHER (%)		
18	Newport Beach-Irvine	E (l-w) M (r/t)	7.8 (l-w)	Flat	90	10	-	S	San Diego Creek
19	Seal Beach-Azusa	S (l-w) VS (r/t)	38.0 (l-w)	Flat	100	-	-	S, N, L, M	San Gabriel River (ocean to mountains)
19A	Seal Beach-Long Beach	E (r/t)	5.6 (l-w)	Flat	100	-	-	S, N, M	Ocean to El Dorado Park
19B	Long Beach-Downey	E (l-w) M (r/t)	9.7 (l-w)	Flat	100	-	-	S, N, M	El Dorado Park to Wilderness Park
19C	Downey-Pico Rivera	E (l-w) M (r/t)	7.7 (l-w)	Flat	100	-	-	S, N, L, M	Wilderness Park to Whittier Narrows Dam
19D	Pico Rivera-Irwindale	E (l-w) M (r/t)	11.4 (l-w)	Flat	100	-	-	S, N, L, M	Whittier Narrows Dam to Santa Fe Dam
19E	Irwindale-Azusa	E(l-w) M (r/t)	7.5 (l-w)	Flat	100	-	-	S, N, L, M	Santa Fe Dam to San Gabriel Canyon
20	Long Beach - Cerritos	E (l-w) M (r/t)	14.0 (l-w)	Flat	100	-	-	S, M	San Gabriel River - Coyote Creek
21	Cypress, La Palma, Buena Park	E-M	14.9	Flat	15	80	5	S, L	Cypress City Tour (loop)
22	Yorba Linda	E (l-w) M (r/t)	8.2 (l-w)	Mod	80	-	20	S, N	El Cajon Trail

1,2 See footnotes on page 9

7

MASTER TRIP MATRIX

TRIP NO.	GENERAL LOCATION	LEVEL OF DIFFICULTY			ROUTE QUALITY			TRIP CHARACT.[2]	COMMENTS
		L.O.D.[1]	MILES	ELEV.	BIKE TRAIL (%)	BIKE LANE (%)	OTHER (%)		
23	Carbon Canyon	S(1-w) S(r/t)	11.2	Mod to Steep	-	-	100	S, N, E	Carbon Canyon Road
24	Fullerton	M-S	13.7	Mod to Steep	-	80	20	S, N, E	Fullerton/Craig Park Loop
25	Anaheim Hills	E (1-w) M (r/t)	7.6 (1-w)	Mod	-	100	-	S, M	Santa Ana Canyon Road
26	Orange	M	13.6	Mod to Steep	-	90	10	S, N, E	Orange/Irvine Park Loop
27	Santiago Canyon	S (1-w) VS (r/t)	12.2 (1-w)	Mod to Steep	-	100	-	S, E	Santiago Canyon Road
28	O'Neill Park Rnch Snta Marguerita	E(r/t) M-S(r/t)	7.0 / 14.0	Mod / Md-Stp	100 / -	- / 70	- / 30	S, N / S, E	O'Neill Regional Park / Mission Viejo to Park
29	El Toro - Laguna Niguel	M (1-w) M (r/t)	15.6 (1-w)	Mod	80	20	-	S, N	Aliso Creek Bike Trail
29A	El Toro - Lagna Hills	E (1-w) M (r/t)	10.0 (1-w)	Mod	100	-	-	S, N	Aliso Creek, Northern Segment
29B	Laguna Hills - Laguna Niguel	E (r/t)	5.6 (1-w)	Mod	40	60	-	S, N	Aliso Creek, Southern Segment
30	Mission Viejo, Laguna Hills	M-S	16.6	Mod	30	70	-	S, N, L	Mission Viejo Bikeway (loop)

1,2 See footnotes on page 9

8

MASTER TRIP MATRIX

TRIP NO.	GENERAL LOCATION	LEVEL OF DIFFICULTY			ROUTE QUALITY			TRIP CHARACT.[2]	COMMENTS
		L.O.D.[1]	MILES	ELEV.	BIKE TRAIL (%)	BIKE LANE (%)	OTHER (%)		
31	Laguna Hills	M-S (1-w) S (r/t)	5.8 (r/t)	Steep	-	100	-	S, E	Lower El Toro Road
32	Lake Forest	E	5.3	Flat	20	80	-	S, N	Serrano Creek Park (loop)
33	San Gabriel Rvr, Coyote Creek, Santa Ana Rvr	S	63.2	Mod	70	20	10	S, N, L, M	Western Orange County Loop
34	Santiago Canyon, Aliso Crk, PCH, Snt Ana Rvr	VS	76.9	Mod to Steep	30	60	10	S, N, L, S/A,E, M	Eastern Orange County Loop
35	Santiago Canyon, Aliso Crk., PCH, San Gabriel Rvr., Coyote Creek, El Cajon Trail, Villa Park	VS	105	Mod to Steep	35	50	15	S, N, L, S/A,E, M	Orange County "Century"

1   **L.O.D.** - Overall trip level of difficulty: VS-very strenuous; S-strenuous; M-Moderate; E-easy; 1-w -one way; r/t-round trip

2   **TRIP CHARACTERISTICS** - General trip features and highlights: S-scenic; N-nature trail; L-landmarks; S/A-sight-seeing attractions; E-elevation workout; M-mileage workout

TRIP DESCRIPTION/TERMINOLOGY

The trip descriptors in the "Master Trip Matrices" are described below in further detail. Several of these same descriptors are also used in the individual trip writeups.

GENERAL LOCATION: The general location of the bike trail is provided in terms of a city, landmark, or general area description, as applicable. The "Master Trip Map" may be useful in conjunction with this general locator.

LEVEL OF DIFFICULTY: The rides are rated on an overall basis as *very strenuous*, *strenuous*, *moderate*, and *easy*, based on elevation gain, trip distance, and condition of the bike route.

A *very strenuous* trip can be of any length, has very steep grades, and is generally designed for bikers in excellent physical condition. It should be noted that even on the most strenuous trip, the bike can be walked uphill for bikers in reasonably good condition. However, rather than suffer this fate, it is recommended that bikers start with the easier trips and work up. Alternately, trips are well enough described such that the biker might plan to ride the easier part of a stressing trip and link up with other easier trips.

A *strenuous* trip has some steep grades and/or relatively long mileage (on the order of 50 miles total). The trip is of sufficiently long duration to require trip planning and strong consideration of weather, water, food, and bike spare parts. Some portions of the trip may be on surfaces in poor condition or on shared roadway.

A *moderate* trip may have mild grades and moderate mileage, on the order of 15-30 miles. The trip is typically of a couple of hours duration and is generally on well maintained bike route.

An *easy* trip is on the order of 10 miles or less, is relatively flat, and is generally on well maintained bike trails or bike paths.

TRIP MILEAGE: Trip mileage is generally computed for the one-way trip length for *up and back* trips and full-trip length for *loop* trips. *Up and back* is specifically used for trips that share a common route in both outgoing and return directions. *Loop* specifically means that the outgoing and return trip segments are on predominantly different routes. *Round trip* is used without distinction as to whether the trip is an *up and back* or *loop* trip. In the trip writeups, the mileage from the starting point or "trailhead" is noted in parentheses to the nearest tenth mile, for example, (6.3).

Obviously, the one-way trips listed can be exercised with a planned car shuttle, ridden as an *up and back* trip, or biked in connection with another bicycle trip listed in this book. For convenience, connections with other trips are noted in the trip writeups or in a separate subsection for that trip titled, "Connecting Trips."

10

TRIP ELEVATION GAIN: The overall trip elevation gain is described in a qualitative fashion. *Flat* indicates that there are no grades of any consequence. Steepness of upgrades is loosely defined as follows: 1) *light* indicates limited slope and very little elevation gain; 2) *moderate* means more significant slope requiring use of low gears and may be ten's of feet of upgrade; 3) *steep* indicates workout-type grades that require low gears and high physical exertion; 4) *sheer* indicates gut-buster grades that require extreme physical exertion (and a strong will to live!).

The frequency of upgrades is divided into the following categories: 1) *single* for flat rides with a single significant upgrade; 2) *periodic* for flat rides where uphill segments are widely spaced; 3) *frequent* where narrowly spaced upgrades are encountered (e.g. rolling hills).

BIKE ROUTE QUALITY: The trip is summarized with respect to route quality in the "Master Trip Matrices" and a more detailed description is given in the individual trip writeups. The following route terminology (which is similar to that used by CALTRANS) is used:

. *Class I* - off-roadway bike paths or bike trails

. *Class II* - on-roadway, separated (striped) bike lanes

. *Class III* - on-roadway, signed (but not separated) bike lanes

If the route is on-roadway and not signed (i.e., not specifically marked as a bike route), it is arbitrarily referred to as *Class X*.

TRIP CHARACTERISTICS: The overall highlights of the bike trip are provided in the "Master Trip Matrices" to assist in general trip selection. The trip may be scenic (*S*), with sweeping vistas, exciting overlooks, or generally provide views of natural or man-made attractions such as cities. Alternatively, the trip may be a nature trail (*N*) or a path through areas which have an abundance of trees, flowers, and other flora. The nature trips or portions thereof are generally on Class I bike routes. The trip may highlight historical or well-known landmarks (*L*) or may have one or more sightseeing attractions (*S/A*). Examples of the former are the Prado Dam on the Santa Ana River (Ride #17A), while the latter might be the Laguna Museum of Art (Trips #9 and #10). Finally, some trips are potentially good workout trips in that there is significant elevation change (*E*) or lengthy mileage (*M*) if the entire trip is taken. Some trips may provide a mix of these characteristics and are so noted. Trips along well-lit Class I routes are so noted in the trip writeups.

Several descriptors are unique to the individual trip writeups. Those descriptors are defined below.

TRAILHEAD : The general location of the start of the bike path is provided for a single starting point. Driving directions to that trailhead are included. Nearby parking is also described in most cases. Always check to ensure that parking is consistent with current laws.

Note that for most trails, there are multiple points of entry beyond the primary point listed. For some of the trips in this book (particularly the river routes), alternate bicycle entry points are noted on maps by arrows (↗) along the bike route. Other alternate trailheads may be found using information obtained from other bikers, or from state or local publications for more popular routes.

WATER: In the "Trailhead" description, some general statements are provided about water availability. In the actual trip description, available water along the route is noted where water is scarce, although the trip should be planned to assume that water stops may not be operational. Particular emphasis is placed on public facilities for water and use of restrooms. Stores, shopping centers, and gas stations also are noted in many instances in the trip writeups, although the availability of water or other facilities in these instances is subject to the policies of those establishments.

CONNECTING TRIPS: Where bike trips can be linked to other trips in the book, they are so noted. *Continuation* trips are those where there is direct linkage at the beginning or end of the trip being described. *Connection* trips are either not directly linked (i.e., a Class X connector is required) or the linkage occurs at the interior of the trip being described. A brief "connector" route description is provided for the *Connection* trips.

BIKE TRIP MAPS: Each ride in the book has an accompanying detailed bike map. A summary of symbols and map features which are used in those maps is provided on the next page.

– – – –	Bike trail in trip description (unless otherwise noted).
· · · · · ·	Alternate bike route (unless otherwise noted).
A B D C	Closed street loops are alternate bike routes (Trips #8 and #18). For example, the unbroken loop A-B-C-D in the figure to the left is all marked bikepath.
SANTA ANA RIVER ∿ ∿ ∿ ∿ o r **SAN DIEGO CREEK** · · · · ·	River or creek when it is a major part of the trip description. The river or creek name is highlighted.
ALISO CYN. WASH ∿∿∿∿∿	River or creek when it is a point of interest.
MAIN ST.	Roadway.
1-ALISO PARK 2-SULFER CREEK	Key trip features. Numbers in key correspond to numbers marked along the mapped route.

/////// IRVINE /////	Nearby City	(///)	Park	□ 5 ▨ 5	Landmark #5
W	Public Water Source	P	Parking	→	Entry Point to Trail
⊢—•	Locked Gate/ Limited Entry	✕✕✕✕✕	Railroad Crossing or Overcrossing	◁▫	School(as a trip point of interest)
⊥▫	Mission	⋊⋉	Gravel Pit	-	-

MAP SYMBOLS AND FEATURES

GENERAL BIKING CONSIDERATIONS

These are a collection of the thoughts that we've had in the hundreds of miles of biking that we have done:

SAFETY: Use common sense when you are biking. Common sense when combined with courtesy should cover most of the safety-related issues. But just to be on the safe side, write to CALTRANS (see the chapter on "OTHER BICYCLING INFORMATION SOURCES") for any of their publications and get some excellent safety information along with it. The four safety "biggies" are: 1) understand bike riding laws; 2) keep your bicycle in safe operating order; 3) wear personal safety equipment as required (helmet is a must, bright or reflective clothes, sunglasses); 4) ride defensively--always assume that moving and parked car inhabitants are not aware that you are there.

Common courtesy is to offer assistance to bikers stopped because of breackdowns. Point out ruts, obstructions, and glass to bikers behind you.

EQUIPMENT: Necessary biking equipment includes a water bottle or two, tire pump, tool kit (typically tire irons, wrench(s), screwdriver), patch kit, and (sorry to say) bike lock. For longer trips, add a spare tube and bike repair manual as well as a light first-aid kit. Bring sunblock and lip salve for extended tours on sunny days. We recommend a bike light even if there are no plans for night biking.

Necessary biking apparel includes a helmet, sunglasses, and clothes which will fit pessimistic weather conditions (particularly for longer trips). On all-day, cool or wet winter outings, we carry a layered set of clothes (this includes long pants, undershirt, long-sleeve shirt, sweater, and a two-piece nylon rain suit). Padded cycling pants and biking gloves are a must for long trips. Lycra clothes are light and extremely functional. For cool and dry days, we may drop the rain suit for a windbreaker (look for a windbreaker that folds up into a fanny pack). For other conditions, our outfits are normally shorts, undershirt, long-sleeve shirt and windbreaker. Laugh if you must, but wait until you find yourself biking home at night, in mid-winter, along a beach with a healthy sea breeze after you spent the day biking in the warm sun (an example of poor trip planning, we admit).

If you are going to get your money out of this book, get an automobile bike rack! The cost of bike racks is cheap compared to most bikes. Besides, it just doesn't make sense to bike fifty miles to take the planned twenty-mile bike trip.

GENERAL INFORMATION: A collection of seemingly random, unconnected, and useless comments are provided which we actually think are "gems of wisdom" based on hard experience:

o Develop and follow a checkoff list for a pre-trip bike examination (tires, brakes, cables, etc.) and equipment (water, food, clothing, tools, spare parts, etc.). It's embarassing to start a trip and realize that you've forgotten your bicycle!

o Check the weather (including smog conditions in urban areas) before going on an extended trip. Select trips and plan clothing accordingly.

o Plan the trip timing to ensure that there is a "pad" of daylight. Night biking just isn't as fun when it wasn't in the original plans. Night biking without the proper equipment is dangerous!

o Trip timing should include allowance for finding parking, trailheads, or connector routes. You never can fully trust authors of bike books!

o Trip conditions and routing are subject to change as a result of weather damage, building and highway construction, bike rerouting, etc. Especially for long trips, research these key elements before departing.

o Plan for afternoon headwinds when heading toward the beach (particularly west-facing beaches). "Pain" is what you feel when the last several miles of your fifty miler is spent bucking the sea breeze.

o Stay out of riverbeds, even concrete ones, unless it is marked part of the route. It may be a very long way to the next exit and it may also rain.

o Some river and creek trails flood out during heavy rains, particularly at river crossings and underpasses. Don't take these trips after heavy rains unless you are willing to plan on many route detours.

o Always take some water, no matter how short the trip. Having water available provides a feeling of security. Being thirsty creates a bad attitude.

o Bring enough water to provide for the contingency that "guaranteed" water spots may be dry.

o The best time of day for most trips on busy thoroughfares is before the rush-hour morning traffic. Morning is also best for rides on narrow country roads. With few exceptions, the best time of the week is the weekend, particularly Sunday.

o The best season for some trips depends on the person. If you want comradery, ride the more popular routes in the summer. If your pleasure is free-wheeling and wide-open spaces, save these routes for other seasons.

o Bring snacks for longer trips. Snacks provide needed energy and attitude improvement when the going gets tough. Having snacks available also allows more flexibility in selecting a "dining out" stop.

o Walk your bike through heavy glass-strewn areas. Lift your bike onto and off of curbs. Trips are more fun when you can ride your bike!

o Bring a map for trips that are not on well-marked bike routes. Once off the prescribed route, it is amazingly easy to lose the sense of direction.

o Maintain a steady pace when taking a long bike ride. For pleasure trips, the pace is too fast if you cannot carry on conversation while biking.

THE COAST

Sunset Beach to Newport Beach Strand: Near Huntington Beach Cliffs

TRIP #1 - SEAL BEACH/SUNSET BEACH TOUR

GENERAL LOCATION: Seal Beach, Sunset Beach

LEVEL OF DIFFICULTY: One way - easy; up and back - easy
Distance - 4.3 miles (one way)
Elevation gain - essentially flat

GENERAL DESCRIPTION: A pleasant tour which concentrates on the beach community setting, this trip starts at the end of the Long Beach Marina, passes along the Seal Beach beachfront, transits a section of highway along the Anaheim Bay National Wildlife Refuge, and ends with a short cruise through the small beach community of Sunset Beach. The trip terminates at Bolsa Chica State Beach (see Trip #4 for the continuation route). This route is Class X through lightly traveled Seal Beach and Class II for about a 1-1/2 mile stretch of Pacific Coast Highway (PCH), as well as within Sunset Beach.

TRAILHEAD: Free public automobile parking is available at the Long Beach Marina along Marina Dr. in Long Beach or along First St. in Seal Beach. From PCH in Seal Beach, turn west on Marina Dr. (2-3 blocks from Main Street in Seal Beach) and continue roughly 0.5 mile to First Street. In another 1/4 mile, cross the San Gabriel River and continue a short distance to the marina parking area near Seaport Village.

Bikers need only a light water supply since there are sources along the way.

TRIP DESCRIPTION: **Seal Beach.** Leaving the marina area and Seaport Village, cross the Marina Ave. bridge over the San Gabriel River (0.1) and turn right at First St. Continue parallel to the San Gabriel River and take in the beautiful view of the marina breakwater and the fleet of pleasure craft. At the end of First St. (0.3), turn left along Ocean Ave. and continue along the beachfront residences to the Seal Beach Pier and Eisenhower Park (0.8). Join the fishermen on the pier or take in the ocean view from the strand.

Continue on Ocean Ave. until it begins curving to the left (northeast) and becomes Seal Beach Blvd. Take a right at PCH (1.7) and start on a small upgrade on a bridge with Anaheim Bay on the right and the U.S. Naval Weapons Station on the left. With some fortune, there may be a large naval ship to view in Anaheim Bay. Continue on a second upgrade to another bridge and at (2.5) admire the view from the highest point of the bridge. Another excellent view of Anaheim Bay is to the right and Anaheim Bay National Wildlife Refuge to the left.

Surfside - Sunset Beach. The trip continues on PCH past the private community of Surfside until a right turn is made at Anderson St. in Sunset Beach (3.0). In a few hundred feet turn left at S. Pacific Ave. and bike along the long, snug row of beach residences. Continue on this Class II bike lane for about 1.3 miles to the bike lane terminus at Bolsa Chica State Beach.

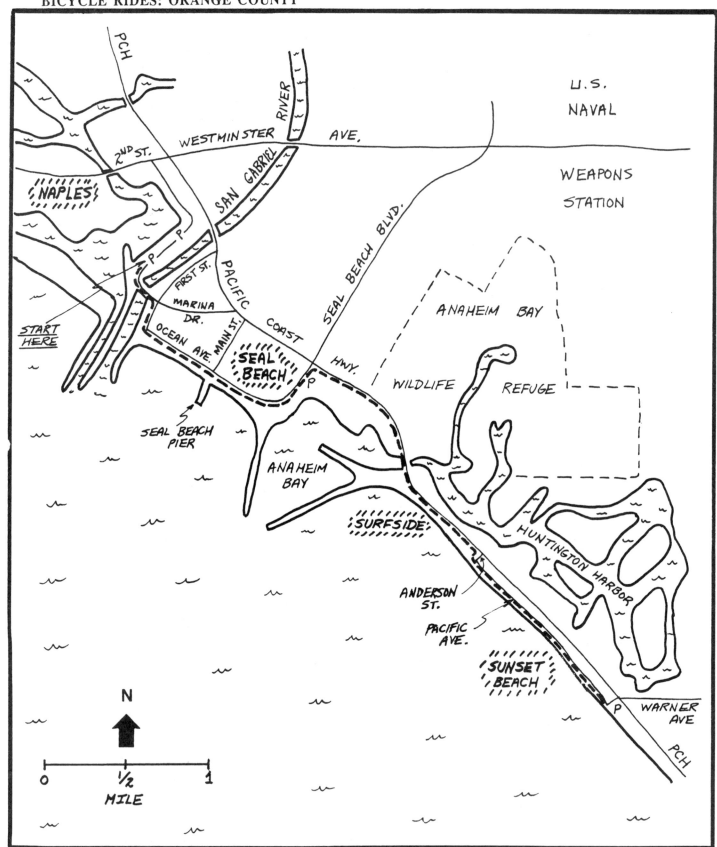

PCH

WESTMINSTER AVE.

SAN GABRIEL RIVER

2ND ST.

NAPLES

U.S. NAVAL

WEAPONS STATION

P
P
P

FIRST ST.

MARINA DR.

PACIFIC

COAST

SEAL BEACH BLVD.

ANAHEIM BAY

START HERE

OCEAN AVE.

MAIN ST.

SEAL BEACH

HWY.

P

WILDLIFE

REFUGE

SEAL BEACH PIER

ANAHEIM BAY

HUNTINGTON HARBOR

SURFSIDE

ANDERSON ST.

PACIFIC AVE.

SUNSET BEACH

N

0   ½   1
MILE

P   WARNER AVE

PCH

TRIP #1 - SEAL BEACH/ SUNSET BEACH TOUR

CONNECTING TRIPS: 1) Continuation with the Sunset Beach to Newport Beach Strand ride (Trip #4) - continue this trip south beyond Bolsa Chica State Beach; 2) connection with the bike route to the Anaheim Bay National Wildlife Refuge (Trip #2) - continue this trip east (away from the beach) on Warner Ave.; 3) connection with the PCH portion of Trip #4 to the Bolsa Chica Ecological Preserve - continue this trip south on PCH from Warner Ave.; 4) connection with the Belmont Shores/Naples area - continue inland along Marina Dr. from the parking area and turn left (west) at 2nd St.

Helmet   No Helmet

TRIP #2 - SUNSET AQUATIC PARK/
HUNTINGTON HARBOR TOUR

GENERAL LOCATION: Huntington   Harbor

LEVEL OF DIFFICULTY: One way - easy; loop - moderate
Distance - 12.0 miles (loop)
Elevation gain - essentially flat

GENERAL DESCRIPTION: The trip first visits the natural Sunset Aquatic Park. From here, this free-form bike ride has no set route. Rather it provides the option to explore the "nooks and crannies" of the northern Huntington Harbor area. The trip meanders through housing areas set along lovely canals, provides many great views of the main channel and boat marinas, and even includes visits to such enjoyable places as little Trinidad Island. There are opportunities to stop and rest at any one of several small parks along the way. The trip through Huntington Harbor is mostly a Class X bike route, but the roadway is generally lightly traveled. There is an option to return to Sunset Aquatic Park via a route along Saybrook Ln. and Edinger Ave. This return route is primarily Class II.

TRAILHEAD: From Pacific Coast Highway (PCH) turn east on Warner Ave., continue about 1-1/2 miles, then turn left (north) on Bolsa Chica St. Continue about 1-1/4 miles to Edinger Ave., turn left (west) and follow the road 1-3/4 miles over a small bridge (1.8). Continue on the road now named Sunset Way East for about 0.2 mile to the marina parking area at Sunset Aquatic Park.

From the San Diego Fwy., exit west at Westminster Ave. and continue about 1-1/2 miles to Bolsa Chica Rd. Turn left (south) and drive two miles to Edinger Ave. Turn right and continue as described above. Another option is to park anywhere along Edinger Ave. and start the trip from there.

From the Garden Grove Fwy., exit south at Valley View St./Bolsa Chica Rd. and drive about three miles to Edinger Ave. Continue as described above.

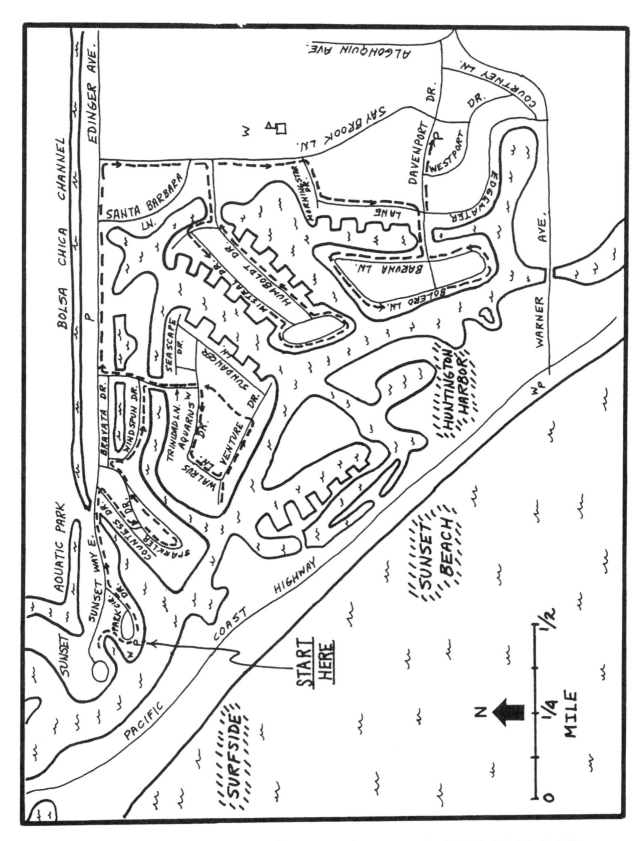

TRIP #2 - SUNSET AQUATIC PARK/ HUNTINGTON HARBOR TOUR

Bikers can load up with water at the Sunset Aquatic Park parking area. Public restrooms are located near the Harbor Patrol building in the park. From this point, water can be had on Trinity Island and at Harbor View Park. There are shopping centers and gas stations along the eastern side of Huntington Harbor, but little in the way of commercial "pit stops" elsewhere in the harbor area.

TRIP DESCRIPTION: **Sunset Aquatic Park.** From the parking/picnic area (a couple of open sites with benches and barbecues), continue west (in the direction of entry) about 0.3 mile to the Harbor Patrol building and the boat launching area. Stop and watch the <u>small</u> cars pulling out <u>big</u> boats and burning up their tires! Ride a little beyond the launch area, lock your bike to the nearby fence, and take a walking tour of the natural (unimproved) Sunset Aquatic Park. There are numerous tide pools, interesting vegetation, and birds of many types. Return to the parking area and continue back across the bridge over the Bolsa Chica Channel (0.9) to Edinger Ave.

Huntington Harbor (northwest). For this reference ride, turn right on Countess Dr. (1.0), make the first left turn (Sparkler Dr.), and continue through a loop which passes between a cozy network of quaint, two-story homes. Just before returning to Edinger Ave., turn right on Bravata Dr. (1.8), then immediately right again on Windspun Dr. Bike on Windspun Dr. to Trinidad Ln. and turn right (2.4). In about 0.1 mile, take in the striking view of the long, home-surrounded canal.

Huntington Harbor (northwest)

21

Trinidad Island. Continue over a small bridge, pass a small playground to the right, and look head-on into the terminus of small, meandering French Park. This is Trinidad Island. Turn right on Aquarius Dr. and continue to the tiny park at the western point of the island (2.9). A small path along the periphery of the island heads in either direction at this point. Turning left, the path continues along the main channel. Continue about 0.5 mile to French Park and wind through this pretty little park back to Trinidad Lane. Return to Edinger Ave. (4.5).

Huntington Harbor (east). Turn right on Edinger Ave. and right again on Saybrook Ln. (5.7). Cruise about 0.3 mile down this pleasant, but busy roadway to Humboldt Dr. Turn right (west) and cross a small bridge; there is a fine view from atop the bridge of the harbor, the nestled harbor "castles," and a cozy little beach (6.1). Tour the quiet island loop following Wayfarer Ln. (to the right), Mistral Dr., the westernmost inner loop, and return to the bridge via Humboldt Dr. (7.7). There are very limited views of the harbor on this loop as the large, and sometimes beautiful residences are packed in side-by-side along the bay shore.

Return across the bridge to Saybrook Ln. and turn right (south). Continue on Saybrook Ln. 0.2 mile to Harbor View Park where there is water and shade (recreation/play areas and tennis courts). Just beyond the park and on the opposite side of the street, turn right (west) on Morningstar Dr. (8.1).

The route is now back on quiet residential streets and continues to Edgewater Ln. (8.2). Turn left on this street and continue to Davenport Dr. (8.5). Turn right (west) and pass over a small bridge; the view from the bridge is almost a copy of that seen from Humboldt Dr. The island loop tour is a cruise through a quiet residential neighborhood on Baruna Ln., around to Bolero Ln. and back to the starting point at the bridge (9.5). Again, there are only scattered harbor views from the island due to blockage by the tightly-packed residences.

Alternate Return Route. The return trip involves following Davenport Dr. to Saybrook Ln. Note that there is parking in the shade near this intersection should there be a desire to start the trip from this end (9.8). Turn left (north) and follow Saybrook Ln. 0.9 mile to Edinger Ave. Turn left again and make a beeline of 1.3 more miles back to your parked car. The total trip mileage is 12.0 miles.

<u>CONNECTING TRIPS:</u> Connection with the beach bikepath to Sunset Beach/Seal Beach (Trip #1) or to the Sunset to Newport Beach Strand (Trip #4) - near the one-way trip terminus (Edgewater Ln. and Davenport Dr.), turn right (south) on Edgewater Ln. and continue to Warner Ave. Turn right (west) on Warner Ave., cross PCH and turn north (Trip #1) or south (Trip #4).

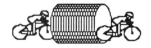

TRIP #3 - HUNTINGTON CENTRAL PARK

GENERAL LOCATION: Huntington Beach

LEVEL OF DIFFICULTY: Loop - easy
Distance - 4.7 miles (loop)
Elevation gain - essentially flat

GENERAL DESCRIPTION: This short and pleasant trip tours both the east and west sections of Huntington Central Park which has over four miles of fine Class I touring without even biking the innermost trails.   The park offers a lovely treed area on the east side with Lake Talbert, the Huntington Central Library, and a duck pond. The east side has less tree cover, but is an equally nice area which sports Lake Huntington, a "frisbee-golf" course, and the Donald D. Shipley Nature Center.   There is a nice eaterie on each side of the park, with Breakfast-in-the-Park on the west side providing lakeside dining under sun umbrellas (we're suckers for this type of environment).

TRAILHEAD: From the San Diego Fwy., exit south at Golden West St. and drive 3-1/2 miles to Slater Ave.   Continue another 1/4 mile and turn left into the east section of Huntington Central Park.

From Pacific Coast Highway (PCH) southbound, drive four miles past Warner Ave. (Huntington Harbor), and turn left at Golden West St.   Continue 2-1/2 miles north passing Talbert Ave.   In another quarter mile, turn right into the park.

From PCH northbound, drive two miles past Beach Blvd. (Huntington Beach) and turn right at Golden West St.   Continue as described above.

Bring a light water supply as water is plentiful.

TRIP DESCRIPTION: **East Section.**   Enter the bikepath and examine the spur trails off to the right which lead to the "Adventure Playground" and a picnic area above the small amphitheater.   Return to the main path and bike into a relatively open area between the library and the amphitheater (0.4).   Turn to the right and follow the park's outermost trail under the tall shade trees.   Continue around Lake Talbert (dry when we visited) and follow a short upgrade to the small loop and parking lot on Slater Ave. (1.6).

Return to the flat and bike past a small play area complete with "merry-go-round" horses anchored in the sand.   Just beyond, the path reaches Golden West St., parallels that road and reaches The Alder Tree, a nice little rest stop for munchies.   Note that there is a street crossing with a crossing guard here (Rio Vista Dr.), which is particularly useful for families who want to cross Golden West St.   However, our reference route continues south and reaches the southwest park edge, follows a 180-degree turn around a duck pond, and passes alongside and below the Huntington Central Library and its beautiful water fountain.   Continue back to the trip origin and turn right on Talbert Ave. Bike to Golden West St. (2.7).

23

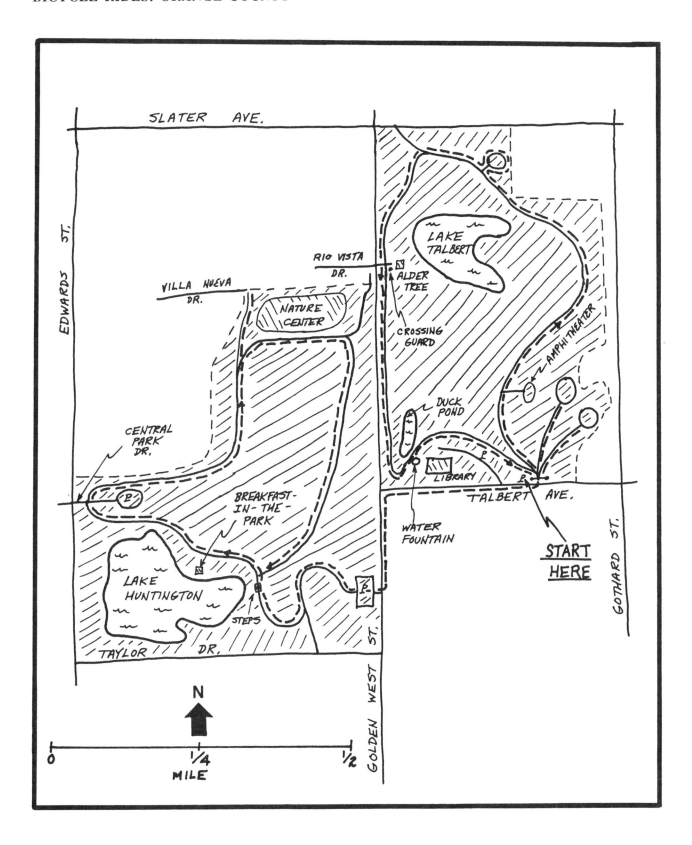

TRIP #3 - HUNTINGTON CENTRAL PARK

West Section. For families, or for bikers who aren't wild about walking/carrying their bikes for short distances, turn right and bike 0.2 mile to the crossing at Rio Vista Dr. and enter the park from the Class I path. Otherwise, turn left and bike 0.2 mile to the parking entry to the more sparsely treed western park section. Pedal through the parking lot onto the Class I path in an area with strange little metal stanchions with chains on them - these are the "holes" that the frisbee-golfers "sink" their frisbees into. This is "disk golf" or "frisbee-golf" country. Stop and watch a group of golfers as they drive through a hole or two.

Continue to the stairway which leads to the lower level of the park (3.2). The options are to carry your bike down the steps or to walk it down a steep incline. Follow the Class I path at the base of the steps to the main western segment loop and turn left. Pedal 0.2 mile to the lakeside and Breakfast-in-the-Park. Continue on the main path another 0.1 mile to the park entry at Central Park Rd.

Cross the road and follow the route past a shaded spur trail which leads to Villa Nueva Dr. In a short distance is the Donald D. Shipley Nature Center, a neat place to learn about the local wildlife (3.8). Bike another 0.3 mile to the junction with the spur trail to Rio Vista Dr. Continue on the shaded main trail another 0.2 mile, passing a large children's play area and returning to the lake area just beyond.

Return Segment. Return via the reference route which means a bike carry up the steps. The alternative is to return via the Rio Vista Dr. crossing and bike through the eastern park segment. The return is about 0.4 mile in either case.

Connecting Trips: Connection with the Sunset Beach to Newport Beach Strand (Trip #4) - pedal 2-1/2 miles to Pacific Coast Hwy. Bike on the highway or the Class I path just beyond in either direction

TRIP #4 - SUNSET BEACH TO NEWPORT BEACH STRAND

GENERAL LOCATION: Sunset Beach, Huntington Beach, Newport Beach

LEVEL OF DIFFICULTY: One way - easy; round trip - moderate
Distance - 13.8 miles (one way)
Elevation gain - essentially flat

BICYCLE RIDES: ORANGE COUNTY

GENERAL DESCRIPTION: Orange County's answer to the South Bay Bike Trail, this trip is entirely along the beach and almost entirely Class I route. This is a very pleasant tour which mixes open areas with great ocean views, together with tight bikepath areas along the well-populated strand. The trip passes three piers, several surfing areas, several state or local parks and beaches, and has numerous locations for food/water/rest stops. Parts of the trip are well populated, particularly near the piers and especially in summertime. The Bolsa Chica State Beach portion of the route is lighted for those folks who like "moonlight" bike rides. An optional partial loop trip is possible by riding portions of Pacific Coast Highway (PCH) on the return leg. This optional leg passes near the Bolsa Chica Ecological Reserve.

TRAILHEAD: Free public parking is available along Pacific Ave. in Sunset Beach, or if one is willing to pay, at Bolsa Chica State Beach. To park at Sunset Beach, turn off of PCH toward the ocean on Warner Ave. and turn right a short distance later at N. Pacific Ave. The state beach entrance is almost 1-1/2 miles further south from Warner Ave. on PCH.

TRIP DESCRIPTION: **Bolsa Chica State Beach to Huntington Beach Pier (5.2 Miles).** The Class I Bolsa Chica State Beach portion of the bike trip begins at Warner Ave. within the state park. Immediately, one has open beach area and a view across San Pedro Channel to Long Beach, L.A. Harbor, and on a clear day, Santa Catalina Island. The roomy bikepath passes the state beach entrance at (1.6) and continues to an area where beach sand has been piled high on either side of the path (2.2). This should give some hint as to what high tide means in this area!

Huntington City Beach

26

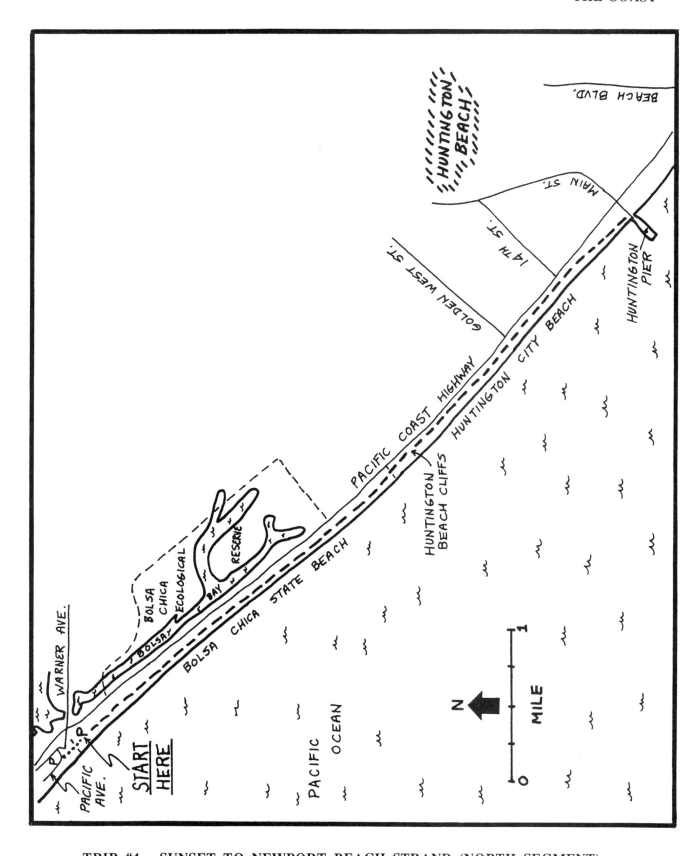

TRIP #4 - SUNSET TO NEWPORT BEACH STRAND (NORTH SEGMENT)

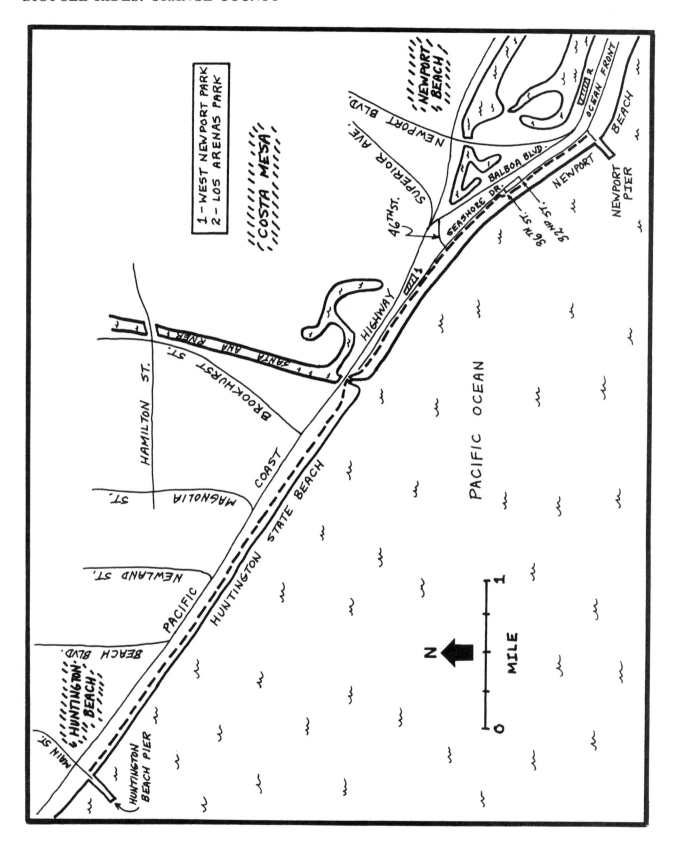

1 - WEST NEWPORT PARK
2 - LOS ARENAS PARK

COSTA MESA

NEWPORT BEACH

PACIFIC OCEAN

TRIP #4 - SUNSET TO NEWPORT BEACH STRAND (MIDDLE SEGMENT)

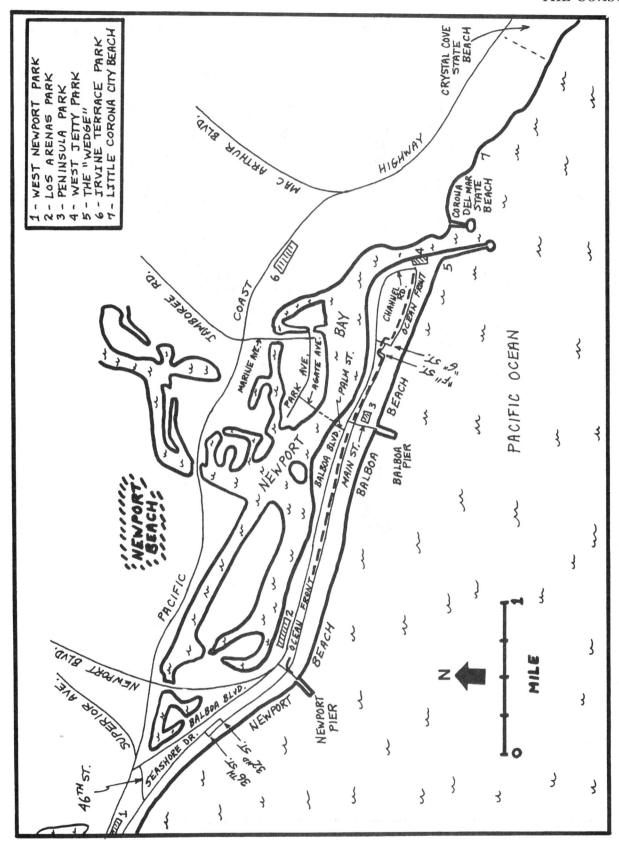

TRIP #4 - SUNSET TO NEWPORT BEACH STRAND (SOUTH SEGMENT)

Just beyond this point, the route climbs gradually and for a short distance to the Huntington Beach Cliffs above Huntington City Beach (2.3). Take a break and hike a short distance to the cliff edge for a guaranteed view of surfer heaven, morning to evening. The route continues on the bluffs and includes a palm tree-lined portion of path, as well as a small park/rest stop.

At (4.7) the path heads downhill and returns to the beach. For the next mile, this area is occupied year round by bathers, swimmers, bikers, walkers and other folks who are interested in being near the Huntington Beach Pier. At (5.2) the path reaches the pier. A short walk to the pier's end leads to some excellent views of the surrounding beach areas, plus the comraderie of fishermen who always seem to be there. On the other side of the pier, stop and check out the surfers riding the waves to the beach, and sometimes under the pier.

Huntington Beach Pier to Newport Pier (5.4 Miles). Continue the trip along Sunset Vista Beach until at (6.1) the route reaches the Huntington State Beach entrance at Beach Blvd. (Hwy. 39). In about two more miles, the state beach ends and the route reaches the Santa Ana River. This is the junction with the Santa Ana River bike route (see Trip #17). Cross the wooden foot bridge and take the right branch of the bikepath a short distance to Seashore Dr. and travel a Class II path along the beachside community homes.

At (9.0) the trip passes the West Newport Park at 56th. St. and at (9.9) reaches 36th St. Take a right turn (toward the beach) and ride a short distance to a Class I bikepath along the strand. On this part of the trip to the end of the bikeway, the biker is effectively sharing the living rooms of all those beach folks living along the strand. The strand path reaches the Newport Pier at (10.6). Try the shops at the pier for some excellent munchies (we are fans of Charlie's Chili) or take a tour down the pier. Another option is to watch the surfers just north of the pier.

Newport Pier to Balboa Penninsula Point (3.2 Miles). If the biker bypasses Newport Pier, there is another chance for a break at Balboa Pier (12.4). In addition to good munchies and a tour of the pier, there are the additional options of shopping at the nearby mall or laying in the grass at Peninsula Park. At about 0.4 mile further down the path, the bike route ends abruptly at the wall of a beach house. Return a short distance to "F" St. and turn away from the beach. Continue a short distance to Balboa Blvd., turn right a short distance later to "G" St., then continue as "G" St. fuses into Ocean Front.

Bike on this pleasant little street on Class X roadway until the street ends at West Jetty Park near Balboa Peninsula Point (13.8). This is the scenic highlight of the trip! Take in the views across the channel to Corona del Mar State Beach, Little Corona City Beach, or across Newport Bay. A short walk out toward the ocean to the West Jetty provides a great view down the coast. Just north of the jetty is "The Wedge," an area with unusual and dangerous currents and tides -- and one of the prize areas for surfers who want to challenge "Mother Nature."

Alternate Return Route: From West Jetty Park, take Channel Rd. toward Newport Bay to its end at Balboa Blvd. Continue on Balboa Blvd. until it meets "F" St., roughly 3/4 mile from West Jetty Park. There are frequent "peeks" between the residences into Newport Bay and of Balboa Island. Continue the incoming bike trip in reverse along the strand. Turn northwest (inland) on 46th St. and travel several blocks to Balboa Blvd. Turn left and in a few hundred feet make a left turn onto PCH.

The remaining return trip can be made on PCH, which is a mix of Class II and Class X routes. However the Class X portion of PCH, for a several mile stretch surrounding the city of Huntington Beach, is a narrow roadway which is filled with both moving and parked cars. The best option on the return leg of the trip is to use the strand bikepath described on the "up" leg between Huntington State Beach (at the Beach Blvd. entrance) and the Huntington Beach Cliffs.

On the PCH return leg, stop at the Bolsa Chica Ecological Reserve, which is just 0.4 mile from the trip origin at Warner Ave. The Reserve is entered via a walking bridge (no bikes) across Bolsa Bay and contains an abundance of bird wildlife over miles of walkways.

CONNECTING TRIPS: 1) Continuation with the bikepath to Seal Beach/ Sunset Beach Tour (Trip #1) - continue this trip north from the trailhead; 2) connection with the bike trip to Sunset Aquatic Park/Huntington Harbor (Trip #2) - continue this trip east on Warner from the trailhead; 3) connection with the Santa Ana River Trail (Trip #17) - from Huntington State Beach, take the bike trail from the north side of the Santa Ana River which passes under PCH; 4) connection with the Newport Beach/Corona Del Mar Tour (Trip #15) and Upper Newport Bay route (Trip #6) - from the junction of PCH and Balboa Blvd., continue southeast on PCH to Tustin Ave. and Jamboree Rd. respectively.

TRIP #5 - MILE SQUARE PARK

GENERAL LOCATION: Fountain Valley

LEVEL OF DIFFICULTY: Loop - easy
Distance - 7.6 miles (outer plus inner loops)
Elevation gain - essentially flat

GENERAL DESCRIPTION: This trip is a family delight! L.A. County has El Dorado Park, but Orange County has Mile Square Park, and there's no major roadway to divide it up. As advertised, it is about a mile on each of its four sides. Besides great Class I bike trails, there are picnic grounds with covered picnic sites, small lakes, playgrounds, basketball courts, tennis courts, handball courts, baseball diamonds, soccer fields, and archery area.

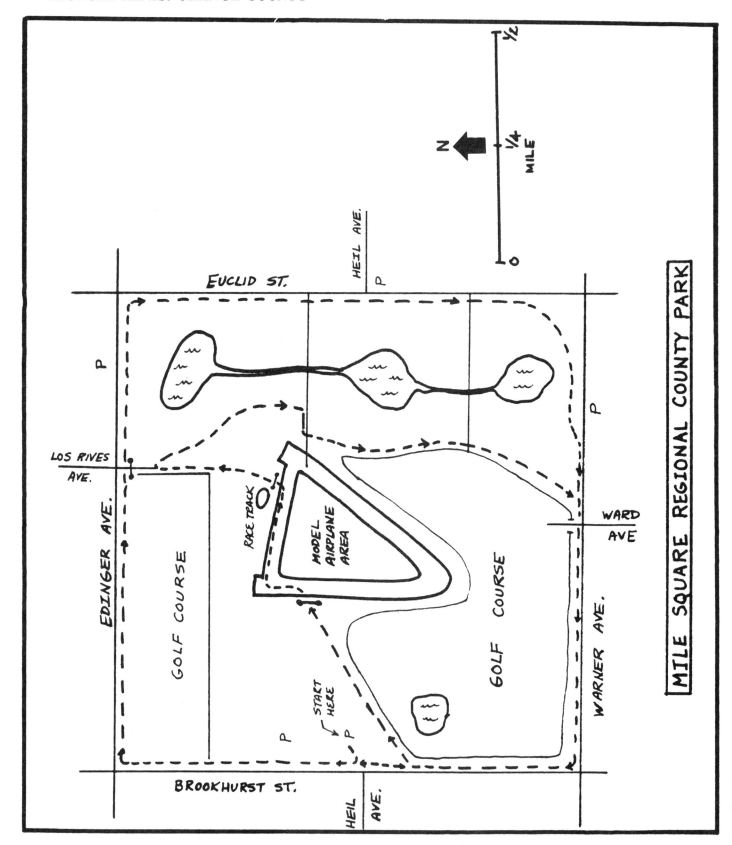

TRIP #5 - MILE SQUARE PARK

The park also sports an adjoining golf course and a model airplane flying area. In addition, there is even a miniature raceway for putting model race cars through their paces. Finally, there's a coffee shop that opens at 5:30 a.m. (who cares!).

The mileage shown is for a fixed route consisting of a tour around the exterior boundary of the park, followed by an "inner loop." The route is actually free-form and at the discretion of the biker. The Class II bikepaths are lightly used and generally in excellent condition. There are water and restroom facilities throughout the park.

TRAILHEAD: From the San Diego Fwy., exit at Warner Ave. and head north about 1/2 mile. For the trip as described here, turn left at Brookhurst St. and continue about 1/2 mile to Heil Ave. There is free parking within the park in this area. There are also numerous places to park free on the park periphery (see the map). There is pay parking within the park off Euclid Ave.

TRIP DESCRIPTION: **Outer Loop.** Return to Brookhurst St. and turn right (north) on the bikepath. Pass the handball courts, tennis courts, and a large open field. There is a fine view of both Mt. San Antonio and Mt. Saddleback from this area on a clear day. Turn right at Edinger Ave. (0.5) and continue along the open field. The route passes a blocked auto entry at Los Rives Ave. (1.2) and the start of a long string of tree-dotted picnic areas shortly afterward. There is a small lake with several bridges over to a small island playground in this area. Continue along the outside park path to Euclid Ave. and turn right (1.6). In the next 0.9 mile along Euclid Ave. are many picnic areas, grassy knolls, scattered tree cover, two additional lake areas, and several automobile roadways into the park.

There is a gradual turn around the southernmost lake and the bike trail begins to parallel Warner Ave (2.6). The route continues past a soccer field, passes through a small parking area, and hugs Warner Ave. In about 0.6 mile, the path crosses the Ward Ave. entry to the golf course and coffee shop. The bikeway turns to a slightly rough surface of asphalt and small gravel for about the next quarter mile, and continues along the golf course to Brookhurst St. (3.5). Turn right, continue along the golf course, and return to the parking area entrance at Heil Ave. (4.0).

Inner Loop. Reverse direction and head back to the junction with an alternate bikepath. Make a sharp left onto that path and continue alongside the golf course, then the baseball fields. Continue alongside the fence, which encloses the old airstrip, to a small entry point (4.4). This strip is used for radio-controlled model cars, high-speed aerodynamic bicycles, and the middle area between strips for model airplanes. Stay to the outside edge of the strip and follow it as it turns east alongside the open field. Near the automobile-blocked roadway (Los Rives Ave. extention) is a small race track for large, radio-controlled, off-road model race cars (4.8).

Turn left onto the extension roadway and, in about 0.3 mile, turn right on the bikepath near the northernmost lake. Continue on the innermost path and pass the archery area (5.4).

33

At the apparent path terminus, follow the roadway heading into the airstrip for a short distance and rejoin the bikeway. Follow the path along the east edge of the golf course, across a small bridge, and return to the soccer field and parking area along Warner Ave. (6.2). To return to the starting point, repeat the exterior park circuit along Warner Ave. and Brookhurst St. (7.6).

CONNECTING TRIPS: 1) Connection with the Santa Ana River Trail (Trip #17C) - take Warner Ave., Heil Ave., or Edinger Ave. east (1 to 1-1/2 miles); 2) Spur trips - there are numerous Class II bike routes in the Fountain Valley/Huntington Beach area which pass through predominantly residential areas.   For example, take Heil Ave. about 1/2 mile west to Bushard St. and head either north or south at that junction.

TRIP #6 - UPPER NEWPORT BAY

GENERAL LOCATION: Newport Beach

LEVEL OF DIFFICULTY: Loop - moderate
Distance - 6.2 miles (loop)
Elevation gain - periodic moderate grades

GENERAL DESCRIPTION: This is a pleasant loop trip with a highlight of natural scenery together with a tour through some varied residential areas. This trip visits the Upper Newport Bay Wildlife Preserve, offering a chance to see a large variety of bay scenery and wildlife.   The bay area roadway is flat, while the residential portion of the trip offers a couple of challenging uphills.   There is an excellent lookout vista at the northern end of Upper Newport Bay.   There are also several excellent spur trips off of this "looper" with an abundance of parks off these spurs.   The trip is almost completely Class II if taken in the counterclockwise direction as written.

TRAILHEAD: Jamboree Rd. begins at Pacific Coast Highway (PCH) in Newport Beach.   It is roughly 2-1/2 miles east of Newport Blvd. (the outlet of the Costa Mesa Fwy.) and 1-1/4 miles west of MacArthur Veteran's Memorial Blvd. Take Jamboree Rd. 1/4 mile northeast to Backbay Dr. and turn left. Continue about 100-200 yards past the Newporter Inn parking lot and turn left into the pay parking area at Newport Dunes Aquatic Park.   There are picnic, recreation, and restroom facilities within the park.   Other options are to use the very limited free parking in surrounding residential areas or to start the trip from the Eastbluff Dr. area.

Load up with water as there are no public facilities directly on this route.   Take a diversion to Eastbluff Village Shopping Center if water is needed.

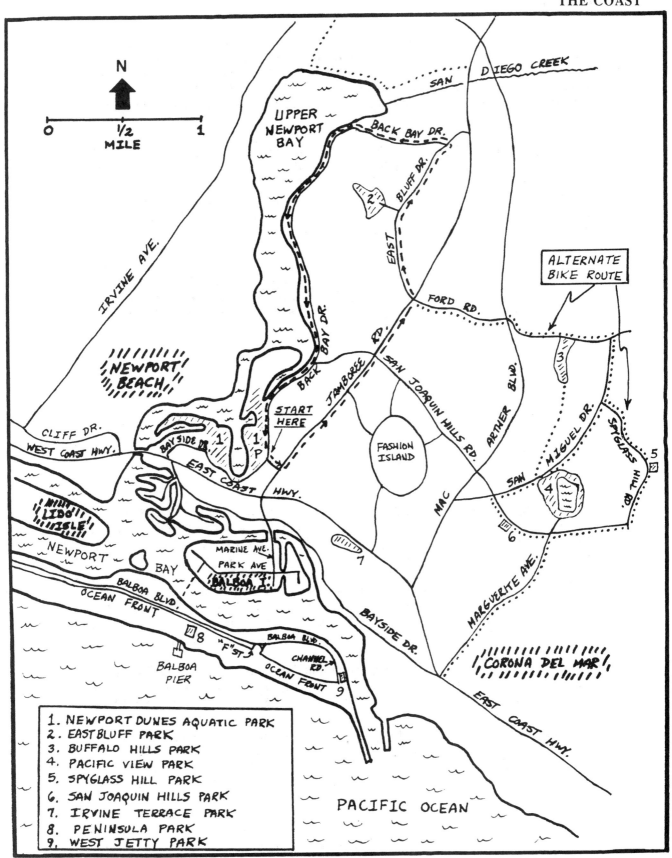

1. NEWPORT DUNES AQUATIC PARK
2. EASTBLUFF PARK
3. BUFFALO HILLS PARK
4. PACIFIC VIEW PARK
5. SPYGLASS HILL PARK
6. SAN JOAQUIN HILLS PARK
7. IRVINE TERRACE PARK
8. PENINSULA PARK
9. WEST JETTY PARK

TRIP #6 - UPPER NEWPORT BAY

TRIP DESCRIPTION: Jamboree Road. Leave the park and continue back on Backbay Dr. to Jamboree Rd. Turn left (north) and head up a grade passing Santa Barbara Dr. (0.4). This is an entrance to Fashion Island Shopping Center. Continue uphill to a plateau at San Joaquin Hills Rd. (0.9), then navigate a steep downhill, followed by another moderate to steep uphill. Near the top of the grade, turn left at Eastbluff Dr. (1.4) and continue through a pleasant residential neighborhood. The route passes a large recreation field at Corona Del Mar High School and then cruises by East Bluff Village Shopping Center (2.1). The bikepath passes along a pleasant palm tree-lined bluff, then heads downhill. Part way down this grade is Backbay Dr. (2.9).

Backbay Drive. At this junction stop and enjoy one of the premier views of the north end of Upper Newport Bay. Bike down a moderate to steep grade on Backbay Dr. and continue along the bay itself. There is a one-way bike lane on the right side of the road only, which continues to the starting point. The route passes a large, open, marshy flat with thousands of birds (3.2) and continues to twist and wind along the bay. There are continuous excellent views into the mud flats, marshes, and open bay.

Back Bay Dr., Upper Newport Bay

In 3/4 mile, the view opens into an expansive sweep, including the high bluffs across the bay. There are numerous turnouts along the way, some of which are occupied by bird watchers and a few tame ducks. There is a series of light "ups and downs" in this area with signs to indicate that the road may be flooded during storms (4.7). The route snakes past a relatively low, but scenic turnout/overlook (5.6) and returns to the park (6.2).

CONNECTING TRIPS: 1) Continuation with the Newport Beach Tour (Trip #7) - at the trip origin, turn right on Backbay Dr.; 2) connection with the San Diego Creek Trail (Trip #18) - at the scenic overlook at Backbay Dr. and Eastbluff Dr., continue downhill on Eastbluff Dr. (stay on the sidewalk) to Jamboree Rd. Turn left at the trail sign at that intersection; 3) spur trip connection - from the starting point, continue south along Bayside Dr., cross PCH and follow the loop back around to Jamboree Rd.

SPECIAL SCENIC CONNECTION: Connection with the Sunset Beach to Newport Beach Strand trip (Trip #4) - bike south on Jamboree Rd., cross PCH and follow the roadway onto Balboa Island. Take the ferry (Agate St.) across the bay to the peninsula.

TRIP #7 - NEWPORT BEACH TOUR

GENERAL LOCATION: Newport Beach

LEVEL OF DIFFICULTY: Loop - moderate
Distance - 23.3 miles (loop)
Elevation gain - periodic moderate to steep grades

GENERAL DESCRIPTION: This jim-dandy biking experience on mixed Class I/II/III bikeway takes a "slice" out of several different Newport Beach areas. The tour leaves from inviting Newport Dunes Aquatic Park, visits the Fashion Island area, tours posh and scenic Spyglass Hill, and passes over San Diego Creek. Next is an eight-mile circuit through a lightly trafficked, modern light commercial area (into Irvine), a westside tour of Upper Newport Bay, visits to sightseer's Galaxy Park and sportsman's Mariner's Park, and a scenic return on Dover Dr. and Pacific Coast Hwy (PCH). The Spyglass Hill area climb and the collection of moderate upgrades throughout the route place this trip at the upper end of a moderate rating.

TRAILHEAD: Jamboree Rd. begins at PCH in Newport Beach. It is roughly 2-1/2 miles east of Newport Blvd. (the outlet of the Costa Mesa Fwy.) and 1-1/4 miles west of MacArthur Veteran's Memorial Blvd. Take Jamboree Rd. one-quarter mile northeast to Backbay Dr. and turn left. Continue about 100-200 yards past the Newporter Inn parking lot and turn left into the pay parking area at Newport Dunes Aquatic Park. There are picnic, recreation, and restroom facilities within the park. Another option is to use the very limited free parking is the surrounding residential area. Pay close attention to local parking laws.

Bring a full water bottle. There are scattered water sources throughout the route, although no public water sources were found in the 8.2 mile northern industrial segment.

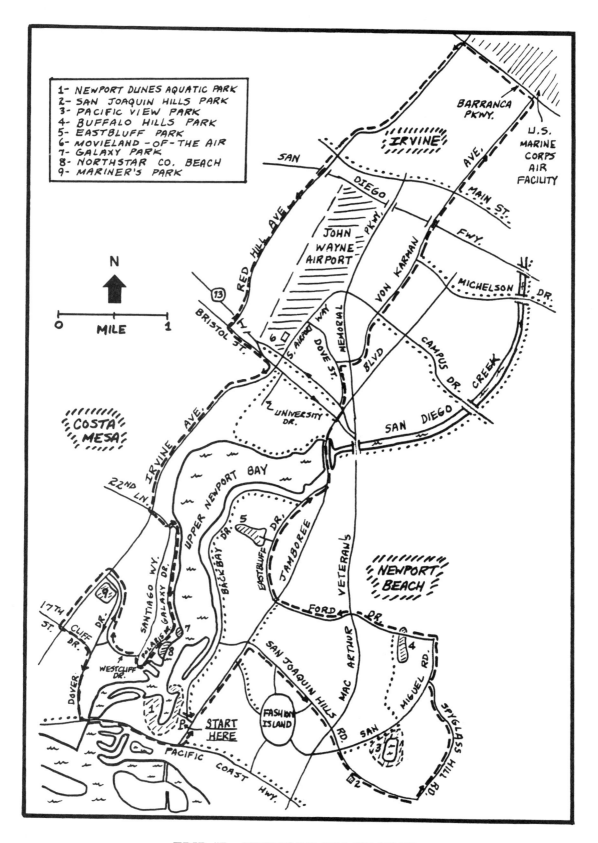

TRIP #7 - NEWPORT BEACH TOUR

TRIP DESCRIPTION: **San Joaquin Hills Rd.** Leave the park and return to Jamboree Rd. and turn left (north). Bike on the sidewalk (marked Class I) through a series of workout roller-coaster grades and turn right at San Joaquin Hills Rd. near the top of the grade (1.0). Pass the gas station and bike on this wide road with plenty of shoulder or use the sidewalk where marked. (Note that there are numerous areas in Newport Beach where signs designate bikeable sidewalks.) The uphill route passes Santa Cruz Dr. (an entry to the Newport Harbor Art Museum), several impressive buildings in the Fashion Island complex, and soon reaches a crest (1.5). There is an excellent view into the canyons to the northeast, as well as a long-distance view to Mt. Saddleback.

The route cruises a residential area and passes Santa Rosa Dr., MacArthur Blvd., and San Miguel Dr. Next is an uphill pedal which passes lawn bowler's paradise at San Joaquin Hills Park. Shortly, the road passes Marguerite Ave. and begins a steep upgrade. During this workout, the biker is treated to the well manicured and flowered Pacific View Memorial Park Cemetery (3.1). The path ends in a short distance at a flat.

Spyglass Hill Rd. Turn left onto Spyglass Hill Rd. and enjoy the prestigious and well-maintained neighborhood while pedaling uphill. Use the Class I sidewalk or the wide road. At the crest is cozy Spyglass Hill Park (actually a children's play area) and just beyond is a downgrade that leads to an open area view near Ridgeline Dr. that will bring tears of joy to your eyes. Spread out before you are Fashion Island, Newport Bay, the surrounding Orange County flatlands, and a long-distance view to Catalina Island. Follow a steep downhill that flattens near San Miguel Dr. and turn right (north) (4.3).

Upper Newport Bay - East. Follow Class II San Miguel Dr. 0.5 mile to its terminus, turn left on mixed ClassII/III Ford Dr., and follow what is a general downgrade through mixed residential/light commercial area to Jamboree Rd. (6.2). Cross Jamboree Rd. on the street now named Eastbluff Dr. and bike 1.3 miles through a well-groomed residential neighborhood, passing the Eastbluff Shopping Center. The bikeway passes along a pleasant tree-lined bluff, then heads downhill and returns to Jamboree Rd.

Bike across the bridge over San Diego Creek on the west side of Jamboree Rd. and meet the Class I bike trail just beyond the north end of the bridge. Turn left and follow that path along the northern periphery of the bay if you desire to take the shorter 15.2-mile Newport Bay loop. However, our reference route continues north on Jamboree Rd. and turns left at Bristol St. (north direction of that divided road) (8.1).

Irvine. At the first intersection, turn right at Dove St. and begin an 8.2-mile arc that passes through light industrial territory with relatively slow and light traffic and plenty of biking room. This portion of the tour is more scenic than expected, particularly for "building watchers" and "sidewalk superintendents." Note that Class I sidewalk biking is allowed where posted. Pedal 0.4 mile to Von Karmen Ave./Newport Place Dr. and turn right onto Von Karmen Dr.

39

Bike northwest on that road past a variety of interesting building architectures and clever landscaping. In succession cross the main intersections at Campus Dr., Michelson Dr., pass over the freeway, and continue to Main St. There are few stoplights on this industrial area tour other than the major intersections. The density of industrial complexes tails off north of the freeway and this bee-line route continues on lightly used roadway to Barranca Pkwy. (11.6). The gigantic hangers and an array of helicopters in the Marine Corps Air Facility are visible from this area.

Turn left and bike on the Class II road 0.7 mile to Red Hill Ave. and turn left again. Pedal past a gas station at MacArthur Veteran's Memorial Hwy. Return 2.7 miles on the Class II route through an array of modern, light commercial complexes, passing over both the San Diego Fwy. and the short Hwy. 73 freeway segment. Along this segment are the Briggs Cunningham Automotive Museum and the John Wayne Airport.

Upper Newport Bay - West. Turn left at S. Bristol St. (15.9) and bike 0.4 mile to Irvine Ave., turn right and pedal downhill past the Newport Beach Golf Course. Near University Dr. on the Class II road is the first peek into Newport Bay. Note that there is a Class I path on the east side of the road in this area. Irvine Ave. winds through some small rolling hills and in 1.3 miles from Bristol St. reaches an open area with a view across the bay with Mt. Saddleback in the background that will "knock your socks off."

Just beyond, pedal to 22nd St./Santiago Way through more small rolling hills. One option is to continue 0.7 mile south to Mariner's Park on Irvine Ave. However, this route turns left at Santiago Way, left again at Galaxy Dr. and proceeds on the latter road through a quiet residential neighborhood. In just short of a mile is little Galaxy Park with benches and a dynamite view of the bay.

Continue on winding Galaxy Dr. which becomes Polaris Dr., and bike past Northstar Ln. (this road leads to a small marina and little Northstar County Beach) (19.2). The road turns sharply right and follows a short and steep uphill to Westcliff Dr. Follow this road 0.4 mile where it changes its name to Dover Dr. (one way northbound) and returns to Irvine Ave. at Mariner's Park (recreation fields, playgrounds, shade and water).

Return Segment. Turn left (south) and bike 0.7 mile to 17th St./Cliff Dr. Free-wheel another 0.7 mile of mostly downhill to PCH (22.0). Follow that Class I path on the east side of Dover Dr. under the west end of the bridge to reach PCH eastbound (got that ?!). The territory on the return segment changes from residential to a mix of open and commercially-developed land and higher density traffic on PCH.

Cross the bridge eastbound on the sidewalk or the Class II path on PCH. There is a fine view from the bridge of both the bay and the boaters below. Docked at the east end of the bridge is the Reuben E. Lee (sternwheeler) floating restaurant. The path crosses Bayside Dr., then follows a 0.4 mile upgrade that provides a grand view of Upper Newport Bay and Newport Dunes Aquatic Park from the crest. In 0.6 mile, turn left on Jamboree Rd., left again at Backbay Dr. and return to the parking area (23.3).

CONNECTING TRIPS: 1) Continuation with the Upper Newport Bay tour (Trip #6) - at the trip origin, turn left at Backbay Dr.; 2) connection with the Newport Beach/Corona Del Mar Tour (Trip #15) - at PCH and Jamboree Rd., bike east on PCH; 3) connection with the Sunset Beach to Newport Beach Strand route (Trip #4) - at Dover Dr. and PCH, bike west on PCH, turn toward the ocean at Balboa Blvd., and turn right at 46th St.; 4) connection with the San Diego Creek tour (Trip #18) - at the south side of the bridge over San Diego Creek, follow the Class I trail on the west side of Jamboree Rd. down below the bridge.

TRIP #8 - IRVINE BIKEWAY

GENERAL LOCATION: Irvine, Tustin

LEVEL OF DIFFICULTY: One way - easy; up and back - moderate
Distance - 11.4 miles (one way)
Elevation gain - essentially flat

GENERAL DESCRIPTION: This trip explores some of the Class II routes within the city of Irvine. The tour includes both rural and light-density urban travel, with a side Class I trip through Hick's Canyon Wash thrown in for diversity. The route is a pleasant, moderate mileage trip with most of the route along Irvine Blvd. and Culver Blvd. The single negative feature of the route is that it encounters a large number of traffic signals. The highlights are Hick's Canyon Wash early in the trip and William R. Mason Regional Park near the trip terminus. There is a multitude of spurs that can be taken off the main route, particularly off Yale Ave.

TRAILHEAD: From the Newport Fwy., exit at Irvine Blvd. and turn east. In about a mile, turn diagonally left on Newport Ave. and proceed about 1/2 mile to La Colina Dr. Turn right and find parking within the local residential area, subject to local parking signs. From the Santa Ana Fwy., exit at Newport Ave. and head northeast about 2.0 miles to La Colina Dr. Turn right and find parking.

Only a light ration of water is needed since there are many parks, gas stations, and shopping centers along the way.

TRIP DESCRIPTION: **Irvine Blvd.** Proceed down La Colina on a Class II residential area bikepath to Redhill Ave. and turn right (southwest). Continue to Irvine Blvd (0.5) and turn left on that busier roadway which parallels a small wash. In a short distance the territory becomes more rural, passing through wide open fields (1.0) and large orange groves. There is an unobstructed view of Mt. Saddleback in the distance and a close-up view of the U.S. Marine Corps Air Facility to the right.

41

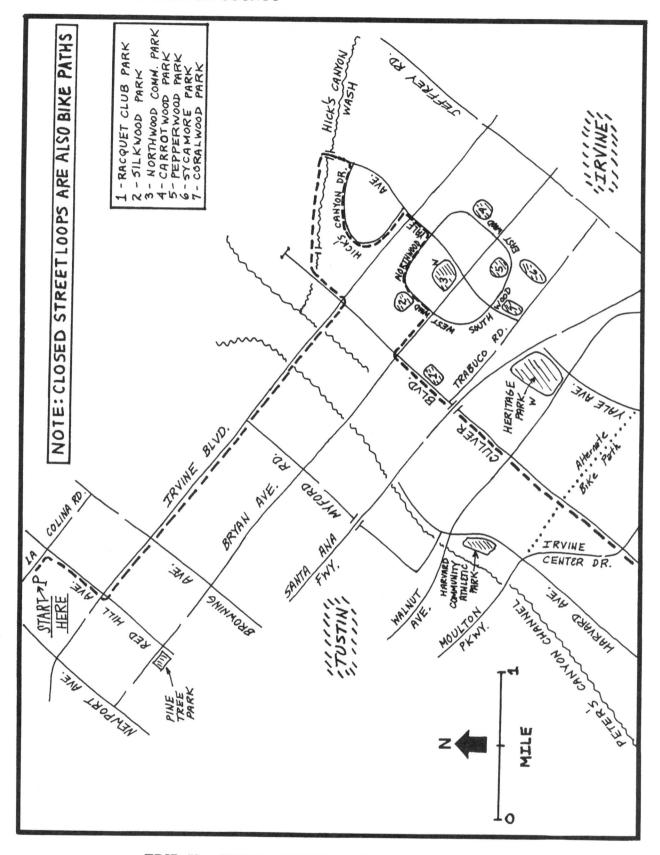

NOTE: CLOSED STREET LOOPS ARE ALSO BIKE PATHS

1 - RACQUET CLUB PARK
2 - SILKWOOD PARK
3 - NORTHWOOD COMM. PARK
4 - CARROTWOOD PARK
5 - PEPPERWOOD PARK
6 - SYCAMORE PARK
7 - CORALWOOD PARK

TRIP #8 - IRVINE BIKEWAY (NORTHERN SEGMENT)

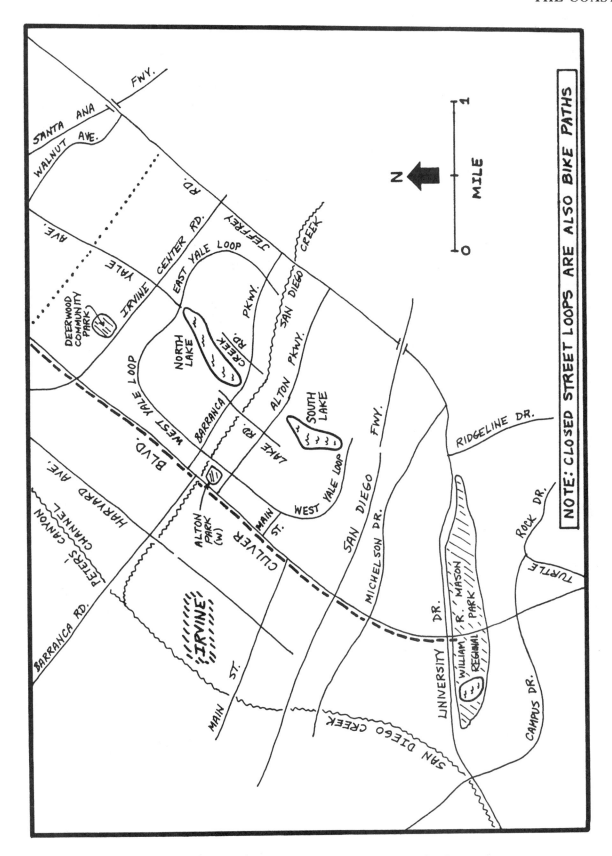

TRIP #8 - IRVINE BIKEWAY (SOUTHERN SEGMENT)

In about a mile, the path crosses Milford Rd. (1.9), passes over Peter's Canyon Channel (2.4) and a lesser channel (2.7). In a short distance, the path crosses Culver Blvd. (2.9).

Hick's Canyon Wash and Yale Ave. Turn left at Culver Blvd. and proceed about 0.2 mile to a little asphalt-covered path to the right (east) alongside an orange grove. Follow this pleasant, semi-secluded path along the tree-lined Hick's Canyon Wash. Pass the first crossing bridge and continue along the path about 0.9 mile to its end. Another crossing bridge brings the biker back to civilization at Yale Ave. (4.0).

North Lake, Irvine

Continue south a short distance and turn right on Hick's Canyon Dr. This is a diversion on a Class II path through a lovely isolated area. Continue around this loop and return to Yale Ave. (4.8). This is the northern section of Yale Ave., a street that probably sports more trip spurs than any other in Orange County. Turn right on Yale Ave. and cross Irvine Blvd., then turn right again on Northwood (5.1). This is part of a one mile Class II loop which is surrounded by pleasant parks. However, our route takes a right turn from Westwood onto Bryan Ave. and continues to Culver Blvd. (6.0).

Culver Blvd. The remainder of the Class II route is a cruise down stoplight "infested" Culver Blvd. The tour crosses Trabuco Rd. (6.5) and the Santa Ana Fwy. (6.6), and in another 0.4 mile passes along a major shopping and business center. The tour passes another major shopping center at Deerfield Ave. (7.8). At this juncture, there is a great view of the mammoth airship hangers at the U.S. Marine Corps Air Facility to the right.

44

The trip proceeds past Irvine Center Dr. (8.0), Warner Ave. (8.5), passes an area of large open fields near Barranca Pkwy., crosses San Diego Creek (9.0), then meets Main St. (9.6) and the San Diego Fwy. (10.1). The setting changes and becomes more rural near Michelson Dr. (10.5). There is an abundance of trees and a park-like setting throughout the surrounding residential areas. In 0.2 mile, the route passes alongside the Rancho San Joaquin Golf Course and shortly therafter crosses University Ave (10.9).

Continue about 0.2 mile further and turn right on a small roadway into the William R. Mason Regional Park. Proceed another 1/2 mile to a lovely lake in the park and take a well-deserved, end-of-the-trip break (11.4). Another option is to continue 0.3 mile past the park turnoff on Culver Blvd. and turn right on Campus Ave. for a tour of the U.C. Irvine campus.

CONNECTING TRIPS: 1) Connection with the San Diego Creek ride (Trip #18) - at Culver Blvd. and Barranca Rd., take the bike trail along the creek; 2) spur trips - there are many fine Class II spur trips as noted on the map. Two particularly nice spurs are the Yale loop and the Eastwood-Northwood-Westwood-Southwood loop.

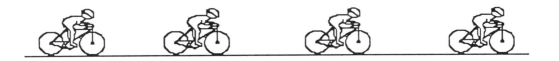

TRIP #9 - LAGUNA CANYON ROAD

GENERAL LOCATION: Irvine, Laguna Canyon, Laguna Beach

LEVEL OF DIFFICULTY: One way - moderate; up and back - moderate to strenuous
Distance - 10.4 miles (one way)
Elevation gain - frequent moderate grades

GENERAL DESCRIPTION: This sun-exposed canyon route starts from Irvine in the Orange County interior and dumps out at breezy Laguna Beach. The first 2.5 miles passes through open agricultural area on lightly traveled Class X roadway. The Class II portion of the trip through Laguna Canyon traverses a series of rolling hills through five workout miles. The remainder of the trip cruises the city of Laguna Beach on Class II bikeway. The highlights of the trip are the canyon vistas and the points of interest near Laguna Beach. The latter include the Irvine Bowl and Irvine Bowl Park, Laguna Beach Museum of Art, Heisler Park, and Laguna Beach itself.

TRAILHEAD: Park in the residential areas south of Irvine Center Dr. between Jeffrey Rd. and Sand Canyon Ave. (Parking previously available off of Laguna Canyon Rd. is no longer legal.) Another option is to park at Irvine Bowl Park and reverse the trip. To find the former parking area, exit the Santa Ana Fwy. at Sand Canyon Ave. Drive southwest about 3/4 mile and turn right on Irvine Center Dr. Just beyond, turn left at Orange Tree. Continue into the residential area and find parking subject to local laws.

45

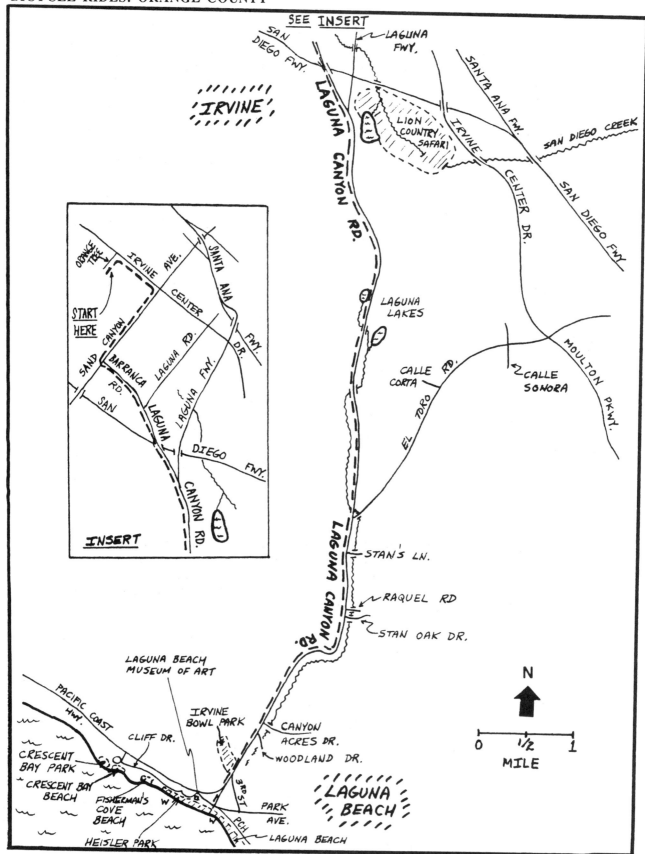

SEE INSERT

LAGUNA FWY.

IRVINE

LION COUNTRY SAFARI

SANTA ANA FWY.

SAN DIEGO CREEK

SAN DIEGO FWY.

LAGUNA CANYON RD.

IRVINE CENTER DR.

SAN DIEGO FWY

LAGUNA LAKES

CALLE CORTA

EL TORO RD.

CALLE SONORA

MOULTON PKWY.

INSERT

ORANGE TREE

IRVINE AVE.

SANTA ANA FWY.

CENTER DR.

START HERE

SAND CANYON

LAGUNA RD.

BARRANCA RD.

LAGUNA FWY.

SAN

LAGUNA

DIEGO

FWY.

CANYON RD.

LAGUNA CANYON RD.

STAN'S LN.

RAQUEL RD

STAN OAK DR.

LAGUNA BEACH MUSEUM OF ART

IRVINE BOWL PARK

CANYON ACRES DR.

WOODLAND DR.

N

0   1/2   1
MILE

PACIFIC COAST HWY.

CLIFF DR.

CRESCENT BAY PARK

CRESCENT BAY BEACH

FISHERMAN'S COVE BEACH

HEISLER PARK

3RD ST.

PARK AVE.

PCH

LAGUNA BEACH

LAGUNA BEACH

TRIP #9 - LAGUNA CANYON ROAD

46

From the San Diego Fwy. southbound, exit northeast at Jeffrey Rd. and continue 1-1/2 miles to Irvine Center Dr. Turn right and proceed 1/2 mile to Orange Tree, then turn right again, proceeding as described above. From the San Diego Fwy. northbound, take the Santa Ana Fwy. junction and exit at Sand Canyon Ave. Continue as directed above.

Bring plenty of water. There are water sources in Laguna Beach only.

TRIP DESCRIPTION: Sand Canyon Road to Laguna Canyon Road.
Leave the parking area and turn right (southwest) on Sand Canyon Rd. Proceed on this popular, flat and open stretch over San Diego Creek (0.3) to Barranca Rd. Turn left and bike through continued flat agricultural area past Laguna Rd. (1.6). The street now named Laguna Canyon Rd. passes over the San Diego Fwy. in another half mile and then meets the Laguna Fwy. terminus (2.5).

Laguna Canyon Entry. The Class II Laguna Canyon Rd. route fuses with the Laguna Canyon Fwy. outlet traffic in an area surrounded by open fields (2.7). In another 0.1 mile, the bikepath starts heading into the canyon opening; the Laguna Reservoir is high on the hillside to the left. There are rolling hills and a small creek along the roadway as the route proceeds into the canyon proper (3.0).

The Canyon Tour. This tour follows a moderate upgrade (3.6) and reaches the top of the grade in an area with a few small shade trees (4.0). In another 0.4 mile, the route passes a small hamlet to the left (east) while to the right are small tree stands and overgrowth. In about 1.3 miles of lightly rolling hills and nearly treeless roadway, the road passes over the outlet creek from North Laguna Lake (5.7). This creek has paralleled the road for about 0.2 mile and will criss-cross under this route all the way into the city of Laguna Beach.

The trip continues over the rolling hills within the canyon and heads up a grade with a "Laguna Beach City Limit" sign near the summit (6.1). At the time of our trip, there was a large number of hawks circling the area. In another mile, the pathway recrosses the creek and meets the El Toro Rd. terminus and a small community to the left (east) (7.1).

In succession, the uphill-downhill route passes Stan's Ln. (7.5), opens up to a view of a ridge-top community to the east, and then passes through a small roadway community with an adjacent cattle grazing area near Raquel Rd. (8.1). The terrain flattens out and passes a park-like area to the east, meets another small community (6.0), then proceeds through a 1.2 mile narrow canyon segment with no other cross-streets. Just beyond Canyon Acres Dr., the canyon opens up to some strong indications that the "big city" is near.

Laguna Beach. The now flat route begins to exit the canyon and passes through heavier residential/commercial areas, then meets the turnoff to the Irvine Bowl and Irvine Bowl Park (10.1). Just beyond is a view into the commercial heart of Laguna Canyon Rd. and a "peek" at the local beach. At (10.4) from the trip start, the bikepath ends at Pacific Coast Highway (PCH) and Laguna Beach Main Beach.

47

The options at this point are to return directly back up the canyon (the round trip may be rugged on a hot day), take a lengthy tour of the city of Laguna Beach, or plop down at the beach. A shadier option is to return to Irvine Bowl Park.

CONNECTING TRIPS: 1) Continuation with the Laguna Beach Tour (Trip #10) - at the trip terminus take PCH to the right (northwest) towards Crystal Cove State Park or left towards Aliso Beach Park; 2) connection with the Lower El Toro Rd. workout (Trip #31) - at the junction with that roadway, head northeast through a strenuous, hilly route; 3) connection with the San Diego Creek route (Trip #18) - from the trip origin, turn left (northeast) on Sand Canyon Rd., left again on Irvine Center Dr. and continue about one mile to Jeffrey Rd. Turn left and find the creek bikeway entry; and 4) connection with the Irvine Bikeway (Trip #8) - from the trip origin, bike to Irvine Center Rd, as above, turn left and continue about 2-1/2 miles to Culver Dr.

TRIP #10 - LAGUNA BEACH TOUR

GENERAL LOCATION: Corona Del Mar - Laguna Beach

LEVEL OF DIFFICULTY: One way - moderate; round trip - moderate to
                              strenuous
                          Distance - 9.1 miles (one way)
                          Elevation gain - frequent moderate to steep
                              upgrades

GENERAL DESCRIPTION: This is one of the finer beach tours, provided that a continuous diet of hills and limited stretches of "tight" biking quarters on Pacific Coast Highway (PCH) aren't a turnoff. There are excellent beach vistas throughout the route in the Crystal Cove State Beach area, at Crescent Bay Point Park and Heisler Park. The bike tour passes through pleasant Laguna Beach and some of the local hillsides and ends at pocket-sized, lovely Aliso Beach. Most of the route is Class II or Class III, although there is a short section near the center of Laguna Beach that rides more like a Class X route.

TRAILHEAD: Proceed south from Newport Beach on PCH. Roughly 1-1/4 miles from MacArthur Blvd., turn right (south) on Seaward Rd. and find parking in that residential neighborhood. From Laguna Beach continue 3/4 mile north beyond the northern boundary of Crystal Cove State Beach to Seaward Rd. (if you pass Hazel Dr., you've gone too far).

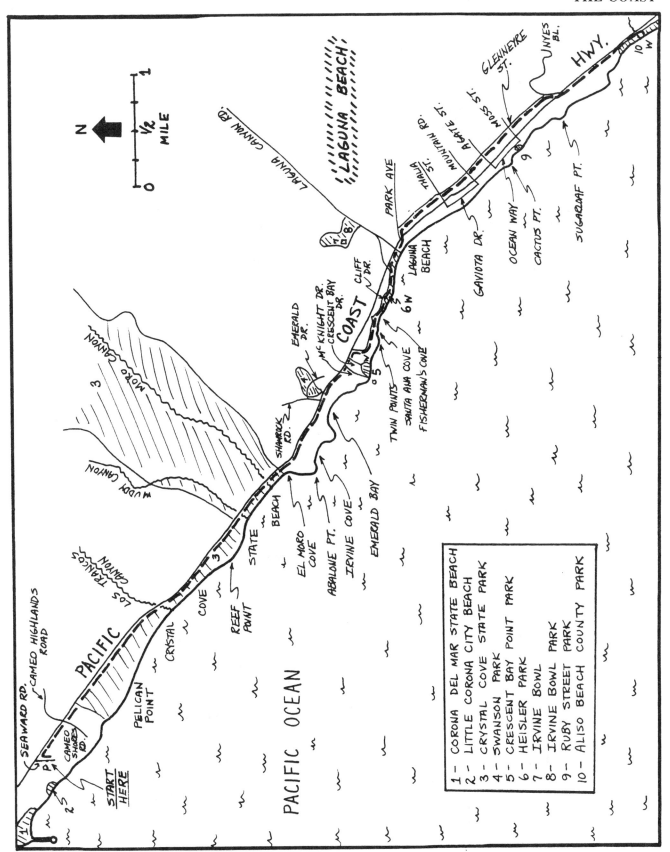

TRIP #10 - LAGUNA BEACH TOUR

TRIP DESCRIPTION: **Crystal Cove State Park.** Return to PCH and turn right (south). This is the start of a Class II route through residential areas. Just beyond Cameo Shores Rd. (0.3) is undeveloped, wide-open land. There are hills to the left (northeast) and the bluffs of Crystal Cove State Park on the ocean side to the right. The roadway passes a park entrance near Pelican Pt. (1.0), Los Frances Canyon (1.5), and then starts a steep downhill. In another 0.1 mile is an entry to the park near the Crystal Cove area followed by a short, steep upgrade. There is a nice peek at one of the many coves in the area near the crest (2.1).

The Hills. In another 0.5 mile, the tour passes near Reef Point. In a short distance, the route heads steeply downhill and provides a spectacular view into El Morro Cove (stop and admire the view). Near the bottom of the grade, there is a roadside snack stand, just at the point where another short, steep upgrade starts (3.3) (those clever devils!). The route continues through steep rolling hills, passing Irvine Cove Way, Bay Dr., and reaching an uphill crest at McKnight Dr. (4.6). Just beyond is Crescent Bay Dr. where our tour diverts to the right (toward the ocean) to take in Crescent Bay Point Park and one of the great vistas along the coast. There is also a water fountain here.

Cliff Drive. The route returns to PCH (5.1) and continues south. In another 0.2 mile, the bikepath leaves PCH and turns toward the beach on Class III Cliff Dr. The short tour along this relatively lightly traveled roller-coaster residential street is one of the premier parts of this trip. The route passes large groups of scuba divers preparing for the trip down to the coves, provides periodic peeks down to those coves, then passes on the city side of Heisler Park (5.9).

This pleasant, long, thin park has a number of fine view points supplied with benches. Stop and watch the scuba divers and scuba school in Diver's Cove. There are nice picnic spots with barbecues and water, too. Beyond is the Laguna Lawn Bowling Green, more park benches with a beach overlook, beach access at the south end of Heisler Park (a great view to the south beaches), and the Laguna Beach Museum of Art (6.3).

Central Laguna Beach. The bike route returns to PCH and heads downhill to the busiest part of town (and some of the tightest Class III bikeway we've seen). The tour passes Laguna Beach at the foot of Broadway; this is the sunbather's Mecca. There is water here and also a pleasant outdoor restaurant next to the beach (The Greeter's Corner Restaurant).

Pacific Coast Highway Alternate Route. In a short distance, the path again leaves PCH and follows Park Ave. two blocks to Glenneyre St. (another block east on Catalina St. is the marked Pacific Coast Bicentennial Bike Route). Do not ride PCH in the next mile or two as it is "flat out" dangerous! Instead, turn right on Glenneyre St. and continue south through a light commercial district with light traffic and plenty of bike room (6.8). The route passes through rolling hills past Thalia St. (7.2), Cress St. (7.5), and tightens down into a small one-lane road through more rural area beyond Caliope St. (7.6).

Beyond Agate St. (7.8) is a steep upgrade and in another 0.5 mile, the path reaches Diamond St. and a bike route junction. Continue on Glenneyre St. if you want some challenging uphill and exciting downhill, passing Alta Vista, Victoria Dr., Nyes Pl., and returning to PCH (8.6). The more standard option is to turn right toward the ocean and return to PCH at this juncture.

Aliso Beach State Park. Beyond Nyes Pl., the route heads downhill past a shopping plaza (left) and mobile home park (right) (9.1). In 0.2 mile, the bike route passes Wesley Dr. (9.3), then follows a steep downhill to the Aliso Beach entrance (9.6). Aliso Beach State Park sports a fishing pier, a fine and lightly-used beach, and a real, live creek that runs through the park to the beach. Best of all, the beach supports a concession stand, water, and restrooms.

Alternate Return Route. On the return trip, follow the bikeway/walkway along the northside of Aliso Creek under PCH. Return by the same route unless there is a desire for some delightful diversions. They are as follows: 1) at Moss St. and PCH, turn west on Moss St. to Ocean Way; follow that pleasant street up on the ocean bluffs to Agate St. Cross PCH at Agate St. and return to Glenneyre St., then proceed to Mountain St.; 2) turn west and recross PCH to Gaviota Dr. (a little road behind a bunch of garages that has limited views at bike access points). Continue on Gaviota Dr. to Thalia St. and again cross PCH, returning to Glenneyre St. The remainder of the trip is a backtrack to the starting point.

CONNECTING TRIPS: 1) Connection with the Newport Beach/Corona Del Mar Tour (Trip #15) - continue one block north on PCH beyond Seaward Rd. to Glen Dr. Continue 0.3 mile to Ocean Blvd. above Little Corona City beach; 2) connection with the Laguna Canyon Road tour (Trip #9) - turn inland (north) at Laguna Beach at Broadway (Hwy. 133) and continue north.

TRIP #11 - LAGUNA NIGUEL BIKEWAY

GENERAL LOCATION: Mission Viejo, Laguna Niguel, Three Arch Bay

LEVEL OF DIFFICULTY: One way - moderate; up and back - moderate
Distance - 6.5 miles (one way)
Elevation gain - frequent moderate grades

GENERAL DESCRIPTION: This tour explores territory ranging from the dry interior hills to the pleasant, breezy west-facing beaches. The route has dry, exposed sections as well as lush, tree-lined segments. There are large undeveloped sections, as well as developed shopping centers at the trip origin, middle segment, and terminus. The one constant of this trip is hilly terrain. There are several nice vista points, particularly late in this trip.

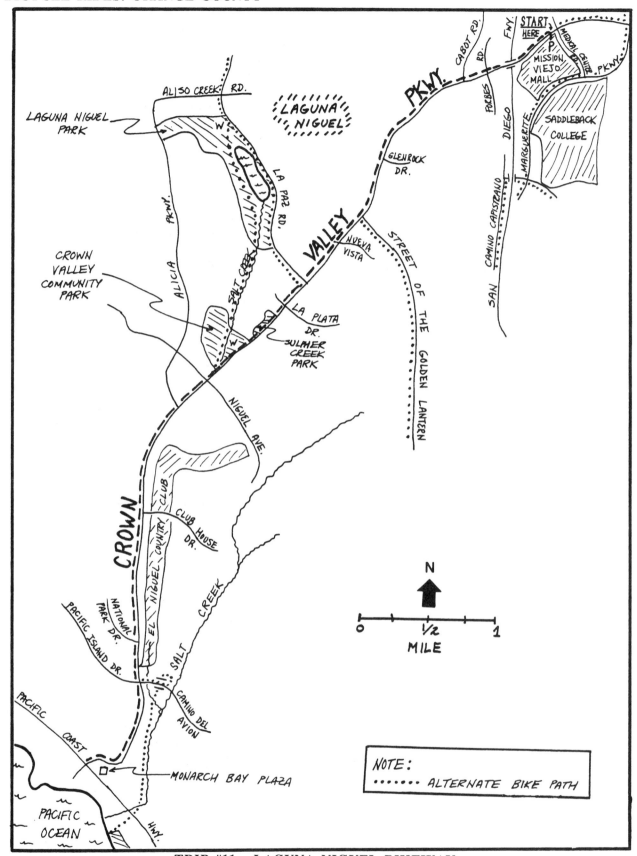

TRIP #11 - LAGUNA NIGUEL BIKEWAY

There are also two excellent spur trips off of the main Class II Crown Valley Pkwy. route. One spur is a hilly workout on the lightly used Street of the Golden Lantern, the other is a Class I hillside route that winds alongside a golf course and lets out at Salt Creek Beach Park.

TRAILHEAD: From the San Diego Fwy., exit east on Crown Valley Pkwy, and proceed about 1/2 mile to Medical Center Rd. (El Regateo to the north). Turn right (south) and find parking within the Mission Viejo Mall.

Bring a moderate water supply and plan to resupply at Crown Valley Community Park near the one-way midpoint.

TRIP DESCRIPTION: Mission Viejo. Exit the Mission Viejo Mall and turn left (west) on Crown Valley Pkwy. For the next 1/4 mile the path remains alongside the mall, heading downhill through pleasant, grassy surroundings. Just beyond the passage over the San Diego Fwy. (0.2), the surrounding territory begins to transition to a drier, less developed look which is more representative of the upcoming journey. The route passes Forbes Rd., crosses over Oso Creek (0.3), then begins to leave "civilization" just beyond Cabot Rd. (0.5).

The Foothills. The path heads uphill reaching the top of the upgrade in about another 0.5 mile. There is a nice view out of the small canyon, back toward Mission Viejo proper, of the distant mountains and foothills. The route continues through this open, exposed, hilly section with dry hills on both sides, passing Glenrock Dr. (1.4), and heading downhill to the Street of the Golden Lantern (1.8). There is a spur trip up this roadway which starts with a steep, steady 0.8 mile upgrade and continues another mile on a new, lightly used road. The area beyond the first 0.5 mile is under residential development and is open and exposed. However, there are some nice views into the hills and canyons, particularly near Sweet Meadow.

Laguna Niguel. In another 0.2 mile, the route passes Nueva Vista where there are new residential developments in the hills to the right (northwest) and a small shopping center to the left. The route passes Adelanto Dr. (2.2), continuing uphill to La Paz Rd., and follows a long downgrade past La Plata to Sulfer Creek Park (2.8). In another 0.3 mile is Crown Valley Community Park. This is a nice shade park with water and restrooms, which is a great place for a rest break. The bike route continues downhill to Niguel Rd. (3.5) and flattens out, reaching Alicia Pkwy. in another 0.3 mile. In this 0.3 mile is a multitude of places to stop and snack, including "The Village" and the Crown Valley Mall.

The hilly route starts uphill just north of Alicia Pkwy. and the surroundings change from one of dry interior to more coastal and treed. The road curves to the south in this area. The tree-lined route reaches the top of the grade at a point above the El Niguel Country Club and Golf Course (4.0). The route "roller coasters" by Club House Dr. (4.4), Laguna Woods Dr. (4.7), and passes through a section with nice views into the surrounding hills. The roadway meets Camino Del Avion (east)/Pacific Island Dr. (west) at (5.6).

Spur Trip to Salt Creek Beach. There is an exceptional spur trip off of Camino Del Avion. Turn east and bike 0.2 mile past a small bridge over Arroyo Salada Creek. Find the bikepath just off of the north side of the road that heads on a steep downgrade under that bridge. There is a great view to the ocean and surrounding territory at this point. The Class I path continues another 1.3 miles down a winding canyon path alongside "The Links at Monarch Bay" Golf Course, passing under Pacific Coast Highway (PCH), and ending at Salt Creek Beach.

Spur Trail to Salt Creek Beach

The Coast. However, our reference route continues on a workout upgrade to a crest at (6.1). As a diversion, cross the roadway for a fine vista that takes in a wide coastal area. Crown Valley Pkwy. begins a long steep descent from this crest with periodic "peeks" at the ocean. In 0.3 mile, the route passes the Monarch Bay Plaza entrance and in onother 0.1 mile, meets PCH (6.5). A half-mile to the north is Mussel Cove and Three Arch Bay.

CONNECTING TRIPS: 1) Connection with the Mission Viejo Bikeway (Trip #30) - from the Mission Viejo Mall, turn right (east) on Crown Valley Pkwy., continue about 1/2 mile to Marguerite Pkwy. and turn left (north);
2) connection with the Aliso Creek Trail/Bikeway (Trip #29) - Option A: Exit Crown Valley Pkwy. at La Paz Rd. or, Option B: Exit Crown Valley Pkwy. at Crown Valley Community Park and ride north on the bike trail.

TRIP #12 - DOHENY BIKEWAY

GENERAL LOCATION: Mission Viejo, San Juan Capistrano

LEVEL OF DIFFICULTY: One way - easy; up and back - easy to moderate
Distance - 6.9 miles (one way)
Elevation gain - essentially flat

GENERAL DESCRIPTION: This is a pleasant trip on predominately Class I and Class II bikeways along Oso and San Juan Creeks. Included in the trip is a segment which passes near historic San Juan Capistrano Mission and a terminus at lovely Doheny State Beach. The route starts at the southern edge of Mission Viejo and cruises the periphery of Laguna Niguel, then visits San Juan Capistrano, Dana Point, and Capistrano Beach. There are several nice parks for rest spots on the lower half of the trip.

TRAILHEAD: From the San Diego Fwy., exit at Avery Pkwy. One option is to drive west a short distance to the end of Avery Pkwy., turn left (south) and find parking on Camino Capistrano. A second option is to drive east on Alicia Pkwy., cross Marguerite Pkwy., and proceed about 0.2 mile to Los Ondas Ave. Turn left and drive 0.1 mile to Coronado Park.

Bring a moderate water supply. There are water stops at the gas station at the Avery Pkwy. terminus and at several parks along the way.

TRIP DESCRIPTION: **Camino Capistrano.** From Coronado Park, return to Class II Alicia Pkwy. and bike on a steep downhill past Plata Dr. (an entrance to Saddleback College) to Marguerite Pkwy. (0.2). Continue on a short Class X stretch across Alicia Pkwy. and turn left (south) at that street's terminus. Proceed south on Camino Capistrano past numerous roadside businesses and fast food stops into a more open countryside (0.5). Here the route clearly becomes Class II.

For the next couple of miles, the surrounding scenery is the hills to the right (west) and the San Diego Fwy. to the left. The route passes the Rancho Capistrano Cemetery (0.7), orange groves, a crossing over the Arroyo Trabuco (1.4), Junipero Serra Rd. (2.3), Oso Rd., and then reaches the northern end of El Camino Real Park (2.7).

El Camino Real Park and Oso Creek. The Class I bikepath travels along the edge of this shaded park. There are park benches, tables, and restrooms. About 1/4 mile further down Camino Capistrano is Mission San Juan Capistrano. However, the marked bike route turns right (west) at La Zanja (Spanish pasta?) St. and proceeds a short distance to a terminus at Avenida De La Vista (3.3). Turn left onto this Class III route and bike through residential neighborhood to a cul-de-sac (3.5).

55

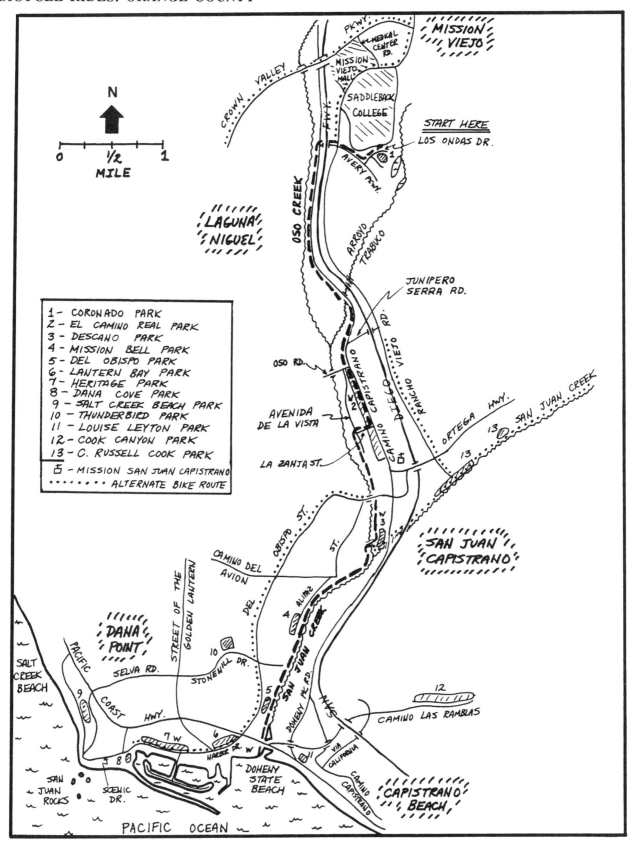

TRIP #12 - DOHENY BIKEWAY

Bike onto the small path that leads to Oso Creek. That Class I bikeway follows the cement-walled creek into a more open valley-like area, passes Del Obispo St. (4.0), and then cruises along a light industrial area to the left (east). In a short distance, the route passes along convenient Descanso Park with its shade trees, grassy rest area, restrooms and water (4.4) and reaches the west side of San Juan Creek.

San Juan Creek. Just beyond, the route crosses the creek on a little bikeway/walkway. This is just upstream of the point where Oso Creek and San Juan Creek joins and takes the name of the latter. There is a long distance view down the creek just beyond this point with a good look at the foothills to the east and west. The bikepath meets several entry points at Via Mistral and beyond (5.0-5.2) and passes alongside Mission Bell Park (5.5). There are additional bike entries at (5.9-6.0) and an increasing housing density along the path. The route passes a large group of condominiums and later the entry to Del Obispo Park (6.5).

Doheny State Beach. Just beyond is a purification plant that has a gas burnoff nozzle that is next to the bikeway (bring hot dogs!). In a short distance, the route passes under Pacific Coast Highway (PCH). There is a stretch here that is sometimes flooded; to reach the ocean requires a backtrack to the nearest entry point. Travel west to Del Obispo and take that street across PCH to the main park entrance.

If the path is not flooded, continue on the trail alongside the marshland (frequently there are ducks in this area). Stop near the beach and enjoy the sweeping view, particularly south (6.9). Finally, take a leisurely spin through Doheny State Beach Park. There are picnic and barbecue areas, shade, water, beach, concession stands, and generally, plenty of people.

CONNECTING TRIPS: 1) Continuation with the Del Obispo Bikeway (Trip #13) - return to the main entrance of Doheny State Beach/Park and turn right (north) at Dana Point Harbor Dr. Continue north across PCH; 2) continuation with the Doheny/San Clemente Bike Route (Trip #14) - from Doheny State Beach/Park, follow the frontage road along PCH south towards Capistrano Beach.

TRIP #13 - DEL OBISPO BIKEWAY

GENERAL LOCATION: San Juan Capistrano - Dana Point

LEVEL OF DIFFICULTY: Loop - moderate
Distance - 17.2 miles (loop)
Elevation gain - periodic light upgrades;
single short, steep upgrade

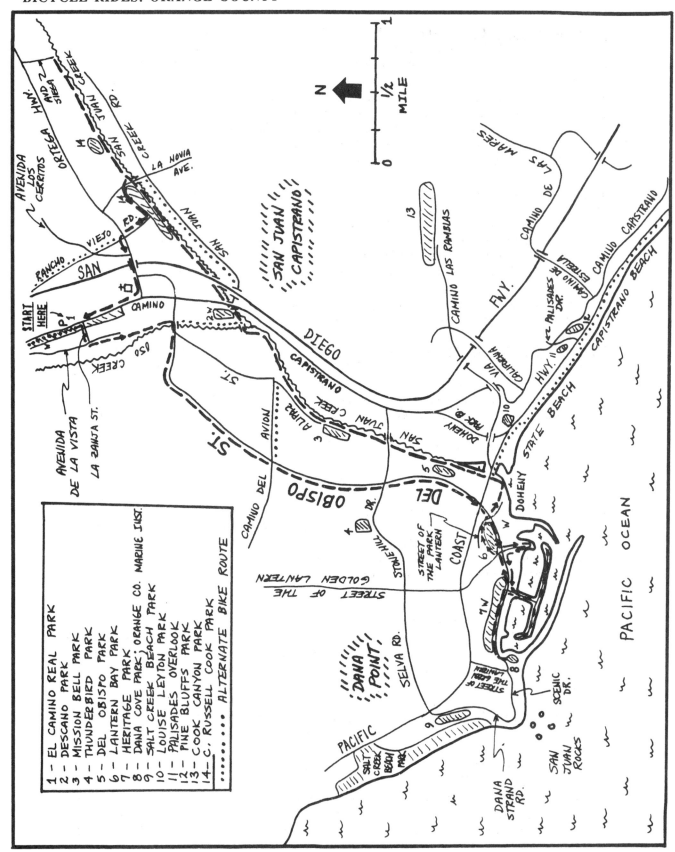

LEGEND

1 – EL CAMINO REAL PARK
2 – DESCANSO PARK
3 – MISSION BELL PARK
4 – THUNDERBIRD PARK
5 – DEL OBISPO PARK
6 – LANTERN BAY PARK
7 – HERITAGE PARK
8 – DANA COVE PARK; ORANGE CO. MARINE INST.
9 – SALT CREEK BEACH PARK
10 – LOUISE LEYTON PARK
11 – PALISADES OVERLOOK
12 – PINE BLUFFS PARK
13 – COOK CANYON PARK
14 – C. RUSSELL COOK PARK
•••• – ALTERNATE BIKE ROUTE

TRIP #13 - DEL OBISPO BIKEWAY

GENERAL DESCRIPTION: This is a "must do" adventure! The outbound leg of this trip is built around the Del Obispo Bikeway with an alternate return leg provided for variety. Most of the trip is on Class I or Class II bikeway. Far and away, the highlight of the trip is the Dana Point Harbor tour at the end of the outbound leg. The route also passes next to Mission San Juan Capistrano. In addition, there is a pleasant cruise on Del Obispo St., several park visits, and a tour into the "far reaches" of San Juan Creek. There are some fine scenic views from atop Lantern Bay Park and some super-duper views from a very strenuous spur trip off Scenic Dr.

TRAILHEAD: From the San Diego Fwy., exit at Ortega Hwy. and head west about 1/4 mile to Camino Capistrano. Turn right (north) and continue 1/4 mile to El Camino Real Park. Find a turn-around point north of La Zanja St. and park alongside the park. From Pacific Coast Hwy. (PCH), turn north at Del Obispo St. (Dana Point Harbor Dr. to the south) and continue 0.5 mile to El Camino Real Park. Park on the opposite side of the street next to the park.

Bring a moderate water supply. There are shopping centers and parks with water scattered about this bike route.

TRIP DESCRIPTION: **Oso Creek.** Ride south and turn right (west) on La Zanja St. Follow the marked Class III route a short distance to Avenida De La Vista and turn left (south). Continue about 0.2 mile through a residential neighborhood (do not even think about that private swimming pool you see along the roadway!) to a cul-de-sac (0.4). Bike onto a small path that leads to Oso Creek. Follow the creek about 0.4 mile on a Class I path and exit at Del Obispo St., heading right (southwest) (0.8).

Del Obispo St. The Class II bike route cruises through an open residential area, passing Alipaz St. and Paseo Terraza (1.2). The roadway curves southward and follows a light upgrade just beyond. There are nearby hills with residences to the right (west) and more distant hills to the left. This type of scenary continues for more than a mile. The route passes Christian Farmer's Market (1.8), Via Del Avion (2.2), and Blue Fin Dr. (2.6). The residential density increases on both sides of the street beyond this point.

In 0.4 mile, the path crosses Stonehill Dr., passing a large shopping center. At (3.5), the route meets Quail Run, where there is a large new condominium community across the road and an entry into Del Obispo Park just beyond. At (3.9) is the busy PCH intersection with its collection of small eateries.

Dana Point Harbor. After crossing PCH, the route becomes Dana Point Harbor Dr. (referred to as Harbor Dr.), passing the Doheny State Park main entrance (left) and the Street of the Park Lantern, with its steep road entry to Lantern Bay Park. Our route continues on Class II Harbor Dr. and passes below the steep bluffs to the landward side of the road. Turn left toward the harbor on the Street of the Golden Lantern (a bike ride on a street with this name has got to be exotic!) (4.3). Proceed to the wharf area and eyeball the numerous pleasure craft tied up there. A short tour to the westernmost edge of the wharf area leads to Proud Mary's, a delightful cafe with outdoor seating under sun umbrellas and a fine harbor view.

59

Return to the boat slips and proceed west on the sidewalk alongside the harbor. Turn left onto Island Way (5.2) and bike on the bridge over to the central island in the harbor. At the island entrance is the Dana Statue, which sits in the middle of a long, thin park on the island's seaward side. The park has benches, grass, barbecue facilities, little roofed picnic shelters, water and restrooms. Grab a bench and watch the boats sail the harbor.

Dana Point Harbor

A tour to the east leads to Delany's Restaurant and the Harbor Patrol Building. There is a nice southward view from the eastern edge of the island (5.9). Heading back across Island Way to the western edge of the island, the biker has a view of the fisherman on the breakwater and a super view west and north to the seaside bluffs (6.7). The route recrosses the harbor on Island Way and returns to Harbor Dr. at (7.3).

Turn left and pass pleasant Heritage Park. The park has all the amenities of the park on the island plus trees, recreation/play area, and a bonafied windsurfer area. The route leads to Dana Cove and the foot of Cove Rd. (7.8). This is an extremely steep road that leads up to some great vista points on Scenic Dr.

Continue on Harbor Dr. and pass the Orange Co. Marine Institute. Visit the old sailing ship docked there. The Harbor Dr. route ends just beyond, at the beginning of the outer breakwater. One can walk onto the breakwater or hike northward along the tight coves from this point.

Lantern Bay Park. Return to the Street of the Golden Lantern (9.0). At the northeast corner of the intersection, follow the short, steep Class I switchback trail up to Lantern Bay Park. There is a 360-degree view from the top of the bluff that takes in the hills to the east, harbor to the south, homes on the bluffs to the west (including a wedding chapel) and condomania to the north. Continue along the south edge of the park on the bikeway/walkway to the Smyth Amphitheater (9.3). This is a mini-amphitheater with a nice scenic view. There was a wedding here on the Saturday we passed through, complete with picolo players in tuxedos!

San Juan Creek. Continue to the Street of the Park Lantern and follow that steep roadway downhill past a restroom to the intersection with Harbor Blvd. Cross the street into the Doheny State Beach/Park entrance and follow the path nearest the beach to the San Juan Creek outlet (9.8).

Stay to the west side of the creek and continue north under PCH. The route passes the entrance to Del Obispo Park (10.3) and then continues uninterrupted along San Juan Creek past the Mission Bell Park entrance (11.1). In another 1.2 miles, the path crosses a bike bridge over Oso Creek just north of the creek junction. There is small Descanso Park dead ahead with shade, grass, water and restrooms.

The bikepath branches at this juncture, left along Oso Creek, and right along San Juan Creek. Take the right branch, passing under Camino Capistrano (12.6) and riding along a wide, green, natural riverbed on continued Class I bikeway. In 0.4 mile is the Paseo Triador cul-de-sac. Follow that road to Calle Arroyo and turn right onto a Class II bikepath. Look for a small walkway/bikeway off to the right that runs through C. Russell Cook Park paralleling Calle Arroyo (13.2). This park path travels beyond a condominium-type development and passes an equestrian staging area and Rancho Viejo Rd. (13.6).

The path jogs to the left (north) at La Novia Ave. and continues as Class I trail along the creek. There is heavy residential development to the north and open fields across the creek to the south. There are horse trails which parallel the bikepath and several bike entry points in this area (13.8, 14.1). At (14.2) the route passes near the unconnected east segment of C. Russel Cook Park, a small shady playground area. In 0.3 mile, the route skirts an athletic field and returns to Calle Arroyo at Via Estenaga. The bikeway passes a large area of horse stables and ends at Avd. Siega (14.8).

Mission San Juan Capistrano. Return to Rancho Viejo Rd. (16.0), turn right, and ride 0.3 mile to Ortega Hwy. This is a short 0.4 mile Class X segment that requires careful biking because of fast-moving traffic. At Ortega Hwy. and Camino Capistrano, turn right (north) and pass Mission San Juan Capistrano. Continue another 0.5 mile to the parking area (17.2).

CONNECTING TRIPS: 1) Connection with the Doheny Bikeway (Trip #12) - at the Descano Park junction, take the westernmost bike trail along Oso Creek; 2) connection with the Doheny/San Clemente Bike Route (Trip #14) - follow the roadway from the Doheny State Beach/Park entrance over San Juan Creek and link up with the bikeway heading south along the beach.

TRIP #14 - DOHENY/SAN CLEMENTE BIKE ROUTE

GENERAL LOCATION: Dana Point - San Clemente

LEVEL OF DIFFICULTY: Round trip - moderate
Distance - 17.1 miles (round trip)
Elevation gain - periodic moderate grades

GENERAL DESCRIPTION: This trip is a mix between a beach route and a city tour. The first half of the trip follows Pacific Coast Highway (PCH) and provides numerous views of surf and sand. The second half of the trip is a loop tour through the heart of San Clemente on El Camino Real (ECR). The return trip includes an alternate return leg on a number of connecting residential roadways.

The highlights of the tour are Doheny State Beach and Capistrano Beach Park near the trip origin, the San Clemente city tour in general, and the pleasant beach at San Mateo Point at the trip's southernmost point. The route is a mix of Class I, Class II, and Class III biking. There are some moderate rolling hills in the San Clemente area and some segments of ECR where there is very limited bike room.

TRAILHEAD: From the San Diego Fwy., exit west on Camino Las Rambles and continue until that roadway fuses with PCH. Continue about 1/4 mile to Dana Point Harbor Dr. (named Del Obispo St. at the northern end of the intersection) and turn left. Continue a short distance and turn left into Doheny State Beach Park. A free parking alternative is to drive up the hill across from the park gate entrance and park at Lantern Bay Park. That roadway is named the Street of the Park Lantern.

Bring a moderate water supply. There are scattered public water sources as noted on the trip map, and other sources such as gas stations in the city proper.

TRIP DESCRIPTION: **Doheny State Beach.** Follow the entrance road south which becomes a frontage road alongside PCH and passes over San Juan Creek. Follow the path to the right which passes alongside a camping area and then enters the north end of Doheny State Beach (0.3). This pleasant stretch has clear ocean views and passes directly alongside the sunbathing area (get my drift?). The Class I path parallels the beach, passes through Capistrano Beach Park, and exits at Beach Rd. (1.1) where it then follows PCH on a Class II path.

Pacific Coast Highway - El Camino Real. The next 1.7 miles is along a stretch of highway with low bluffs to the east and rows of bushes which block the sea view to the west. At this point, PCH meets Camino Capistrano where a nice ocean view opens back up. The road name becomes El Camino Real at this point.

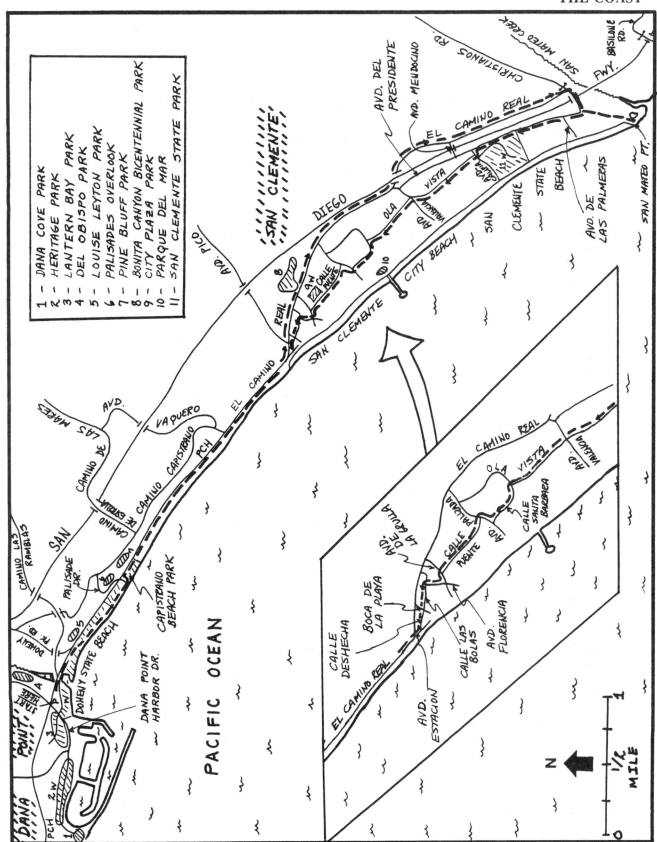

TRIP #14 - DOHENY/ SAN CLEMENTE BIKE ROUTE

There is a small shopping center to the east and a snack bar on the beachfront (2.8). The route returns to the surrounding cliffs for another 0.6 mile, then enters the San Clemente City limits at Avd. Estacion.

The route changes to Class III at this juncture. Shortly, the bikepath begins a long, steady upgrade through a heavy trafficked commercial district (4.1). There are portions of the next two miles where bike room on ECR is very restricted. The uphill passes the entry to Bonita Canyon Centennial Park at El Portal (4.6), levels out somewhat, passes Avd. Palizada, and crests near Avd. Del Mar (5.1). There is a view of the lovely hillside residential community from this area. After another more moderate upgrade, the path reaches its highest point near Paseo De Cristobal (5.7).

In 0.2 mile at Avd. Valencia, the road splits into ECR and Avd. Del Presidente. Our route forks left on ECR and passes under the San Diego Fwy. (6.0). This entire section to the PCH terminus is more residential, has lighter traffic, and more bike room (this section is Class II quality, but not marked). The bikepath parallels the freeway on small rolling hills with predominantly downhill riding. ECR passes Avd. Mendocino (6.5) and reaches it's terminus at Christianos Rd. (8.0).

San Mateo Point. The trip route follows Christianos Rd. west over the San Diego Fwy. Just beyond the southbound on-ramp is a small path/roadway entrance that is blocked to automobiles. Follow that route south and downhill 0.3 mile and take the junction west at that point (the southbound bikeway continues on to the south gate of Camp Pendleton). Follow this junction path another 0.4 mile to a lovely and lightly used beach and a fine overlook/vista near San Mateo Point (8.7). If your timing is right, you may even see one of the high-speed AMTRAK passenger trains pass by on the elevated railway near the beach.

Avd. Del Presidente. Return to Christianos Rd. and turn left (toward the ocean). This is the terminus (or origin) of Avd. Del Presidente (9.4). The Class II path heads moderately and generally uphill past Avd. De Las Palmeras (9.7), the entry to a nice private residential area. The road parallels the San Diego Fwy. and continues uphill past Avd. Vista De Oceano (9.9), then passes alongside the north edge of San Clemente State Park. There is a bike entry from this roadway into a large, pleasant, forrested park (with campsites) (10.4). Our route continues along Avd. Del Presidente through rolling hills to Via Califia.

San Vicente Residential Route. One option at this junction is to continue another 0.7 mile on this Class II route on Avd. Del Presidente and turn south on Avd. Valencia. However, our route turns left (south) at Via Califia and in a short distance turns right at Ola Vista, a pleasant, quiet residential street through rolling hills. At Avd. Valencia, our route follows the Pacific Coast Bicentennial Bike Route (11.3). The route (as shown on the detail map) follows in order: Ola Vista, left on Calle Santa Barbara, right on Calle Seville, right on Avd. Palizada, left on Calle Puente, left and downhill on Avd. De La Grulla, right and downhill on Avd. Florencia, left on Calle Los Bolas, left on Boca De La Playa, right on Calle Deshecha, and right on Avd. Estacion, returning to ECR (13.7).

Along the way, the bike route passes markets near Avd. Santa Barbara and Avd. Victoria. It also passes the road access to the Municipal Pier on Avd. Del Mar near Calle Seville, and a nice rest and water stop at City Plaza Park along Calle Puente.

El Camino Real - Pacific Coast Highway. The return route is Class III along ECR until the automobile roadway narrows to one lane and the bike lane expands. The path remains Class II until the left turn entry at Beach Rd. back into San Clemente Beach Park (16.0). The path repeats the outgoing route in reverse and returns to Doheny State Beach (17.1).

<u>CONNECTING TRIPS</u>: 1) Connection with the Doheny Bikeway (Trip #12) - from Doheny State Beach, bike to the outlet of San Juan Creek and follow the bikepath on the north side of that creek; 2) connection with the Del Obispo Bikeway (Trip #13) - return to the Doheny State Beach entrance, turn right (north) on Dana Point Harbor Dr. and continue across PCH; 3) continuation with the San Clemente to San Diego ride (Trip #16) - continue south beyond the San Mateo Point turnoff discussed in this trip text.

TRIP #15 - NEWPORT BEACH/CORONA DEL MAR TOUR

<u>GENERAL LOCATION</u>: Newport Beach - Corona Del Mar

<u>LEVEL OF DIFFICULTY</u>: Round trip - moderate
Distance - 10.1 miles (round trip)
Elevation gain - periodic moderate grades

<u>GENERAL DESCRIPTION</u>: This is a fine coastal tour that provides a number of vistas and other scenic attractions. This is a mixed class route with a significant amount of Class X on relatively lightly-traveled roadways. The outgoing bikepath travels Pacific Coast Highway (PCH) just north of Lower Newport Bay, then ducks inland to visit Ocean Blvd. on the bluffs above the Corona Del Mar beaches. The return leg is on Bayside Dr. right alongside the bay. There are numerous spur tours into the islands along the bay, the Newport Strand or Upper Newport Bay.

<u>TRAILHEAD</u>: From PCH heading south, continue 0.4 mile beyond the Newport Blvd. overpass and turn left at Tustin Ave. Continue to Avon St., turn right (east) and continue about one block to free public parking. From PCH heading north, continue about 1.1 miles beyond Dover Rd. and turn right at Tustin Ave. Continue as described above.

Bring a moderate water supply. There is water on Ocean Blvd. near the trip mid point.

65

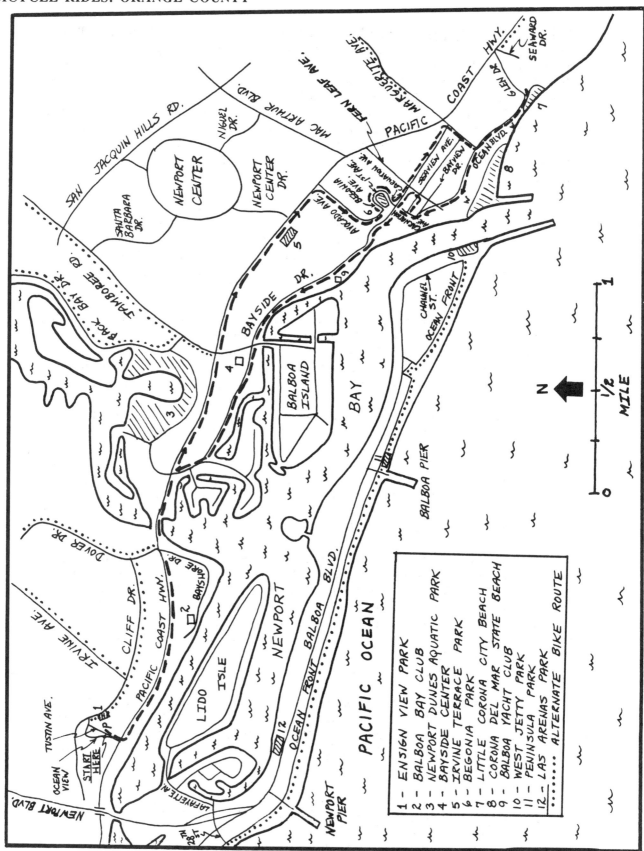

1 - ENSIGN VIEW PARK
2 - BALBOA BAY CLUB
3 - NEWPORT DUNES AQUATIC PARK
4 - BAYSIDE CENTER
5 - IRVINE TERRACE PARK
6 - BEGONIA PARK
7 - LITTLE CORONA CITY BEACH
8 - CORONA DEL MAR STATE BEACH
9 - BALBOA YACHT CLUB
10 - WEST JETTY PARK
11 - PENINSULA PARK
12 - LAS ARENAS PARK
····· ALTERNATE BIKE ROUTE

TRIP #15 - NEWPORT BEACH/ CORONA DEL MAR TOUR

TRIP DESCRIPTION: **Pacific Coast Highway/ Lower Newport Bay.**
To start the trip, walk up the steps just north of the parking area and enjoy the vista from Ensign View Park. Next, bike back to PCH and turn left (east). The next half-mile is Class X and best spent riding very carefully on PCH or using the wide sidewalks if the car traffic gets tough. The path soon becomes Class II. The route passes the exclusive Balboa Bay Club (0.8) and a nice view of Fashion Island in the distance opens up directly ahead. In 0.3 mile, the path crosses Bayshore Dr. Just beyond, the path reaches the bridge over Newport Bay. There is a diversion under the bridge which takes the biker to Dover Dr. on the opposite side of PCH.

Cross the bridge on the sidewalk or on the Class II path on PCH. There is a fine view from the bridge, including a chance to look from the top down onto boats passing under. The Reuben E. Lee (sternwheeler) floating restaurant is docked near the bridge on the east end. The path crosses Bayside Dr. (1.8) and starts uphill. Near the crest, there is a grand view of Upper Newport Bay and Newport Dunes Aquatic Park (2.2)

Next the route passes private Promentory Dr., then Jamboree Rd. In this tree-lined section of bikeway, the biker has a choice of using the marked sidewalk path or the Class II bikeway on PCH; this option continues for about 0.5 mile. The bikepath crosses Malabar Dr. (an access to cozy Irvine Terrace Park) (3.0), then Newport Center Dr. which is one of several entrances to Fashion Island (3.3). Continue 0.2 mile and turn right (south) on Avocado Ave. This is the beginning of a Class X segment on lightly-traveled roadway which continues up to the loop return to PCH.

Corona Del Mar. In 0.2 mile, at the start of a small upgrade, cross the road and ride up the sidewalk in this short, one-way section. The road curves left and becomes Pacific Dr., continues a short distance, curves right and becomes Begonia Ave. (3.9). There is a park bench here and a fine view down a small canyon to the ocean.

Just beyond, the route swings around Begonia Park (Begonia Ave., right on First St., right on Carnation Ave.). Begonia Park appears to be the home of the Itsy-Bitsy Bathing Suit Frisbee Throwers Society (I.B.S.F.T.S.)! Continue downhill on Carnation Ave. and turn left (southwest) at Bayside Dr. (4.1). To the right are bluffs and an overlook to be visited later. Continue another 0.5 mile with some uphill through a residential neighborhood and turn right on Marguerite Ave. Bike 0.2 mile to Ocean Blvd. and the highlight segment of the trip (4.8).

Ocean Blvd. Turn left (southwest) on Ocean Blvd. and continue 0.2 mile to a small grassy vista point that has a fabulous overlook of Corona Del Mar State Beach, the Newport Harbor breakwater and beyond. There is a water fountain here. Continue another 0.2 mile to the end of Ocean Blvd. at Poppy Ave. There is an equally fine view into Little Corona City Beach and southward. Return to Marguerite Ave. (5.5) and continue past Jasmine Ave., the entry to the state beach. In another 0.1 mile is Heliotrope Ave. with a grassy overlook point which is directly above hillside residences. Just beyond is another mini-park (with water fountain) and another pretty vista point. From here, there is an excellent view down the breakwater and into Lower Newport Bay (5.8).

Just beyond, Ocean Blvd. fuses into Bayview Dr. which turns right and becomes Carnation Ave. Continue down to the end of this street for an interesting overlook of the harbor, Begonia Park and Carnation Ave. (6.1). The two Carnation Ave. segments used to be at the same level until that "terrible quake of '38" (just kidding!). Backtrack to Seaview Ave., then turn left on Fern Leaf Ave. and follow a steep downhill to Bayside Dr.

Bayside Drive. Turn left (northwest) (6.4) and cruise downhill a short distance on a tight roadway with the coastal bluffs to the right. The first view of the marina is at (7.1), followed by a transition back to a residential area (7.3), then a return to a marina setting near the classy looking Bahia Corinthian Yacht Club. The area returns to residential as the route passes Jamboree Rd. (7.7), and in 0.2 mile reaches the Bayside Shopping Center. The palm-tree surrounded Gladstones 4 Fish Restuarant, with its unique exterior, is tucked away at the shopping center edge.

The bike route passes alongside a canal with the lovely Balboa Island homes, each with its own boatslip, across the water. In 0.3 mile is the Balboa Yacht Basin road entry and at (8.5) the route returns to PCH. Continue across the bridge and carefully ride the narrow Class X segment back to Tustin Ave. and the starting point (10.1).

CONNECTING TRIPS: 1) Connection with the Sunset Beach to Newport Beach Strand tour (Trip #4) - continue northwest past Tustin on PCH and take the southside walkway up to Newport Blvd. Cross the bridge and continue to Ocean Front; 2) connection with the Upper Newport Bay ride and Newport Beach Tour (Trips #6 and #7, respectively) - turn north on Jamboree Rd. and continue 1/4 mile to Back Bay Dr.; 3) connection with the Laguna Beach Tour (Trip #10) - from the end of Ocean Blvd., continue on Poppy Dr., turn left at Glen Dr. and continue to PCH.

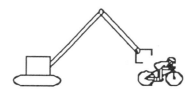

TRIP #16 - SAN CLEMENTE TO SAN DIEGO

GENERAL LOCATION   San Clemente, Camp Pendleton, Oceanside, Carlsbad, La Jolla, San Diego

LEVEL OF DIFFICULTY One way - strenuous
Distance - 67.2 miles (one way)
Elevation gain - periodic moderate-to-steep grades; sheer grade at Torrey Pines State Reserve

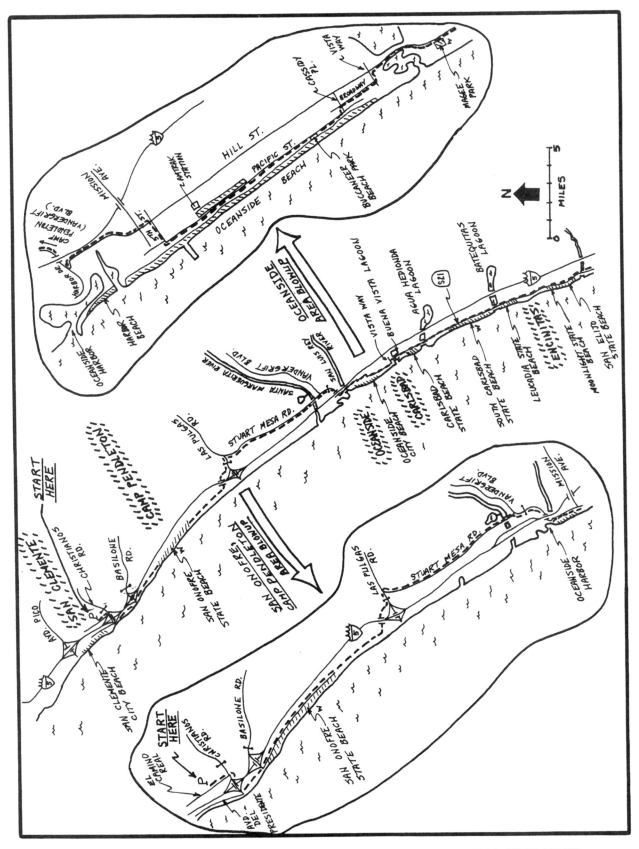

TRIP #16 - SAN CLEMENTE TO SAN DIEGO (NORTHERN SEGMENT)

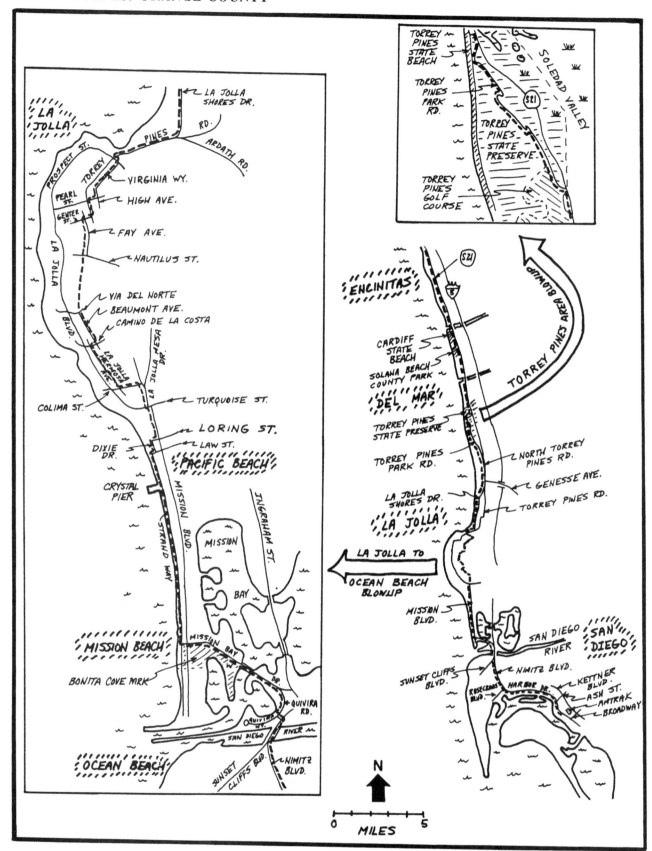

TRIP #16 - SAN CLEMENTE TO SAN DIEGO (SOUTHERN SEGMENT)

GENERAL DESCRIPTION: Few trips that we've ridden have the variety and natural scenic beauty of this coastal tour. The entire route described follows the Pacific Coast Bicentennial Route with most of the route on Class I and Class II roadway. This classic visits the seaside bluffs of San Onofre State Beach, the hilly roads through Camp Pendleton, and cruises along the beaches of cities from Oceanside to Del Mar. Next is a breathtaking scenic ride into the Torrey Pines State Beach area followed by a breathtaking (huff-puff) sheer climb into the lovely woodlands of the Torrey Pines State Reserve. The trip winds up with a brief La Jolla city tour, a pedal on the periphery of both Mission Bay and San Diego Bay, and ends near the Cruise Ship Terminal area of San Diego proper.

There is an option to start this trip from Santa Ana or Oceanside and take the AMTRAK on the return leg. Refer to the detailed trip description.

TRAILHEAD: From the San Diego Fwy. exit at Christianos Rd. and drive north of the freeway to El Camino Real. Find parking subject to local traffic laws. If an over-night trip is planned, do not park on El Camino Real; an option is to park in a nearby residential area.

Bring a couple of filled water bottles, particularly on hot days. There are scattered public water sources at parks and commercial businesses along the route.

TRIP DESCRIPTION: San Onofre. Return to Christianos Rd. and pedal to the Class I trail entry just west of the southbound freeway on-ramp. Follow the Class I road along the rolling terrain of the oceanside bluffs. In one mile, the route passes through a fence and follows a Class II frontage road, then crosses over the northernmost Camp Pendleton entry at Basilone Rd. The path continues on a bridge over the railroad tracks (2.5), passes the main entrance of the San Onofre power generating station, and reaches the entry to San Onofre State Beach (4.0).

For the next three miles, the bicycle path bee-lines through the park, passing RV's, tent campers, canyon hiking trails to the beach, and numerous water and restroom stops. If time permits, hike down one of the marked, scenic canyon trails. At the park's southern end, pass through the motorized vehicle barrier and bike on the Class I section of old Hwy. 1.

Camp Pendleton. Continue along the top of the ocean bluffs, pass below an automobile vista point, and follow the path through a tunnel under the freeway (9.3). For the next 1-1/2 miles, the Class I roadway passes through flat and arid terrain with the freeway fading in the distance. This stretch provides the feeling of real isolation (barring the numerous passing bikers). At trail's end, turn left at Las Pulgas Rd. and check in at the Camp Pendleton entrance gate (11.2). Just beyond the gate, turn right onto Stuart Mesa Rd., pass Camp Flores (Boy Scouts of America) in one-half mile, and stay on Stuart Mesa Rd. by turning right.

The next three miles is in rolling hills with a particularly tough upgrade near the end of this stretch. In the middle section, the road passes the main Los Flores area at Nelson Dr. (Avoid the menacing tank parked there!)

Pass the road to the Cook overcrossing and stay to the right at the intersection with Hammond Rd. (16.1). Pedal past the large fields of cultivated flowers, continue alongside a canyon on a steep downgrade, pass the surrounding salt marches, and then pump an equally steep upgrade to the Stuart Mesa Rd. intersection with Vandergrift Blvd. (19.1). Turn right on the latter street and bike a one-mile upgrade of varying levels of steepness to Wire Mountain Rd. Pass that street, exit the Camp Pendleton main gate, cross San Rafael Dr., and continue under the freeway (20.7).

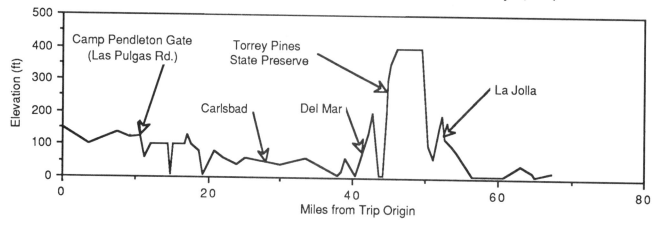

Oceanside. The street name is now Harbor Dr. At the first intersection turn hard left and bike up to Class II Hill St. (the prettier but less direct route is to follow the winding Harbor Dr. to Pacific St. and turn left), continue 0.8 mile to 6th St. and cross the railroad tracks. Pedal to Pacific St. and turn left. Bike on that Class III road (including the southward jig-jog at 5th St) through a coastal residential community. There are periodic views of the nearby beach plus cozy little Buccaneer Beach Park.

Turn left on Cassidy St., right on Broadway, left again on Vista Way (all are Class III), and right again on Class II Hill St. (25.1). This set of maneuvers occurs over a short 0.6-mile stretch, but serves to avoid a busy Hill St. segment. This is the beginning of a 16-mile stretch on California Hwy. S21. Cross Buena Vista Lagoon, the first of several scenic lagoons on this trip segment, and enter Carlsbad.

Carlsbad to Del Mar. Pass Magee Park (water), and cruise an area with several popular, but contrasting, dining establishments (posh Neimans, quaint Ollie's Oyster Bar, and Norby's:Danish Bakers with outdoor dining). In a short distance is the entrance to Carlsbad State Beach. Pass Tamarack Ave. and enter an area with the fisherman working the Agua Hedionda Lagoon to the left and sunbathers and surfers doing their thing on the ocean side. The scenery in the southern Carlsbad area is exceptional, particularly because the bikeway is directly on the oceanfront.

The road passes Cannon Park at Cannon Rd., then Palomar Airport Rd., and continues alongside South Carlsbad State Beach (water, restrooms, camp sites) for the next 2-1/2 miles. The main entry to this beautiful beach is at Poinsettia Ln. Pass across picturesque Batiquitos Lagoon and enter Leucadia as the tree-lined road turns inland. Pass a series of inviting lunch stops and deli's, Leucadia Blvd. (33.6), Leucadia Park (with water), and enter Encinitas.

The Class II road passes the Moonlight State Beach entry at Encinitas Blvd., Kypling's Restaurant in the Lumberyard (with a delightful music band playing outdoors when we passed through), and the palacial Indian grounds of Swamis City Park. Hwy. S21 returns to the beachfront and passes San Elijo State Beach (water) at Cardiff-by-the-Sea. There is an exceptional view of the coastal cliffs to the south from this area. The bikeway is two-way, Class II, although there is Class I path on the opposite side of the street.

Continue on the bridge over the expansive San Elijo Lagoon with Cardiff State Beach on the opposite side. Follow a short upgrade away from the ocean to Solana Beach. We couldn't resist stopping at the Coast Carbo Station ("Power Sandwiches" and "Energy Drinks") along the highway. Cross over the lagoon created by the San Dieguito River, take in the post card view of the Del Mar Racetrack just inland, and enter the city of Del Mar (40.5).

South Del Mar, Highway S21

Just beyond 27th St., start a one-mile upgrade heading inland and enjoy the periodic views of the city below. The grade is steep for a quarter mile, then lessens to a steady, mild uphill. The road passes several posh inns and Del Mar Heights Rd. (42.7), then reaches its high point just beyond.

Now all the work pays off! Follow a steep downgrade that opens up to one of the trip's premier spectacles -- the view across Soledad Valley and lagoon and also the forrested hills of the Torrey Pines State Preserve in the distance. Return to sea level at the gigantic seaside-lagoon play area. Follow the bikeway into Torrey Pines State Beach. (An option is to continue on Hwy. S21 at this point; this option is faster, but far less scenic.)

Torrey Pines State Preserve. Follow a steep upgrade which gets even steeper beyond the first curve. In this segment is some of the most difficult sustained biking that we have done. In 0.6 mile of sheer upgrade is the North Grove area with several foot trails leading into the surrounding forest. Continue a steep uphill through the lovely forrested preserve, then pass the ranger station and a fantastic overlook of La Jolla. Start another upgrade (350 feet elevation gain in the first mile) which soon flattens significantly. The path angles back towards the highway and offers some nice inland views. Pedal along the Torrey Pines Memorial Golf Course and reach the top of this extended pull 1.9 miles from the beach. Return to S21 (North Torrey Pines Rd.) and follow the rolling hills along the golf course past Science Park Rd., the Scripps Clinic, and reach Genesee Ave. (47.0)

La Jolla. Veer right and bike downhill on the Class II tree-lined road. Pass Torrey Pines Scenic Dr. (the turnoff to the San Diego Glider Port and the Salk Institute), bike alongside the University of California, San Diego campus, and in another 0.9 mile turn right again at La Jolla Shores Dr. In 0.6 mile on this Class III road, pass Horizon Way and begin a steep and winding downgrade on the lovely treed highway. There is a fine vista just beyond Horizon Way. The road passes the Scripps Aquarium and Museum and in 0.3 mile reaches a flat (49.7).

In 0.6 mile, turn right at Torrey Pines Rd. and follow a workout Class II uphill for 0.9 mile to the crest at Prospect Pl. Turn left and bike a short, steep uphill to Virginia Way. (The route described for the next 2.6 miles is the low traffic option). The well-marked Class III route passes through a residential neighborhood and in succession turns left on High Ave., right on Pearl St., left on Girard Ave., right on Genter St., left on Fay Ave. and right on Nautilus St. Bike a short distance to a Class I path, continue 3/4-mile on that rural bikeway, and turn left at Beaumont Ave. Pedal to Camino De La Costa, turn right and then left again on La Jolla Hermosa Ave.

Pacific Beach. To reach the beach, turn left on Colima St., right at La Jolla Mesa Dr. (which becomes Mission Blvd.), right on Loring St., left on Dixie Dr., and right on Law St. This places the biker at the northern end of the Class I Strand Way on the ocean (56.4).

Bike south 1.9 miles to Ventura Pl. on this scenic and well-populated path. The strand bikeway passes Crystal Pier and cruises both the Pacific Beach and Mission Beach areas. A word of caution! We arrived at 5:00 pm on Saturday night; we had to leave the super crowded strand (walkers, bikers, skaters, skate boarders, wind surfers ---- OK, just kidding!) and followed the back alley known as Strand Way (58.8).

Mission Bay. Bike on Ventura Pl. past the amusement park and continue east on what is now Mission Bay Dr. Turn left into Bonita Cove Park (water, restrooms, shade, scenic harbor views) and bike on the Class I trail that parallels Mission Bay Dr. to a point just short of the bridge over Mission Bay Channel. Follow the small road up to the bridge. The scenic views from all bridges in this area are exceptional. Reenter the main road and follow the Class II route over the bridge, turning right into Quivira Rd. Bike around Quivira Basin to the junction where the road becomes Quivira Way and turn left onto Sunset Cliffs Blvd.

Ocean Beach to Point Loma. Bike on the bridge over the San Diego River and observe the myraid of bikepaths through the area (60.7). Stay with the fast-moving traffic for the few hundred yards needed to turn left at Nimitz Blvd. (We found no easy or low traffic route to this intersection.)

Follow this Class II divided roadway about two miles through primarily residential territory being very wary of cars entering and exiting Nimitz Blvd. north of Tennyson St. The route turns sharply left at North Harbor Dr. at the Nimitz Blvd. terminus.

San Diego Bay. Pedal on the sidewalk alongside the Fleet Anti-Submarine Warfare School (where in my younger Navy days, I learned that, "A collision at sea can ruin a man's entire day."), then observe the cement-bound U.S.S. Recruit "floating" majestically along the north side of the highway. Pass over the bridge and on the opposite side, follow the Class I bikepath that meanders through the cozy mile-long thread of Spanish Landing Park. There are scattered water and restrooms, tree shade, and benches from which to observe the comings and goings in the bay.

Proceed around the Sheraton Hotel (65.2) and cross Harbor Island Dr., returning to a Class I path along the harbor. Bike alongside the San Diego International Airport, pass the U.S. Coast Guard Station, cross Laurel St., and take in the view of the San Diego City skyline. The bikeway rounds the bend of the harbor heading south, passes by the old windsailer Star of India (now a museum) and reaches the trip end point at the Cruise Ship Terminal (and a few eateries) in a short distance. (67.2).

The AMTRAK Option. Park at either the Santa Ana or Oceanside AMTRAK stations (these have baggage stops), bike to San Diego, and take the train on the return trip. The San Diego station is near the intersection of Kettner Blvd. and "C" St. The biker's "special" presently leaves at 4:45 pm on the weekend (be there 45 minutes early). Call AMTRAK at 800-872-7245 for the latest information before starting the trip.

<u>**CONNECTING TRIPS**</u>: Continuation with the Doheny/San Clemente Bike Route (Trip #14) - at the trip origin, bike north on El Camino Real.

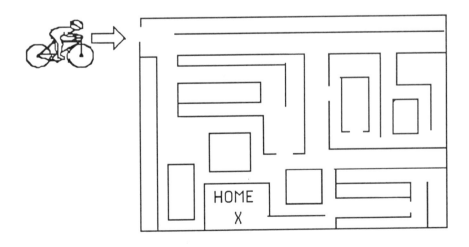

THE RIVERS

San Diego Creek Outlet

TRIPS #17A-#17C - SANTA ANA RIVER TRAIL

This moderate-to-strenuous level Santa Ana River trip from Prado Dam to Huntington Beach (61.2 strenuous miles round trip) is broken up into three sections. The general area map for the entire trip is provided below. Almost the entire route is Class I path with horse trails paralleling much of the bikeway. There are two places where the bikepath crosses the Santa Ana River bottom (Katella Ave. and 17th St.) and several areas where the path is very near the water (e.g., Orangewood Ave.). In high water situations, the nominal route is blocked by locked fences. The biker must return to and cross highways, as necessary, in these instances.

Trip #17A explores the most northerly section of the bikepath starting below Prado Dam, visiting Featherly Park, and ending at Yorba Regional Park. Trip #17B starts at Yorba Regional Park, passes through a short, scenic treed section early in the route, and terminates at Anaheim Stadium or El Camino Park. Trip #17C starts at El Camino Park, passes along Centennial Regional Park and the Mesa Verde Country Club, and lets out at the Pacific Ocean in Huntington Beach.

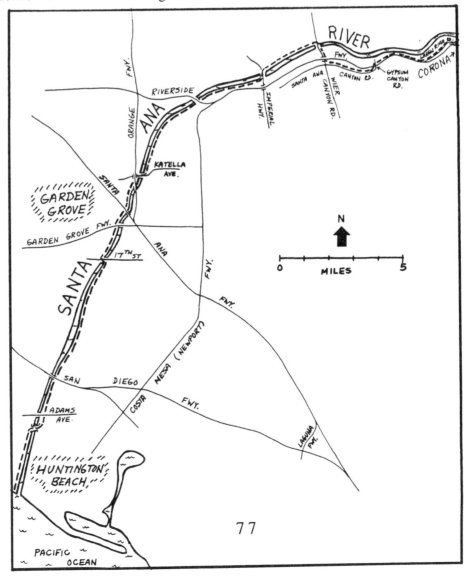

77

TRIP #17A - SANTA ANA RIVER: GREEN RIVER ROAD TO YORBA REGIONAL PARK

GENERAL LOCATION: Prado Dam, Anaheim Hills, Yorba Linda

LEVEL OF DIFFICULTY: One way - moderate; up and back - moderate
Distance - 7.2 miles (one way)
Elevation gain - periodic moderate grades

GENERAL DESCRIPTION: At the top end of the Santa Ana River Trail, this mixed Class I-III route starts just south of the Prado Dam at Green River Rd. and ends at Yorba Regional Park. Along the way are a few rolling hills, a horse ranch, a mini-motorcross area for children, pleasant Featherly Regional Park, and a short tour of Santa Ana Canyon Rd. Allow time for bicycle tours of Featherly and Yorba Regional Parks, which have an abundance of bikepaths or bikeable roadways. For bikers interested in a more lengthy workout, the trip can be extended north along Green River Rd. toward the city of Corona or continued south along the Santa Ana River.

TRAILHEAD: From the Riverside Fwy., exit at Green River Rd. and park north of the freeway where there are gas stations, a mini-market and a restaurant.

Bring a moderate water supply. There is water at Featherly Regional Park near the halfway point and Yorba Regional Park. If extending the trip north or south, bring additional water, as the nearest water supplies are several additional, exposed miles away.

TRIP DESCRIPTION: **Green River Country Club and Golf Course.** From the parking area, bike south on Class III Green River Rd. and begin an immediate moderate to steep downgrade. At 0.3 mile, the route begins a moderate uphill, passing a trailer park and reaching the crest near and at the level of the Riverside Fwy. (0.7). The path meets the entrance of the Green River Country Club, a little road on a bridge over the river that is taboo to bikers (1.0). Continue straight ahead to a Class I bikepath that travels directly alongside this very narrow stretch of the Santa Ana River. Further up the trail, stop and look back into a fine view of the Santa Ana Mountains. This stretch of the route also provides some nice peeks into the Green River Golf Course.

Featherly Regional Park. The path proceeds up a moderate grade and reaches Coal Canyon Rd. in another 0.2 mile. To the right is the Triple H Ranch, where there are several corrals with some extremely beautiful horses. The bike trail proceeds directly south along the asphalt bikepath and passes a mini-motorcross bicycle park in another 0.3 mile (2.2). For the next mile, the Class I path continues alongside trees, scrub, and a multitude of other flora and fauna that indicate the river is nearby. At (3.2), the bikepath reaches the fenced Featherly Regional Park boundary and in another 0.2 mile, passes a quarter-mile tent camping section of the park. At (3.6) the trail reaches Gypsum Canyon Rd.; a right turn here leads into the entrance to Featherly Regional Park.

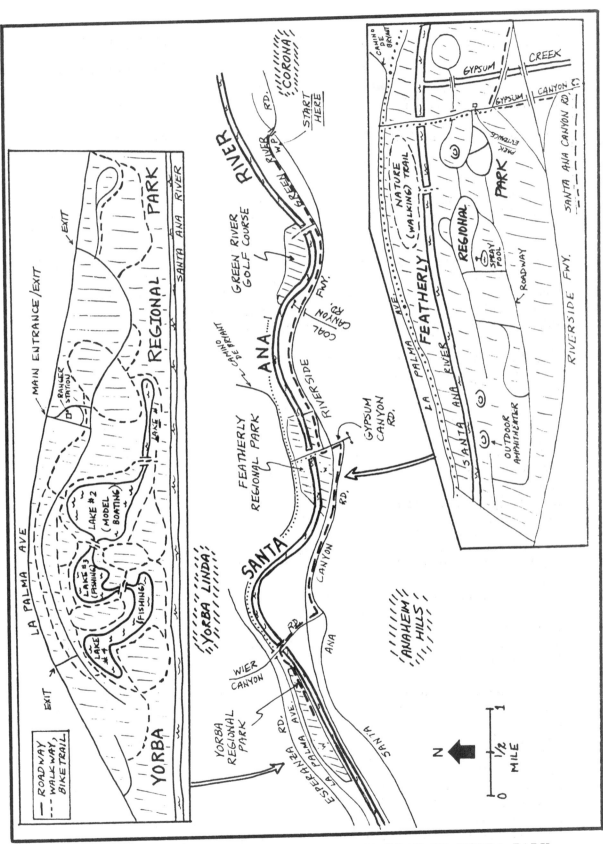

TRIP #17A - SANTA ANA RIVER: GREEN RIVER ROAD TO YORBA PARK

Yorba Regional Park, Santa Ana River

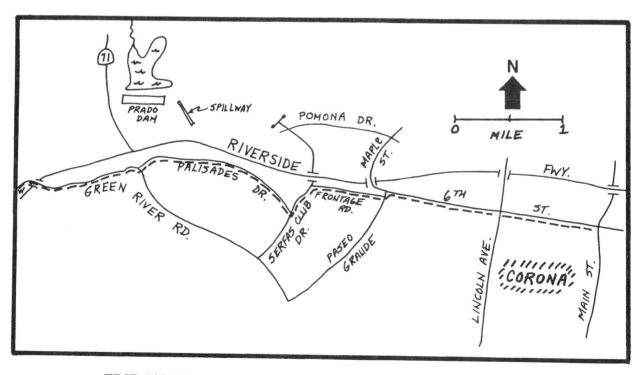

TRIP #17 EXTENTION: GREEN RIVER ROAD TO CORONA

Santa Ana Canyon Rd. At Gypsum Canyon Rd., the reference route proceeds under the Riverside Fwy. (last shade for awhile), and turns right onto Class II Santa Ana Canyon Rd. (3.8). Note that there is an option to turn north and cross the Santa Ana River on Gypsum Canyon Rd. (opened 4/90); after crossing, follow the Class I trail along the north bank to Yorba Regional Park. However on the reference route, bikers have a 0.4-mile moderate uphill pump to a flat, then another steady uphill which crests at Riverside Dr./Longwood St. (5.6). There is a fine view into Yorba Linda and back into the Santa Ana Canyon from this point.

Yorba Regional Park. The path turns right at Wier Canyon Rd. (5.9), passes under the Riverside Fwy., and jogs left at La Palma Ave. (6.6). Continue along the walkway on the south side of La Palma Ave. for a short distance and take the first bike trail right into Yorba Regional Park. Ride around the park's east edge to the Santa Ana River Bike Trail. At the junction, there is a dirt path to the left which might be entertaining for balloon tire bikers (7.1). However, our route goes right and proceeds into the park via the first entry trail.

CONNECTING TRIPS: 1) Continuation with the middle segment of the Santa Ana River Trail (Trip #17B) - continue south past Yorba Regional Park and across Imperial Hwy. to the south side of the river; 2) connection with the Santa Ana Canyon Rd. route (Trip #25) - continue west on Santa Ana Canyon Rd. at its intersection with Wier Canyon Rd.; 3) connection with the El Cajon Trail (Trip #22) - turn north on Wier Canyon Rd. at its intersection with La Palma Ave. Cross the bridge, turn right on New River Rd. then right again at Esperanza Rd. Continue into the foothills to the trail near Ave. Barcelona.

TRIP #17B - SANTA ANA RIVER: YORBA PARK TO EL CAMINO PARK

GENERAL LOCATION: Yorba Linda, Placentia, Orange

LEVEL OF DIFFICULTY: One way - easy; up and back - moderate
Distance - 10.0 miles (one way)
Elevation gain - essentially flat

GENERAL DESCRIPTION: This section of the trip starts at Yorba Regional Park which, in itself, could serve as a nice area for a family bike trip. The trip joins the Santa Ana River Trail at any one of several points from within the park, passes through a lovely area of trees and grassy knolls for several miles, and then transitions into an open, exposed route for the remainder of the trip. In the latter section are a gigantic open mining pit, Anaheim Stadium, and the terminal point at shaded El Camino Park.

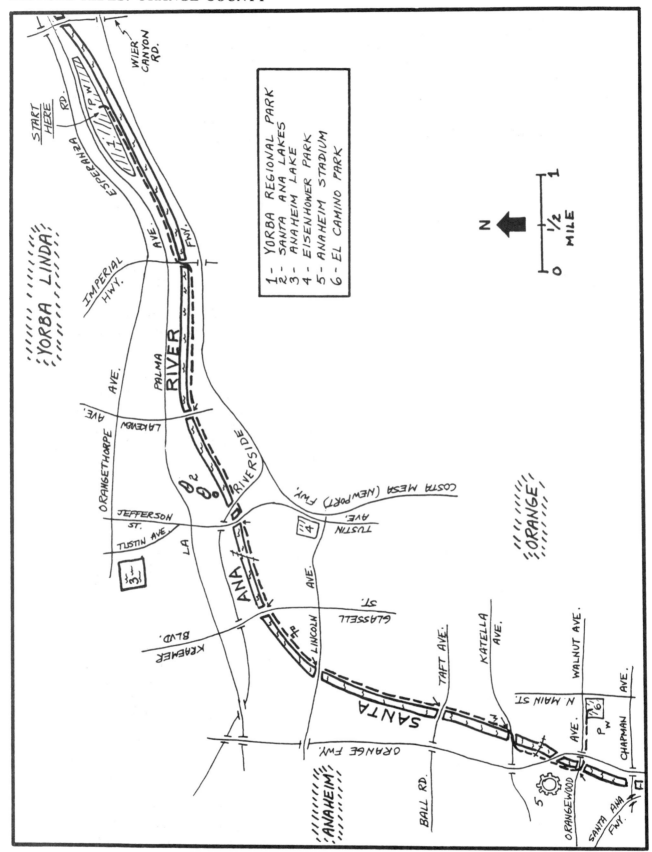

TRIP #17B - SANTA ANA RIVER: YORBA PARK TO EL CAMINO PARK

TRAILHEAD: From the Riverside Fwy., take the Imperial Hwy. exit and travel 1/4 mile north to La Palma Ave. Turn right (east) and travel about one mile to free parking at the baseball diamonds/soccer fields south of the roadway. Better yet, pay a small fee and park within the Yorba Regional Park itself; the entrance is about another 3/4 mile further on La Palma Ave.

From Imperial Hwy. north of the Riverside Fwy., continue south past Orangethrope Ave. (Esperanza Rd. to the east). In another quarter mile, turn left (east) on La Palma and continue as before.

Only a moderate water supply is needed. There are both water and restroom facilities at the beginning of the trip (at the park) and near the end (at a small restroom directly on the bikeway). There is also a small market stop along the way.

TRIP DESCRIPTION: **Yorba Regional Park to "The Rest Stop."** There are bikepaths around the lakes and throughout Yorba Regional Park (see the detailed map accompanying the prior ride). Follow the park bikepath nearest the river and take one of the many paved or direct paths across to the river trail. Within the first mile from the main parking area within the park, there is marshland along the river with many birds.

Continue along the natural riverbed and cross from the north to the south levee at Imperial Hwy. (2.1). The route passes through a pleasant area with grassy knolls, trees, bushes, a few joggers, and even a few horseback riders (on a paralleling path). At (3.9), pass under Lakeview Ave. and at (4.9) the Riverside Fwy. Stop and check out the man-made water holding basins in the riverbed--they're cleverly constructed. At (5.1), pass an exit through a fence which leads to a little market that has soft drinks and other "stuff" on ice. Do the entire Santa Ana River and you will know why we call this "The Rest Stop!"

Anaheim Stadium and El Camino Park. The river starts heading in a southerly direction in this area. The route passes under Glassell St. (6.2) and continues alongside a gigantic open mining pit in another 0.3 mile. The path crosses under Lincoln Ave. (7.0) and Ball Rd. (8.3) while traveling through an industrial area.

At (9.1), there is a small restroom stop right along the bike trail. Just beyond this point, the route crosses the river bottom at Katella Ave. (9.3). Shortly after, the bikepath travels alongside Anaheim Stadium and under the Orange Fwy. (9.7). In 0.3 mile is Orangewood Ave. In a short distance, an exit to the north and a right turn at Stadium Way will lead to Anaheim Stadium. For our reference trip, however, an exit to the south and an additional 0.5 mile pedal leads to El Camino Park.

CONNECTING TRIPS: 1) Connection/continuation with Trips #17A or #17C along the Santa Ana River Trail - follow the described route to the Santa Ana River and turn north (Trip #17A) or continue south from the trip terminus (Trip #17C); 2) connection with the Santa Ana Canyon Trip (Trip #25) - at the trip origin, ride to Wier Canyon Rd. (east) or Imperial Hwy. (south) on the Santa Ana River Trail. Cross under the Riverside Fwy. and head in either direction on Santa Ana Canyon Rd.

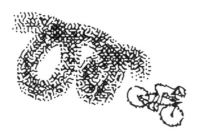

TRIP #17C - SANTA ANA RIVER:
EL CAMINO PARK TO PACIFIC OCEAN

GENERAL LOCATION: Orange, Garden Grove, Costa Mesa, Huntington Beach

LEVEL OF DIFFICULTY: One way - easy; up and back - moderate
Distance - 13.4 miles (one way)
Elevation gain - essentially flat

GENERAL DESCRIPTION: The first part of this section of the Santa Ana River Bike Trail is a tree-lined route along a portion of the riverbed that is lush meadowland. The route passes near several golf courses, as well as a couple of small parks and the large and pretty Centennial Regional Park. In between some of these lovely sights is a lot of concrete and industry backed up along the river. The trip lets out at a pleasant stretch of Huntington Beach at the southern end of Huntington State Beach.

TRAILHEAD: From the Santa Ana Fwy., exit at Katella Ave. and head east 3/4 mile to State College Blvd. Turn right (south) and make a left turn in 0.4 mile at Orangewood Ave., then continue one mile to El Camino Park. There is parking closer to the river on the side streets off Orangewood Ave.; however, read the parking signs carefully if you park here. From the Orange Fwy., exit at Orangewood Ave. and proceed east about 0.5 mile. From the Garden Grove Fwy., exit at Main St. and proceed north about 1-1/4 mile to Orangewood Ave. and turn left.

Fill a water bottle at the park. There are facilities at a couple of nearby stops along the trip south, or travel one mile north (see Trip #17B) where there is a restroom along the Santa Ana River bikeway.

TRIP DESCRIPTION: **Lower Santa Ana River Meadowland.** From El Camino Park, travel one-half mile west on Orangewood Ave. to the entrance point on the west side of the river. Continue south and pass Chapman Ave. (1.0), the Santa Ana Fwy., and the Garden Grove Fwy. (1.8). Just beyond this point is one of the prettiest stretches of the trip. The river bottom is a rich meadowland for the next 1-2 miles and the bikepath meanders through a surrounding mini-forest. Pass Garden Grove Blvd., which is an exit to luscious River View Golf Course (2.2). Shortly after, the trail passes a small park with a children's play area, barbecue facilities and a biker's rest stop (water, restroom).

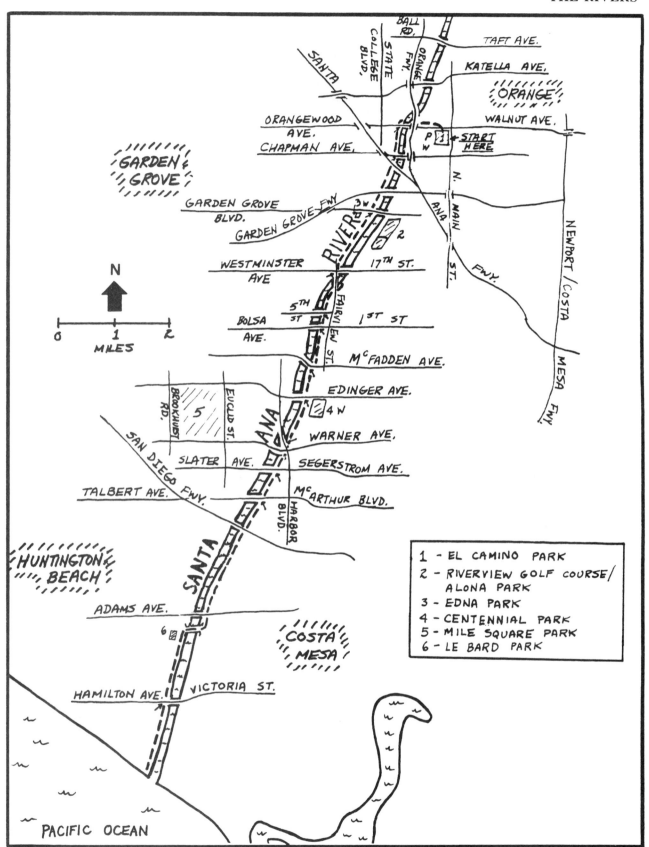

1 - EL CAMINO PARK
2 - RIVERVIEW GOLF COURSE/ ALONA PARK
3 - EDNA PARK
4 - CENTENNIAL PARK
5 - MILE SQUARE PARK
6 - LE BARD PARK

TRIP #17C - SANTA ANA RIVER: EL CAMINO PARK TO PACIFIC OCEAN

Centennial Regional Park. At 17th St., the bikepath crosses the river bottom (3.4). From this point to the ocean, the river is one long concrete waterway. The route passes under Fairview St. (3.8), 5th St., McFadden Ave., and Edinger Ave. (6.0). Shortly after Edinger and about 200 yards off the bikepath, there is lovely Centennial Regional Park with its little lakes, birds, and shady gazebos. There is bikepath throughout the park, as well as restroom facilities.

Continue south past Harbor Blvd. (6.9), Warner Ave., and pass one of the steepest underpasses of the river bikeway system at Slater Ave. (7.6). Next is the crossing under Talbert Ave. At (8.1), traverse a tunnel under the San Diego Fwy. (be watchful for broken glass) and pass a grassy rest area next to the path. The route becomes more scenic as it cruises alongside the Mesa Verde Country Club (9.4), passes under Adams St., and by the site of Fairview Regional Park (10.7).

Lower Santa Ana River Near Adams Ave.

The Coast. In about a mile, follow the wooden bike bridge across the river to the west side; there is a small park/playground a few hundred yards beyond the crossing and off the trail at Le Bard Park (10.9). Continue south and pass Victoria St./Hamilton Ave. (11.9), the "fragrant" Orange County Sanitation Treatment Plant (12.9), and a small bridge over a separate channel just north of Pacific Coast Highway (PCH) (13.3). In another 0.1 mile, pass under PCH and enter Huntington State Park at the junction with the Sunset Beach-Newport Beach Strand bikepath.

CONNECTING TRIPS: 1) Continuation with the Sunset Beach-Newport Beach Strand route (Trip #2) - at the terminus of the Santa Ana River Trail, turn south and pass over the bridge/bikeway toward Newport Beach or turn north and head towards Sunset Beach; 2) connection with Mile Square Regional Park (Trip #5) - turn west at Edinger Ave. or Warner Ave. and turn into the park in about one mile at Euclid St.

TRIP #18 - SAN DIEGO CREEK

GENERAL LOCATION: Newport Beach, Irvine

LEVEL OF DIFFICULTY: One way - easy; up and back - moderate
Distance - 7.8 miles (one way)
Elevation gain - essentially flat

GENERAL DESCRIPTION: This pleasant trip follows San Diego Creek upstream starting from its confluence with upper Newport Bay. The creek is soil-lined for the most part and contains marshes, water pools, and mud flats at low water, particularly along the lower creek segment. The route passes near a state wildlife preserve, the University of California, Irvine Campus, two parks, and an attractively-developed residential area. There are numerous spur trips off the main route. The trip is nearly 100% Class I on well-maintained bike surfaces.

TRAILHEAD: From the intersection of Pacific Coast Highway (PCH) and Jamboree Rd. in Newport Beach, drive north on Jamboree Rd. for about three miles to Eastbluff Dr. Find parking on that street or in the adjoining residential areas subject to local traffic laws. From the San Diego Fwy., take the Hwy. 73 exit in Costa Mesa and continue until the highway fuses into Bristol St. Continue about one mile further on Bristol St. to Jamboree Rd., turn right (south) and drive about one-half mile to Eastbluff Dr. Turn right on Eastbluff Dr., head up the hill and find parking as described above. From the Costa Mesa (Newport) Fwy., exit south at Bristol St. Once on Bristol St., follow the directions above.

Bring a moderate water supply. There is one public water stop about half way through the trip. Also, there is a commercial zone near the turnaround point on Barranca Pkwy.

TRIP DESCRIPTION: **Upper Newport Bay to U. C. Irvine.** From the intersection of Eastbluff Dr. and Jamboree Rd., follow the bikepath on the west side of Jamboree Rd. down to San Diego Creek. The trail turns sharply to the right and parallels the creek, passing under Jamboree Rd. (0.3). The bikeway proceeds into the quiet, open, natural area above the soil-lined river bed and passes over a small wooden bridge (0.5). In another 0.1 mile is the MacArthur Trail junction. There is a sign with a map of the local streets and trails, one of several along the route.

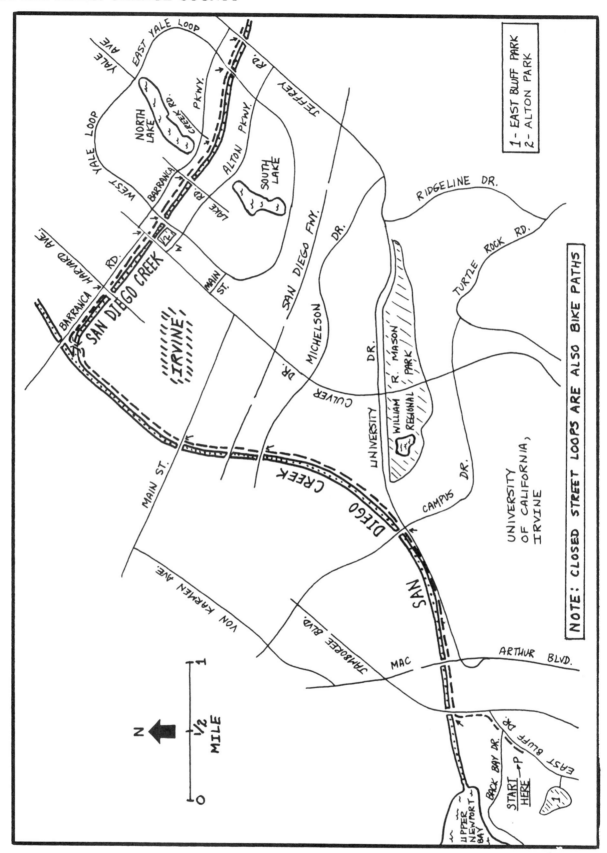

TRIP #18 - SAN DIEGO CREEK

The trail passes under MacArthur Blvd and then meets the California Rd. junction (1.1). To the left, on the other side of the creek bank, are the man-made ponds of the State Wildlife Preserve. To the right is the California Rd. entry along the periphery of the U.C. Irvine campus. The route passes under Campus Dr. (1.6) and begins a slow turn to the north away from University Dr. There is a junction off to the right which leads to the William R. Mason Regional Park.

The Marshlands to Peter's Canyon Channel. On the San Diego Creek route, there is a marshy area that seems to be a favorite for a variety of birds and even a few ducks (1.8). The route passes alongside the San Joaquin Country Club/Golf Course and then jig-jogs on a bridge over a small wash (2.8). In turn, the route passes under Michelson Dr., the San Diego Fwy., and Main St. (3.5) through some of the more open territory of the trip.

In roughly a mile from Main St., the bike trail crosses a bridge to the opposite side of San Diego Creek near a creek junction (4.4). The path to the left follows the Peter's Canyon Channel, while our route takes us right (east). There is a great view of the gigantic airship hangers at the U.S. Marine Corps Air Facility in this area.

Alton Park. In about 0.7 mile, the route crosses Harvard Ave. at the traffic light, then continues back along the channel. There is a steep undercrossing at Culver Dr. (which may be flooded during storms) and, in 0.2 mile, another undercrossing at West Yale Loop (5.9). To the right (south) is pleasant little Alton Park and a water fountain. Note that West and East Yale themselves are part of a 3-4 mile circular bike loop.

Condomania to the Jeffrey Road Terminus. The route continues to an area where a few condominiums are built up alongside the creek with a lovely church across the water (6.2). In 0.2 mile, the bikeway crosses under Lake Rd. (a short spur takes the biker to North Lake) and enters another condo area alongside the creek. The trail then passes under Creek Rd. (6.8), continues along a pleasant eucalyptus-lined stretch, passes the East Yale Loop bikepath, and goes under Jeffrey Rd. through a small tunnel. The trail abruptly terminates at the other side of the road in a wooded turnaround area (7.8)

Alternate Return Routes. There are several ways to complete the return trip. One is to head north on Jeffrey Rd. to Barranca Pkwy. on the Class II bikepath and follow Barranca Pkwy. through this pleasant residential/ commercial area of Irvine. This path returns to San Diego Creek at Culver Dr. Another option is to head north on East Yale Loop on a Class II bikepath and follow the West Yale portion of the loop back to San Diego Creek. Other options are to continue further south of the West Yale Loop and take other spurs off that path.

CONNECTING TRIPS: 1) Continuation of the Upper Newport Bay route (Trip #6) - return to the trailhead and go uphill 0.2 mile to Back Bay Dr.; 2) connection with the Irvine Bikeway (Trip #8) - on the return leg, turn either north or south on Culver Dr.

TRIPS #19A-#19E - SAN GABRIEL RIVER TRAIL

The San Gabriel River Trail is probably the premier single river trail in this book. The route captures Southern California from the sea through the inland valley to the mountains, all in one continuous 38 mile shot. Taken in the winter after a cold storm, this trip is one of the best in every sense. The general area map is provided below with the San Gabriel River highlighted by a dark arrow.

The first segment (#19A) explores the river outlet near Seal Beach, a wildlife area to the north, and ends at super El Dorado Park. The connection segment (#19B) visits no less than five parks along the way and finishes at Wilderness Park in Downey. The next northerly segment (#19C) leaves Wilderness Park, travels alongside some of the finest San Gabriel river bottom, and ends at one of the highpoints of the entire tour, the Whittier Narrows Recreation Area. Trip #19D starts at that fabulous recreation area and ends at another, the Santa Fe Dam Recreation Area. The most northerly segment (#19E) leaves from that dam and ends in the foothills at the entrance to San Gabriel Canyon.

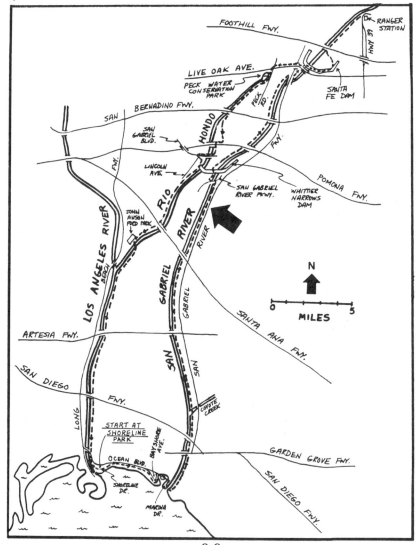

TRIP #19A - SAN GABRIEL RIVER: SEAL BEACH TO EL DORADO PARK

GENERAL LOCATION: Seal Beach - Long Beach

LEVEL OF DIFFICULTY: One Way - easy; up and back - easy
Distance - 5.6 miles (one way)
Elevation gain - essentially flat

GENERAL DESCRIPTION: This is the starting segment of one of the most varied and interesting trips in this book, the San Gabriel River Trail. This is a completely Class I bike route that starts at the scenic lower section of the San Gabriel River near the the Long Beach Marina and winds up at classic El Dorado Park.   The early part of the trip provides a look at "recreation city" with   water, boats, water skiers, and jet skiers.   The trip transitions into a nature area that is rich in wildlife and ends in a park that is so inviting that it could serve as a separate family excursion.

TRAILHEAD: Free public parking is available at the Long Beach Marina along Marina Dr. in Naples or along First St. in Seal Beach.   From Pacific Coast Highway (PCH) in Seal Beach, turn west on Marina Dr. (2-3 blocks from Main Street in Seal Beach) and continue roughly 0.5 mile to First St.   In another 1/4 mile, cross the San Gabriel River and continue a short distance into the marina near Seaport Village for parking.   The trailhead is located at Marina Dr. at the east end of the bridge over the San Gabriel River.

Only a light water supply is needed for this short trip.   There are public water sources at the trip origin and terminus.

TRIP   DESCRIPTION: **The Scenic Lower River Segment.** The first part of the trip provides views of boaters, water skiers, and an interestingly-developed shoreline.   The natural river basin then passes PCH (0.4), the Westminster Ave. access, and the Haynes Steam Plant (electricity generation).   At (2.2), a small alternate Class I bikepath leads off to the east along a 1.2-mile shaded route to Seal Beach Blvd.   In this stretch of the river, up to the concrete portion (3.5), one has views of the large bird population that includes pelicans, egrets, and the ever-present seagulls.   The trip passes under the Garden Grove Fwy. (2.3) and San Diego Fwy. (3.5).   In this portion of the bikepath are many "freeway orchards" -- those freeway-locked areas under the power poles that are used for growing containerized plants.

The River Crossing and El Dorado Park. In 0.4 mile, the trip crosses a signed bikeway/walkway bridge across the river.   Do not miss the bridge unless you've decided to change plans and see Coyote Creek (Trip #20).   Once across the bridge, there are views across the river to the El Dorado Golf Course and El Dorado Park West.   At 0.7 mile from the bridge crossing, the route reaches Willow St. and skirts the edge of the Nature Study Area which is the south end of El Dorado Park East (5.0).   Shortly afterward, the bikepath reaches Spring St. and the entry to Areas I and II of the park (5.6).

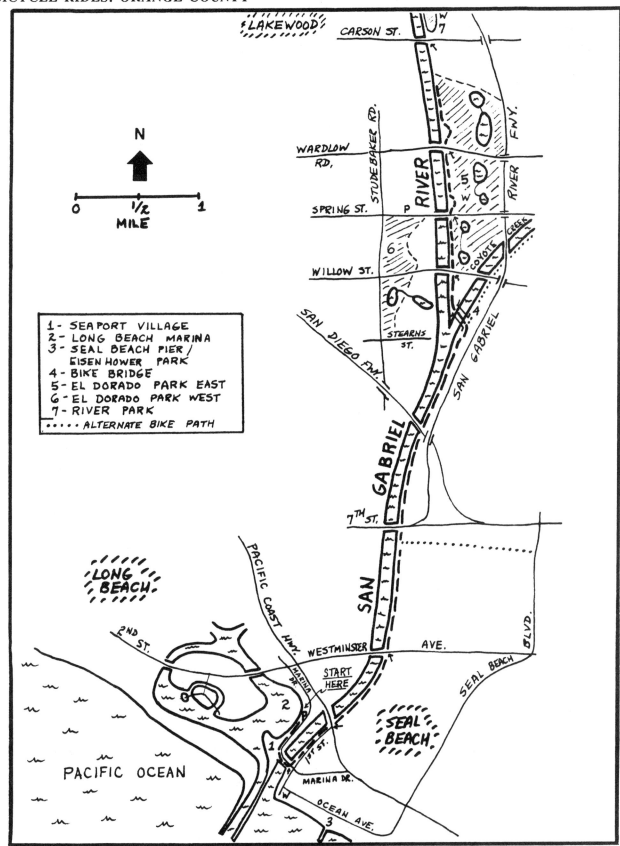

TRIP #19A - SAN GABRIEL RIVER: SEAL BEACH TO EL DORADO PARK

There is a myriad of bikepath options just within the park. This portion of the trip is worth a good exploration effort in itself.

CONNECTING TRIPS: 1) Connection with the San Gabriel River Trail (Trip #19B) - continue north beyond El Dorado Park toward Wilderness Park; 2) connection with the Coyote Creek Trail (Trip #20)- at the eastern end of the bike bridge across the San Gabriel River, stay on the eastern river bank.

TRIP #19B - SAN GABRIEL RIVER: EL DORADO PARK
TO WILDERNESS PARK

GENERAL LOCATION: Long Beach, Lakewood, Cerritos, Norwalk, Downey

LEVEL OF DIFFICULTY: One way - easy; up and back - moderate
Distance - 9.7 miles (one way)
Elevation gain - essentially flat

GENERAL DESCRIPTION: This is a segment of the Class I San Gabriel River Trail that has direct access to five major parks. In particular, this trip should not be completed without a tour of El Dorado Park. In addition, River Park provides a pleasant diversion from the river route, and Wilderness Park is a fine rest stop with a small pond/lagoon to dip the toes into before returning to the trip origin. There are also horse corrals and equestrian trails alongside the bike route in some sections. This is a fine workout section as the bike and foot traffic is very light.

TRAILHEAD: From the San Diego Fwy., turn north on Palo Verde Ave. and drive 0.9 mile to Spring St. Turn right (east) and continue about 0.8 mile to free parking along Spring St., just west of the bridge over the San Gabriel River. Other options are to continue over the bridge and park in the Nature Center parking area (turn south at the park entrance), or to continue up Spring St., make a U-turn, and return to the Area II park entrance to the north (right). The latter two options are pay parking.

From the San Gabriel Fwy., turn west on Willow St. (Katella Ave. in Orange County), continue about one mile to Studebaker Rd. and turn right (north). Continue about 0.3 mile to Spring St. and turn right (east). Follow the parking instructions above. For direct entry at Area II (pay parking) from the southbound San Gabriel Fwy., just take the Spring St. exit and turn right into the park entrance.

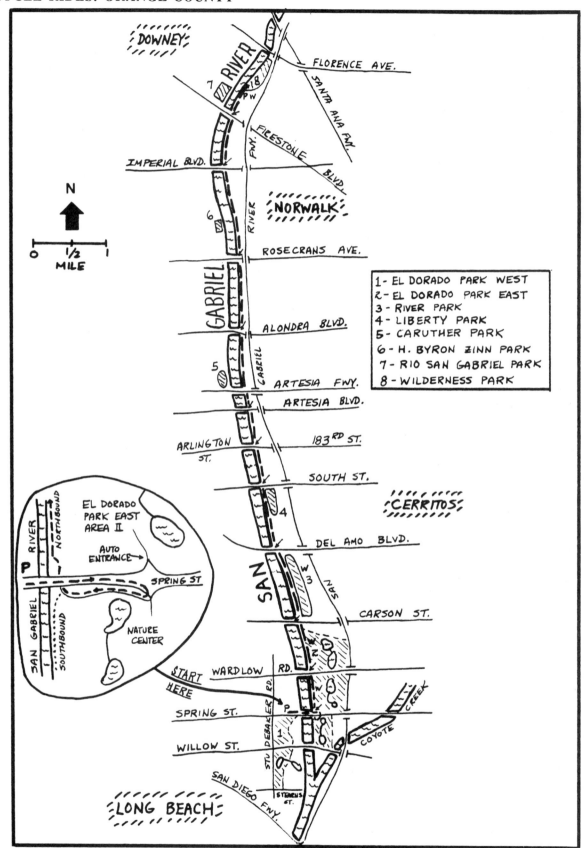

N

0 ½ 1
MILE

1- EL DORADO PARK WEST
2- EL DORADO PARK EAST
3- RIVER PARK
4- LIBERTY PARK
5- CARUTHER PARK
6- H. BYRON ZINN PARK
7- RIO SAN GABRIEL PARK
8- WILDERNESS PARK

TRIP #19B - SAN GABRIEL RIVER: EL DORADO- TO WILDERNESS- PARK

Bring a light water supply. There is plenty of water and many restroom facilities at the parks along the way. El Dorado Park is a particular delight! Bring some barbecue food and enjoy the munchies at the park after a "tough" bike ride.

TRIP DESCRIPTION: El Dorado Park. From the parking area on Spring St., ride over the bridge and turn right (south) at the Nature Center entrance. Make another sharp right and continue parallel to Spring St. (but in the opposite direction) along the Nature Center roadway. Continue 0.2 mile to the fence along the San Gabriel River Bike Route. Rather than passing through the fence entry, follow the roadway as it turns to the right and passes under Spring St. The road enters Park Area II.

Stay to the left rather than bike into El Dorado Park. Pass through the fence and head right (north) along the San Gabriel River Trail (0.6). The first part of the trip parallels Park Area II. The path leaves the river again and follows the roadway under Wardlow Rd. (1.1). Again, stay to the left and pass through a fence which returns the biker to the river trail (the other option is to bike through Park Area III and rejoin the trail 0.5 mile later). The path continues alongside a stand of trees and passes the end of Park Area III (1.6) near the weapons firing range.

River Park. The route passes a pedestrian bridge which crosses over to De Mille Junior High School and then passes Carson St. (2.0). For the next 0.7 mile, the biker cruises alongside fun River Park. The park boasts tree cover, horse stalls and corrals, horse trails, a little footbridge leading to a connecting alternate bike trail (which reconnects near Del Amo Blvd.), baseball diamonds, and water (near the baseball fields). The shady park area ends near Del Amo Blvd. (3.0).

The Middle Trip Section. For the next half mile, the trip highlight is the clever (and in some cases, not so clever) graffiti on the concrete river walls. In 0.8 mile, the route reaches little Liberty Park, which is effectively a grassy rest area. Just beyond the park is South St. (3.8), followed by a passage below 183rd St. through a narrow tunnel (4.5). (Slow and keep an eye peeled for oncoming bikers in the tunnel.) The route then passes more horse stalls.

The path dips down into the riverbed to cross under Artesia Blvd. (4.9). If the biker misses the marked route, there is an option to walk (crouch) the bike under the roadway. There is a short section where the bikes must be walked across a railroad crossing, followed by passage under the Artesia Fwy. (5.3). The first of many spillways in the river area is near this junction.

The trail passes the Cerritos Ironwood Golf Course; nearby is the pedestrian bridge across the river that leads to Caruther's Park (5.6). However, the reference path stays on the east levee and enters a several mile pleasant residential stretch beyond Alondra Blvd. where there are horses in many of the backyards (we even spotted a llama). The route passes Rosecrans Ave. (7.0), another walk bridge over the river, and a new bridge under construction that is part of the Century Fwy. (7.8). In 0.3 mile, the path reaches Imperial Hwy. and later dips down into the river below a railroad tressel (8.7).

95

Wilderness Park. At (9.0), the bike trail passes Firestone Blvd. In a short distance, the route reaches the transition to a natural river bottom after 11 solid miles of concrete. There is Rio San Gabriel Park across the river and a small spillway. There is some excellent river bottomland north of this area (see Trips #19C and #19D). In about 0.7 mile, the trip reaches a refreshing terminus at Wilderness Park. This is a half-mile strip of park that offers water, restrooms and shade just for starters. There are also sports and recreation areas, playgrounds, a small pond, and a lovely decorative water fountain.

CONNECTING TRIPS: Continuation with the San Gabriel River Trail south to Seal Beach (Trip #19A) from the trip origin, or north to the Whittier Narrows (Trip #19C) from the trip terminus.

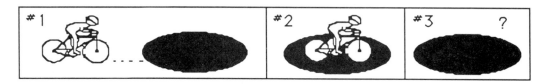

TRIP #19C - SAN GABRIEL RIVER:
WILDERNESS PARK TO LEGG LAKE

GENERAL LOCATION: Downey, Santa Fe Springs, Whittier, Pico Rivera

LEVEL OF DIFFICULTY: One way - easy; up and back - moderate
Distance - 7.7 miles (one way)
Elevation gain - 50 feet (Whittier Narrows Dam)

GENERAL DESCRIPTION: This is a pleasant segment of the San Gabriel River Trail that starts at Wilderness Park, visits Santa Fe Springs Park, and ends at the trip highlight in the Whittier Narrows Recreation Area. A short diversion at Whittier Blvd. also leads to Pio Pico State Historical Park. The Whittier Narrows area sports a ride on the dam, a visit to a wildlife refuge area, and a trip at the terminus to relaxing Legg Lake. This is one of the few river segments that is predominantly natural river bottom and there are some lush areas that beckon for rest stops. This is 99% Class I trail (one street crossing) with light bike traffic south of the Whittier Narrows Dam.

TRAILHEAD: From the San Gabriel River Fwy., exit west on Florence Ave. A short distance west of the freeway, turn left (south) on Little Lake Rd. This roadway also leads back onto the southbound freeway; therefore, in a few hundred feet, turn right onto Little Lake Rd. proper. Continue on this roadway to the free parking area at Wilderness Park. From the Santa Ana Fwy., exit west on Florence Ave. Pass under the San Gabriel Fwy., and follow the directions above.

Bring a moderate water supply. There is no enroute water supply between Santa Fe Springs Park and the Whittier Narrows Recreation Area (Legg Lake, Nature Center).

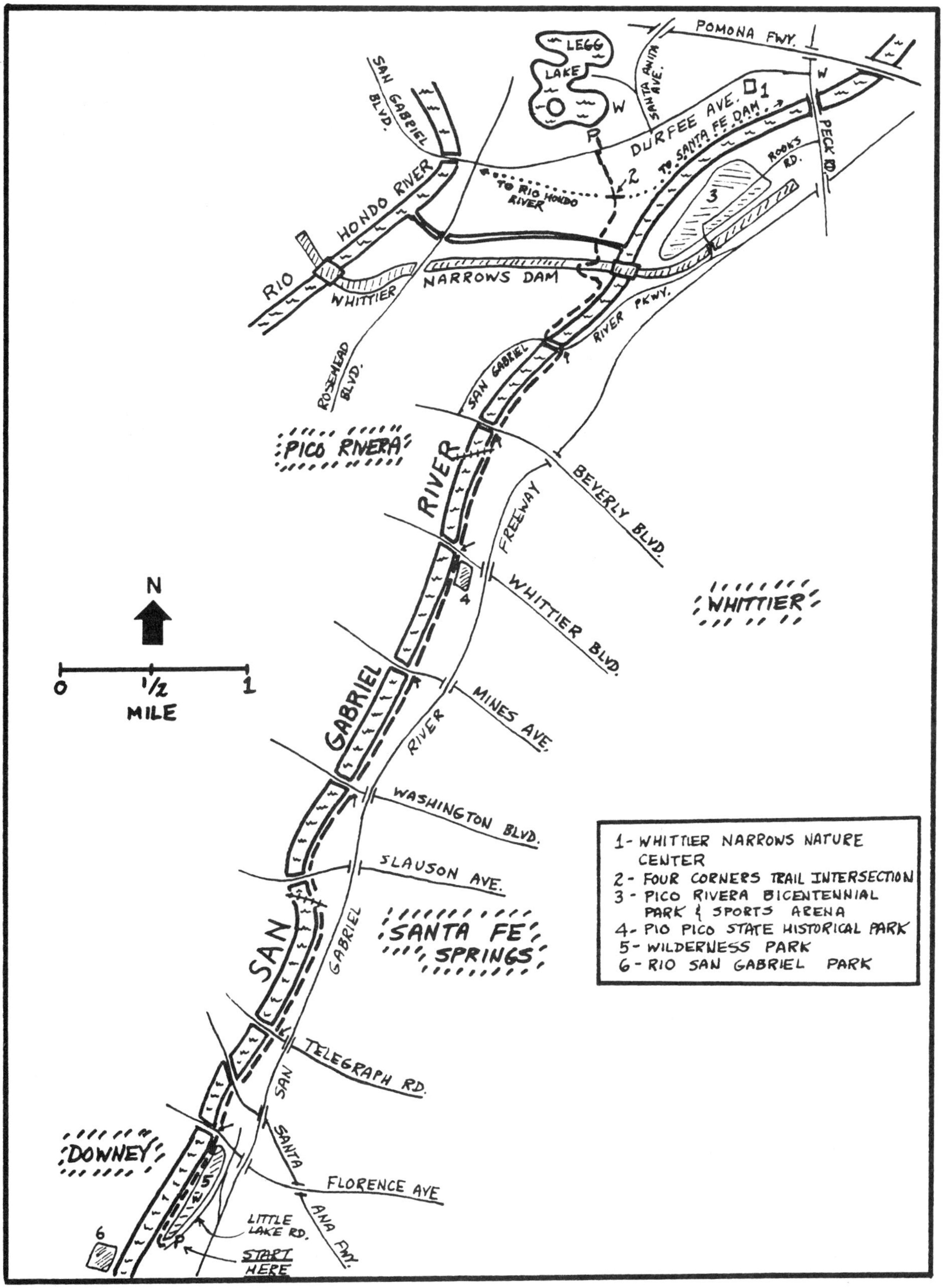
POMONA FWY.
LEGG LAKE
SANTA ANITA AVE.
SAN GABRIEL BLVD.
DURFEE AVE.
TO SANTA FE DAM
PECK RD.
ROOKS RD.
TO RIO HONDO RIVER
RIO HONDO RIVER
WHITTIER NARROWS DAM
ROSEMEAD BLVD.
RIVER PKWY.
SAN GABRIEL RIVER
PICO RIVERA
BEVERLY BLVD.
FREEWAY
WHITTIER BLVD.
WHITTIER
N
0 1/2 1
MILE
MINES AVE.
RIVER
WASHINGTON BLVD.
SLAUSON AVE.
SAN GABRIEL
SANTA FE SPRINGS
TELEGRAPH RD.
SAN SANTA ANA FWY.
DOWNEY
FLORENCE AVE
LITTLE LAKE RD.
START HERE
1- WHITTIER NARROWS NATURE CENTER
2- FOUR CORNERS TRAIL INTERSECTION
3- PICO RIVERA BICENTENNIAL PARK & SPORTS ARENA
4- PIO PICO STATE HISTORICAL PARK
5- WILDERNESS PARK
6- RIO SAN GABRIEL PARK

TRIP #19C - SAN GABRIEL RIVER: WILDERNESS PARK TO LEGG LAKE

TRIP DESCRIPTION: **Wilderness Park to Santa Fe Springs Park.** From the south end of the parking lot, skirt the south edge of Wilderness Park and follow the path to the river entry. Turn right (north) and continue past Florence Ave. (0.2) and the first of many spillways 0.2 mile further. There are some trees and a great deal of brush along the path, and the riverbed is built up into holding basins. At (0.7), the tour reaches Santa Fe Springs Park, where there are play areas, shade, recreation fields, and restrooms. Fill up with water here if you are running low.

The Railroad Route and Pio Pico Historical Park. About 0.4 mile from the park, the route crosses Telegraph Rd. At (1.4) the bikeway passes the highest (about six feet) spillway on this segment of the river. In this area, there is a stand of eucalyptus trees and a collection of horse stalls tucked between the river and the San Gabriel Fwy. At (2.1), the route passes under a railroad tressel. Soon after another railroad track comes in from the east and parallels the bike route for several miles. There is a high liklihood of having a train for company on this stretch.

In a short distance the route passes under another railroad tressel which, in turn, lies below the highly-elevated Slauson Ave. overpass (2.3). The riverbed and greenery in the riverbed continue, while there is brush and railroad tracks to the right. At (3.0) is Washington Blvd. and the beginning of a long, exposed stretch of bikeway. At (4.7) the bikepath meets Whittier Blvd.; it is a 0.2-mile diversion to the right (east) to visit Pio Pico Historic Park.

Our route trucks onward and reaches a point where the riverbed begins developing into a mini-forest. This continues up to the Whittier Narrows and beyond and is one of the lovliest stretches of the river. At (5.3), the path heads under another railroad tressel; the paralleling railroad tracks fuse with that track and the merged track leaves the river heading east. In another 0.2 mile is Beverly Blvd. Further north is a spillway with a large enough collecting basin to support a flock of young water frolickers. There is also a view into Rose Hills at this point.

Whittier Narrows Dam. The trip reaches a junction where the trail changes from asphalt to dirt at San Gabriel River Pkwy. (6.1). The dam is viewable at this point. Continue ahead if you have a wide tire bike and a desire to see Pico Rivera Bicentennial Park and Sports Area. Otherwise, return to the roadway and cross the river to the west side. This is the "advertised" route to the Whittier Narrows Dam. Continue north and observe the lush tree-filled river bottom. The route passes the Pico Rivera Golf Course (6.7) and makes a hard left at the dam base. From this point, there is a short, steep path up to the top of the dam (6.9). Stop and take in some of the excellent sights viewable from this area.

Whittier Narrows Nature Center. Continue down the meandering concrete bikeway on the backside of the dam. The path crosses a water run-off channel and reaches the marked Four Corners Trail Intersection (7.2). Continue straight ahead and pedal another 0.4 mile through the lush bottomlands to Durfee Ave. Turn right (east) and continue a few hundred feet to the Legg Lake parking area within the Whittier Narrows Recreation Area (7.7).

CONNECTING TRIPS: 1) Continuation with the San Gabriel River Trail south to El Dorado Park (Trip #19B) - from the trip origin, bike south; 2) continuation with the San Gabriel River Trail north to Santa Fe Dam (Trip #19D) - from the Four Corners Trail Intersection, turn right (east) at the junction.

TRIP #19D - SAN GABRIEL RIVER:

LEGG LAKE TO SANTA FE DAM

GENERAL LOCATION: Whittier Narrows, El Monte, Baldwin Park, Irwindale

LEVEL OF DIFFICULTY: One way - easy; up and back - moderate
Distance - 11.4 miles (one way)
Elevation gain - 50 feet (Santa Fe Dam)

GENERAL DESCRIPTION: This is one of our favorite segments of the river trips. The San Gabriel River in the Whittier Narrows region is river stomping at its best; there are trees, thickets, clear running water and readily visible wildlife in and around the river. The Whittier Narrows Recreation Area offers a wildlife sanctuary, Legg Lake, vista points from the top of the dam, and a diversion trip to the Pico Rivera Bicentennial Park and Sports Area. The Santa Fe Dam Recreation Area offers an expansive, pleasant picnic and recreation area at the edge of the lake, as well as superb lookout points from the top of the dam. Set aside a few hours and fully explore these territories. The best time to take this trip is within several days of a cold winter storm when the snow level in the nearby mountains is low. The route is nearly 100% Class I.

TRAILHEAD: From the Pomona Fwy., exit at Rosemead Blvd. south, travel about 0.8 mile to San Gabriel Blvd./Durfee Blvd. and turn left. Continue on Durfee Ave. 0.6 mile and turn left into the pay parking area at Legg Lake. Find a tree under which to park your car. Bring four quarters for the parking area fee.

Bring a moderate water supply. There are rest and water stops directly on the route and at the Santa Fe Recreation Area terminus.

TRIP DESCRIPTION: **Whittier Narrows Recreation Area.** Leave the parking area and cross Durfee Ave. a few hundred feet west of the parking area. Pass through the signed gate and pedal down a small asphalt road through an area surrounded by bushes, plants, trees, and brush. In a short distance is a junction; to the left through a sometimes-locked gate is the Whittier Narrows Nature Center. However, our route proceeds to the right and meets the Four Corners Trail Intersection (0.5). There is a nice view into the backside of the Whittier Narrows Dam from this area.

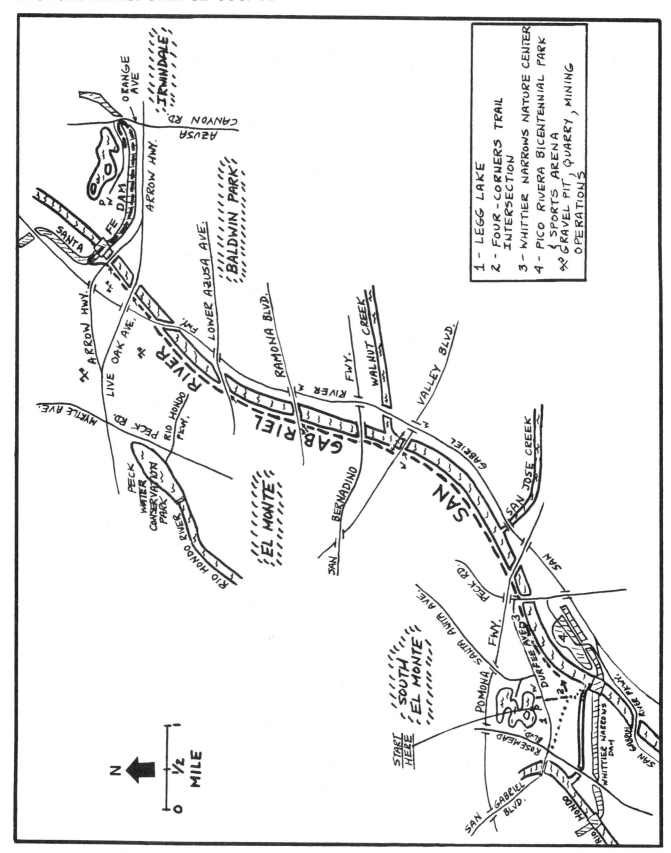

TRIP #19D - SAN GABRIEL RIVER: LEGG LAKE TO SANTA FE DAM

Turn left (east) and follow the path as it turns northward and rejoins the San Gabriel River (0.7). There are permanent horsetrails to the left (west) and also "find-your-way" paths in the lush river bed; both are well used by horseriders, the latter accompanying our path for the next couple of miles. In this area, there are excellent views of Rose Hills to the east.

The Unofficial Recreation Area/San Jose Creek Confluence. The route passes the first of many spillways that stair-step their way up the river (1.4). Small children slide down the rounded portion of the spillway into a holding basin below and even a swimming dog might be seen. In another 0.4 mile is Peck Rd. and a second spillway with a large pool backed up behind it. (There are gas stations and restaurants not too far from the river at this exit.) The trail passes the Pomona Fwy. (2.0) and then the third spillway, which has some fishermen and a few swimmers using the upstream water pool. In 0.3 mile is the confluence with San Jose Creek and one of the most used unofficial recreation spots on the river. There are inner-tube riders, swimmers, fishermen, horses with riders crossing the river, and even some off-road bicycling.

The Middle Segment. At (2.7) is a small rodeo ring where bikers have a free chance to watch the trainers work with horses or, with luck, to watch a mini-rodeo. Just beyond is one of the highest spillways on the river (about ten feet) with a holding basin stretched across the river on the downstream side. The route continues alongside residential areas, passes Mountain View High Athletic Field (3.9) and reaches Valley Blvd. (4.1). There is a small bike rest stop here with a simple pipe water fountain. On a clear day, there is a striking view into the San Gabriel Mountains.

The bikepath travels under a railroad bridge and later meets the Walnut Creek junction (4.3). From this point north, the water level drops significantly and the river bed is much less interesting. At this junction, to the left (west) of the trail, is a corral that holds brahma bulls and a buffalo. Continuing onward, the bikeway passes the San Bernardino Fwy. (4.7) and then meets another biker rest area at Ramona Blvd. (5.6).

The Gravel Pits. At (6.5), the route passes the first of several large gravel dredging operations (to the right). In 0.2 mile, the trip passes Lower Azusa Rd. There is a large, open, water-filled gravel pit to the left (west) (5.9), followed by a "granddaddy" gravel pit across the river to the right (6.4). There are several above-ground mining operations in this area.

Santa Fe Dam and Recreation Area. At (7.5), the path crosses under the San Gabriel River Fwy. and stares directly into the Santa Fe Dam face. The route passes a power station (7.0), Live Oak Ave. and appears to dead-end at Arrow Hwy. (8.8). Follow the signed path left and continue to the base of the dam. Pass through the bike entry opening in the fence and continue up a short, steep grade to the top of the dam (9.2).

From the top of the dam in winter are views into the San Gabriel Mountains that are awe-inspiring! There are also views into the San Jose Hills to the southeast and Puente Hills to the south. The cities of the foothills are spread out all the way to the western horizon.

101

There is a trail left (northwest) that dead-ends near the west levee terminus. However, our route goes right and continues another 1.9 miles along the top of the dam providing other fine views, including those down into the Santa Fe Recreational Area. The dam trail ends at the bike trail access gate and proceeds 0.2 mile further to the auto access road to the recreation area (Orange Ave. which is named Azusa Canyon Rd. south of Arrow Hwy.). The mileage at this point is (11.4).

Atop Santa Fe Dam

The recreation area itself is a charmer. To get there, make a hard left onto the automobile roadway access just downhill of the auto pay gate. There are bikepaths and a slow moving, lightly travelled roadway that can be linked into a couple of miles of biking route. The entire park is built alongside a lake and comes equipped with picnic areas, swimming area with a sand beach, playgrounds, fire pits, shaded pogodas (group area at the western end of the lake), boat rental and a snack bar. Also, there are dirt bicycle roadways beyond the west end of the lake. (Note that, as we sadly found, there is no reasonable entry back up to the top of the dam coming from this direction.) By the way, there are also restrooms and drinking water here.

CONNECTING TRIPS: 1) Continuation with the southbound San Gabriel River Trail to Wilderness Park (Trip #19C) - from the Four Corners Trail intersection, head south and over the Whittier Narrows Dam; 2) continuation with the northbound San Gabriel River Trail to the San Gabriel River Canyon (Trip #19E) - at the recreation area automobile access, continue north (nearly straight ahead) and follow the bike trail signs.

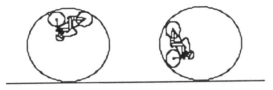

TRIP #19E - SAN GABRIEL RIVER:SANTA FE DAM TO SAN GABRIEL CANYON

GENERAL LOCATION: Irwindale, Azusa

LEVEL OF DIFFICULTY: One way - easy; up and back - moderate
Distance - 7.5 miles (one way)
Elevation gain - 50 feet (Santa Fe Dam)

GENERAL DESCRIPTION: This 100% Class I trip starts downstream of the Santa Fe Dam, then climbs onto and follows the dam levee.   The route continues from the dam upstream to the San Gabriel River terminus at the Los Angeles National Forest Information Center in San Gabriel Canyon.   Along the way, the path traverses the Santa Fe Dam Nature Area, where there is a natural river bottom cactus garden.   There are also spectacular close-up views of the foothills and surrounding mountains.   These views are absolutely great after a cold winter storm.   The stretch north of the dam is little used and makes for a good work-out trip.

TRAILHEAD: From the San Gabriel River Fwy., exit east on Live Oak Ave. and continue 0.9 mile to the junction with Arrow Hwy., making a U-turn onto Arrow Hwy.   Drive back in almost the reverse direction about 0.8 mile to the free parking near the dam outlet.

Another option is to use pay parking in the Santa Fe Dam Recreation Area. This is particularly useful if the biker wishes to avoid riding up onto the dam and wants to start from the recreation area.   Exit on Live Oak Ave. (east) as above, but continue one mile past the junction of Live Oak and Arrow Hwy. Turn left (north) at the Recreation Park entrance at Orange Ave. (named Azusa Canyon Rd. to the south).

TRIP DESCRIPTION: From the free parking area, pedal to the bike entry through the fence to the west of the spillway near the dam base.   Follow the bike trail signs and pedal up the steep roadway to the top of the dam (0.2). From the top, there is a great 360-degree view.   Most prominent are the San Gabriel Mountains to the north and the San Jose Hills and Puente Hills to the southeast and south, respectively.   The view into the mountains is a real "heart grabber" when the snow level is down to low elevations and the sky is clear.

There is a route to the left (northeast) that dead-ends near the west levee terminus.   Our route goes right and travels another 1.9 miles on the dam top, providing more interesting views, including a look down into the Santa Fe Dam Recreation Area (see Trip #19D).   The dam trail ends at a bike access gate and proceeds 0.2 mile further to the pay gate and automobile access road into the recreation area (2.3).

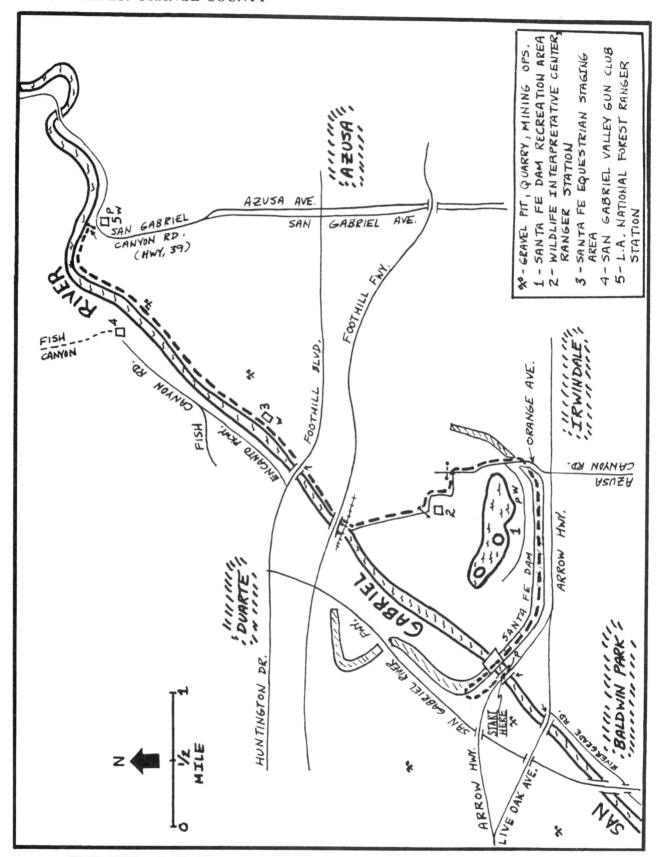

TRIP #19E - SAN GABRIEL RIVER: SANTA FE DAM-SAN GABRIEL CANYON

Head downhill and turn sharply left below the pay gate to visit the developed park (southern) section of the Santa Fe Dam Recreation Area. However, our route follows the signed bike route and proceeds straight ahead.

Northern Santa Fe Dam Recreation Area. Follow the roadway to the dead-end at a nice little walled park-like area (2.8). Turn left and continue following the well-marked road 0.2 mile until it turns right (north) again. In another 0.2 mile, the route reaches the Wildlife Interpretive Center; there are both picnic and tent camping areas near the roadway intersection (3.2). Turn left again and proceed a few hundred feet to the ranger station. There are two bike route options at this point, plus marked walking/nature trails which tour the wildlife area. All routes head west and meet an old north-south asphalt roadway in a short distance. Follow the bike trail marker and turn right (north) on that old road.

The roadway passes through an interesting ecological area which is surrounded by a wide variety of cactus. At (3.8), the roadway reaches the top of a small rise; from this point is a nice view which includes a good look at the surrounding bottomland, the backside of the Santa Fe Dam, and a view north to the Foothill Fwy. In 0.4 mile, the bikepath returns to the San Gabriel River and shortly thereafter passes under the Foothill Fwy. (4.3).

The Gravel Pits. At (4.8), the bikeway passes a trans-river passenger cable car. In 0.1 mile is Huntington Dr./Foothill Blvd. Next is the Santa Fe Equestrian Staging Area where there are restrooms and water (5.2). There is a large above-ground gravel mining/processing works in the background. The river bed is boulder- and brush- filled with a spillway breaking the continuity of the scene every half-mile or more.

At (5.5), the path goes by an old closed-off railroad bridge. There is a budding residential area across the river with the homes continuing up into the nearby foothills. There are more gravel operations along the roadway to the right (east) with one sand and gravel operation lying right next to the trail (6.1). The route also passes a large water-filled gravel pit (6.5).

San Gabriel Canyon Entrance. The trail heads into a progressively more well-defined canyon environment. At (6.8), the route passes Fish Canyon in the hills to the left (west). There is an exquisite series of waterfalls (wintertime) several miles back into the canyon called Fish Falls. (Sorry, this is hiking country only.) At this point on the bike trail, there is also a firing range, the San Gabriel Valley Gun Club. The hills echo the sounds, providing a "Gunfight at the OK Corral" aura.

Just beyond, the trail dead-ends at a fence (7.5). A small trail to the right leads to Hwy. 39 and the L.A. National Forest Ranger Station. There is water and parking here should the biker want to start from this direction.

CONNECTING TRIPS: 1) Continuation with the San Gabriel River Trail south to Whittier Narrows (Trip #19D) - cross Arrow Hwy. and bike east a few hundred feet (in front of the spillway); 2) continuation with a very strenuous Class X "gut-buster" up San Gabriel Canyon Rd. - we observed a few hearty bikers working their way up the several miles of continuous steep grade.

TRIP #20 - COYOTE CREEK TRAIL

GENERAL LOCATION: Long Beach - Seal Beach/Cerritos

LEVEL OF DIFFICULTY: One way - easy; up and back - moderate
Distance - 14.0 miles (one way)
Elevation gain - essentially flat

GENERAL DESCRIPTION: Another of the river trails, this is a 99.44% pure Class I route. The trip starts at the scenic lower section of the San Gabriel River outlet near the Long Beach Marina and proceeds to the Coyote Creek junction. The Coyote Creek path is well maintained, but lightly used. The 9.1-mile Coyote Creek section is not highly scenic, unless one enjoys "window shopping" into backyards of the adjoining homes and apartments. It is a fine workout bikeway, however. The trip passes alongside Cerrito's Regional County Park (which is a convenient and pleasant rest point) and passes under Artesia Blvd. Next is a 2.5-mile recent extention through commercial area to a terminus at Foster Rd. A short ride from here leads to shaded Frontier Park.

TRAILHEAD: Free public parking is available on Marina Dr. in Long Beach or along First St. in Seal Beach. From Pacific Coast Highway (PCH) in Seal Beach, turn west on Marina Dr. (2-3 blocks from Main Street in Seal Beach) and continue roughly 0.5 mile to First St. In another 1/4 mile, cross the San Gabriel River and continue a short distance along the marina for parking. The trailhead is located at Marina Dr. at the east end of the bridge over the San Gabriel River (near Seaport Village).

Bikers should have a filled water bottle since the trip is waterless up to Cerritos Regional Park. An option is to ride south about 0.3 mile from the trailhead to use restrooms at the beach. The side trip may also serve as a very pleasant scenic diversion. After the ride, Shoreline Village at the marina edge may serve as a nice dining spot, watering hole, or place to shop.

TRIP DESCRIPTION: **The Scenic Lower Segment.** The first part of the trip provides views of boaters, water skiers, and an interestingly-developed shoreline. The natural river basin then passes the PCH access, the Westminster Ave. entry (1.2), and the Haynes Steam Plant (electricity generation). At (2.2), a small diversion Class I path leads off to the east along a 1.2-mile shaded route to Seal Beach Blvd. In this stretch of the river, up to the concrete portion at about (3.5), one has views of a large bird population that includes pelicans, egrets, and the ever-present seagulls. The trip passes under the Garden Grove Fwy. (2.3) and San Diego Fwy. (3.5). In this portion of the path are many "freeway orchards" -- those freeway-locked areas under the power poles which are used for growing containerized plants.

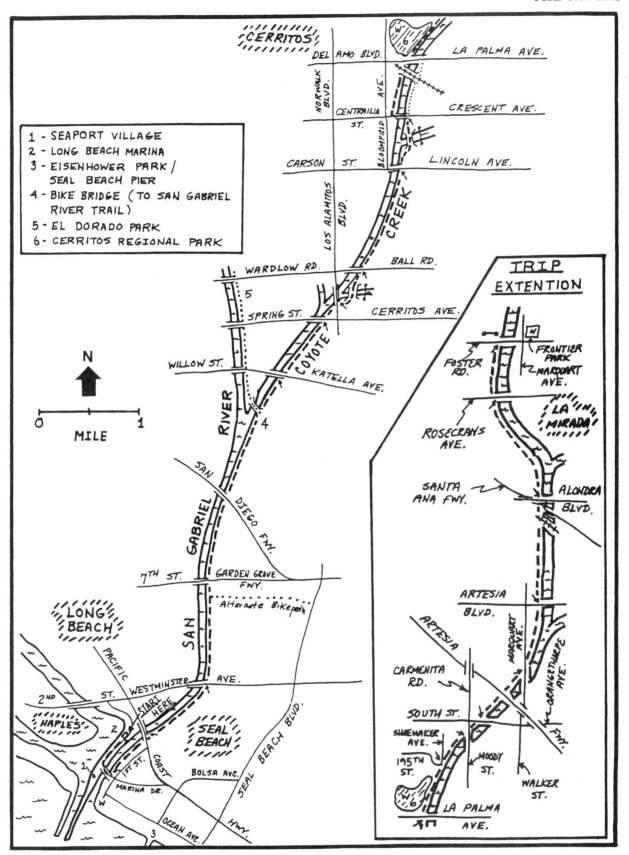

1 - SEAPORT VILLAGE
2 - LONG BEACH MARINA
3 - EISENHOWER PARK /
    SEAL BEACH PIER
4 - BIKE BRIDGE (TO SAN GABRIEL
    RIVER TRAIL)
5 - EL DORADO PARK
6 - CERRITOS REGIONAL PARK

TRIP #20 - COYOTE CREEK

Coyote Creek. At (3.9), a marked bridge over the river takes bikers to the connecting portion of the San Gabriel River Bike Trail (Trip #19A). However, at this junction, our route continues along the east side (stay to the right) of the channel and passes the Katella Ave. entry, the San Gabriel River Fwy., and the Cerritos Ave. access (5.2). Nearby, the channel junctions to the north (no easy access at this junction was found on the return trip), although our reference route stays along the east side of the channel. Two additional small channel junctions to the east were encountered at (5.6) and (7.3). However, both junctions are closed off by locked gates and the main Coyote Creek path crosses those junctions via small overpasses. The Los Alamitos access is at about (5.6). Pass Ball Rd., a small walking-only bridge across the creek at (6.3), Lincoln Ave., and bike to Crescent Ave./Centrailia St.

Exit the bikeway and cross to the west bank. Continue 1/2 mile to La Palma Ave./Del Amo Blvd. and pass alongside Cerritos County Regional Park. There is water within sight of the bikeway plus a park complete with restrooms, recreational fields, and a limited amount of shade. Pedal along a residential area and pass under Moody St./Carmenita Rd., then South St./Orangethorpe Ave. (Note the fast food establishments and gas stations to the west.) (9.2).

In a short distance, bike under the Artesia Fwy. and pass alongside residential developments (with scattered shade trees), biking past Walker St./Marquart Ave. The path veers left (due north) along the La Canada Verde Creek fork and continues another 0.4 mile to Artesia Blvd. The channel dips under the Santa Ana Fwy. and Alondra Blvd. on a recently opened 2.5-mile path extention through a strictly commercial zone. The bikeway passes alongside the Santa Fe Springs Drive-in Theater (12.3), then beelines 1.7 miles to a terminus at Foster Rd.

CONNECTING TRIPS: 1) Continuation to lower and middle portions of the San Gabriel River tour (Trips #19A and 19B) - take major access streets west over the San Gabriel River Fwy. noting that distance between Coytote Creek and the San Gabriel River increases the further north one goes on Coyote Creek; 2) connectors to the lower portion of this trip along the San Gabriel River are described in Trip #19A.

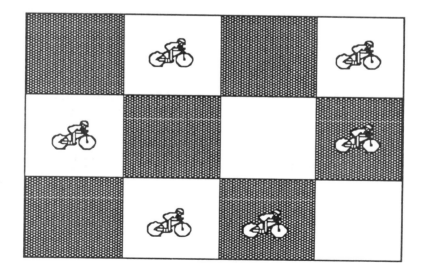

THE INLAND TRAILS

Aliso Creek Trail: El Toro Community Park

TRIP # 21 - CYPRESS TOUR

GENERAL LOCATION: Cypress, La Palma, Buena Park

LEVEL OF DIFFICULTY: Loop - easy to moderate
Distance - 14.9 miles (loop)
Elevation gain - essentially flat

GENERAL DESCRIPTION: This is a pleasant cruise primarily on Class II city streets that explores several inland Orange County cities. The tour leaves pleasant and tiny Eucalyptus Park and follows a lightly travelled loop through mostly residential and some light industrial areas. There are two enjoyable Class I loops within the larger tour. Other highlights are Cypress College and El Rancho Verde Park and Bicycle Path The route described can be linked with numerous other Class II and Class III routes in the area.

TRAILHEAD: From the Garden Grove Fwy., exit north on Valley View St. and drive 1-3/4 miles to Orangewood Ave. Turn left and continue a short distance to Eucalyptus Park.

From the San Gabriel River Fwy., exit east at Katella Ave./Willow St. Continue east three miles to Valley View St., turn right and drive one-half mile to Orangewood Ave. Turn right again and continue to the park.

Bring a filled water bottle. There are scattered water sources along the way.

TRIP DESCRIPTION: Northbound. Leave the park and bike east on Orangewood Ave. Once across Valley View St., pass Maplegrove Parks North and South (athletic courts, grass, shade, water) and in another 0.4 mile continue past Manzanita Park (trees, athletic courts). Turn left (north) at Knott St. and bike 0.3 mile to the end of the housing tract. Turn left and bike 1.0 mile along a wash on the Class I path, returning to Valley View St. (2.5).

Turn right and cruise north on the sidewalk 0.5 mile to Cerritos Ave., turn left onto the Class II street, turn right in a short distance on Walker St. (the eastern edge of the Los Alamitos Race Course) and left again on Class II Ball Rd. There is a small shopping center and gas station at this intersection (3.9). Continue west on Ball Rd. to Moody St. and begin a pleasant, sporadically shaded 1.5 mile Class I partial loop on the large sidewalk. The path turns right at Denni St. and right again at Orange Ave. returning to Moody St. (5.4). Continue north on Moody St. for 1.8 miles and turn right just past Sharon Dr. onto the Class I bikepath below the power poles.

This is the westernmost edge of the El Rancho Verde Park and Bicycle Path, a laid-back two-mile stretch of mixed Class I path/grass, the last one mile for balloon tires only. Our reference route follows the (lighted) first mile; there are water fountains along the path at the baseball field near the half-way point and just across Walker St. Continue to the end of the Class I path at Valley View St. (8.2).

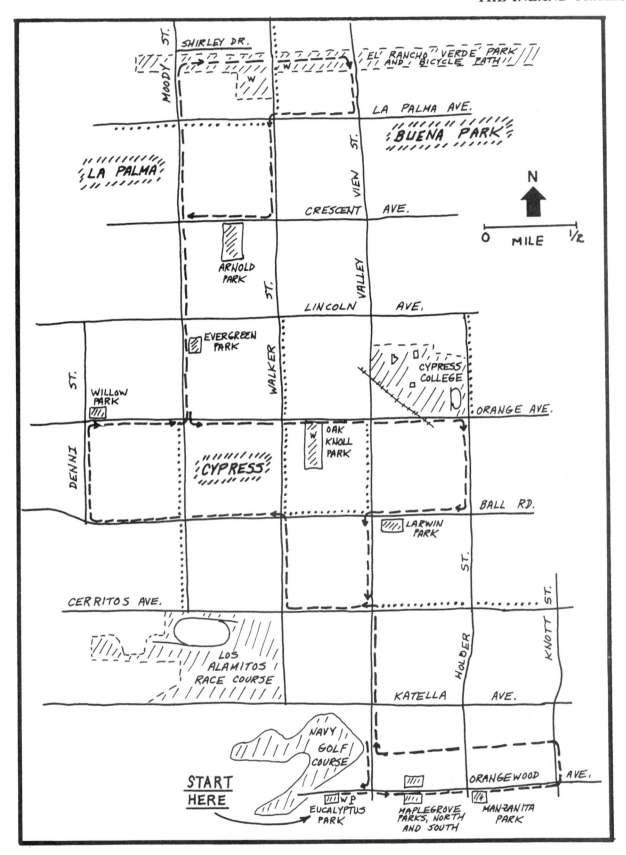

TRIP #21 - CYPRESS TOUR

Southbound. Follow Class X Valley View Ave. a short distance to La Palma Ave., turn right (west), left on Walker St., and right on Crescent Ave. All streets in this short 1.8 mile zig-zag stretch are Class II. Continue on Crescent Ave. between the tennis courts to the north and the sports complex of Arnold Park to the right. At Moody St., turn left (south) (10.0).

Return on Moody St. to Orange Ave. and turn left, passing the Cypress Community Center/Oak Knoll Park with its recreation field, water and restrooms. At 1.5 miles from the Moody St./Orange Ave. intersection, pass the expansive lawns of the Cypress College campus and turn right on Holder St. Follow Holder St. 0.5 mile to Ball Rd., turn right and return to Valley View St. (13.5). Bike 1.4 mile south, turn right at Orange Ave., and return to Eucalyptus Park. (14.9).

CONNECTING TRIPS: 1) Connection with the Western Orange County Loop (Trip #33) - at La Palma Ave. and Valley View St., bike east on the former street; 2) connection with the Coyote Creek ride (Trip #20) - bike west on Lincoln Ave. at its intersection with Moody St.

TRIP #22 - EL CAJON TRAIL

GENERAL LOCATION: Yorba Linda

LEVEL OF DIFFICULTY: One way - easy; up and back - moderate
Distance - 8.2 miles (one way)
Elevation gain - periodic moderate grades

GENERAL DESCRIPTION: This delightful trip roams through some of the most pleasant residential neighborhoods in Orange County, particularly for bikers who are horse lovers. The primarily Class I route meanders along the general route of the old El Cajon Canal (now the Anaheim Union Canal). The trip is segmented as follows: 1) 3.6 miles through a rural residential setting (several road crossings required); 2) a diversion onto a Class X roadway on Kellogg Dr. followed by a Class I passage through the Yorba Linda Country Club; 3) return to a Class X roadway downhill and along Esperanza Dr; and 4) a final 1.8 mile Class I roadway through a new, rural residential neighborhood near Yorba Linda Blvd. and Esperanza Rd. This is a particularly fine trip for nosy people who like to peek into backyards.

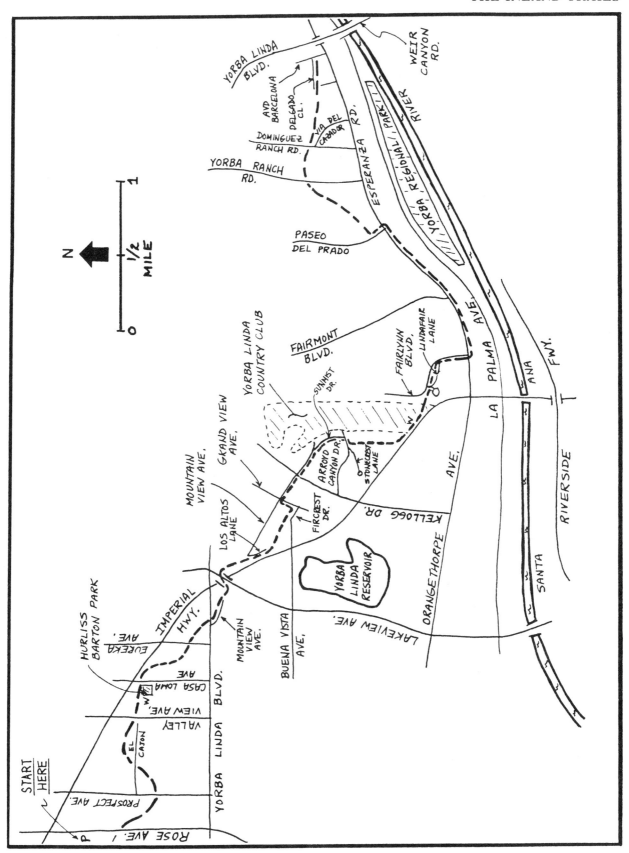

TRIP #22 - EL CAJON TRAIL

TRAILHEAD: From the Orange Fwy., exit east at Yorba Linda Blvd. Continue about 2.2 miles and turn left on Rose Dr. Continue 0.6 mile just past Verna Ln. (right hand side only) and look for the asphalt bike trail. If you pass Bastanchury Rd., you've gone too far. Find parking near the trailhead subject to the local parking laws.

From the Riverside Fwy., exit north at Tustin Ave. Continue 3-1/2 miles as Tustin Ave. becomes Rose Dr. and meets Verna Ln. Park as described above.

Bring a moderate water supply. There are only two water fountains that we found along the bikeway.

TRIP DESCRIPTION: **Trailhead to Hurliss Burton Park.** The trail has a short spur to the west of Rose Dr., however, our route starts from the east side. Proceed along a eucalyptus-lined path and a mini-orange grove through a pleasant residential neighborhood. Cross Prospect Ave. (0.3) and enjoy a quarter mile of "pure" horse country (both sights and smells). Cross El Cajon Ave. (0.6) and continue through a fenced trail area that borders many residential backyards (we saw a wedding reception and also some young children jumping from the roof into a swimming pool in this stretch!). The path crosses Valley View Ave. (1.0), a small tank farm, and then crosses Casa Loma Ave. (1.3). There is small, pleasant Hurliss Barton Park just to the right at the crossing, with shade and water.

Hurliss Barton Park to the Imperial Highway Crossing. The route parallels Imperial Hwy. for a short distance, then loops back away from the roadway and crosses the canal on a little wooden bridge (1.6). The path cruises along a eucalyptus-lined section, crosses Eureka Ave. (1.9), and switches to a colorful oleander-lined section. The route crosses Yorba Linda Blvd. and parallels Mountain View Ave., climbing to a small, scenic crest (2.3). Next is the Lakeview Ave. crossing; half a mile south (right) from this junction is the Yorba Linda Reservoir with several miles of jogging-, equestrian-, and balloon tire riding- trails.

However, our route continues left on Lakeview Ave. and crosses a bridge over Imperial Hwy. (2.5). Once across, the path heads steeply downhill, then levels off near a residential area at Los Altos Ln. (2.8). The path winds around an equestrian staging area, then passes a small commercial zone near Fircrest Dr. At (3.0), the path crosses Grand View Ave., turns left, proceeds one block and continues right along Mountain View Ave. (3.4).

Yorba Linda Country Club and Golf Course. In 0.2 mile, the Class I path ends at Kellogg Dr. Continue across that roadway onto a short, testy grade to Sunmist Dr. and turn right. Follow that road on a milder grade through a plush neighborhood to its terminus at Arroyo Canyon Dr. (4.1). Turn right and look for the little asphalt continuation trail in a short distance. Follow the path downhill while taking in the views of the Anaheim Hills and the Santa Ana River flood plain. At 0.3 mile from Arroyo Canyon Dr., the path reaches a point above Imperial Hwy. (4.3), then continues downhill to the Yorba Linda Country Club and Golf Course. Traverse the golf course near the fence, cross a small golf cart path (with a nearby water fountain), and pass over the canal on a little concrete strip.

There is a trail junction just beyond this point (4.8). The tree-shaded trail left travels along the golf course and dies out at Brookmont Dr (this is a pleasant diversion ride). Our route goes straight ahead up a steep hill, with an expansive view to the south and southeast at the top of the grade. The trail winds around the hill, passes through a packed dirt stretch, and meets little Lindafair Ln. Cross that street and continue on the trail 0.2 mile to Fairlynn Blvd.

El Cajon Trail Near Yorba Linda Golf Course

Esperanza Road. Continue 0.3 mile downhill on Fairlynn Blvd. to Esperanza Rd. and turn left. Follow that Class X roadway 1.2 miles to Paseo Del Prado and turn left. Climb a short grade and turn right in about two blocks onto the asphalt bikepath (6.9). In another 0.2 mile, the trail travels along a cactus-lined hillside, followed by a cruise alongside the backyards of several residences.

At (7.6) the bike trail crosses Yorba Ranch Rd., travels along a lovely tree-lined section, passes some tennis courts, and soon reaches Dominguez Ranch Rd. (7.8). The route continues on a Class I trail through this newer residential neighborhood passing in succession Via Del Conejo, Via Del Bisconte, Avd. Antigua, and terminates near Avd. Barcelona just north and west of the junction of Yorba Linda Blvd. and Esperanza Rd. (8.2). If time permits, try a freeweeling tour through the well laid out residential community.

CONNECTING TRIPS: 1) Connection with the Santa Ana River Trail (Trip #17A north or Trip #17B south) - continue east on Class X Esperanza Rd. under the Wier Canyon Rd. overpass and walk your bike across the open field to the right (south) to La Palma Ave. Turn right and continue to Yorba Regional Park; 2) connection with the Fullerton Tour/Craig Park route (Trip #24) - continue from the trip origin three miles west on Bastanchury Rd.; turn right (north) and proceed one mile to the Craig Park entrance. This road is on a Class X roadway with some sections having very narrow shoulder; and 3) connection with the Carbon Canyon Workout (Trip #23) - at the trip origin, bike north 1-1/2 miles on Rose Dr. to Valencia Ave., turn right, and continue 0.4 mile to Carbon Canyon Rd.

Biking   Worldwide

TRIP #23 - CARBON CANYON WORKOUT

GENERAL LOCATION: Carbon Canyon

LEVEL OF DIFFICULTY: Up and back - strenuous
Distance - 11.2 miles (up and back)
Elevation gain - continuous moderate to
steep grades

GENERAL DESCRIPTION: This is a rugged uphill workout which starts from Carbon Canyon Park and proceeds to the Carbon Canyon Rd. summit, 700+ feet elevation gain in 5-1/4 miles. The trip is a canyon-watcher's delight with nice unobstructed views (which also means that there is little in the way of surrounding tree cover). The return is a free-wheeling adventure which is nothing short of exciting. This is biking away from the "big city" with interesting terrain, varied plant life and tree cover, and relative peace and quiet. There is a striped divider section on the entire roadway to the summit, although this is not a sanctioned Class II bikepath.

TRAILHEAD: Exit the Orange Fwy. at Imperial Hwy. and drive east 1-3/4 miles to Valencia Ave. Turn left and continue one mile to Carbon Canyon Rd., turn right and proceed 1-1/4 mile to Carbon Canyon Regional Park.

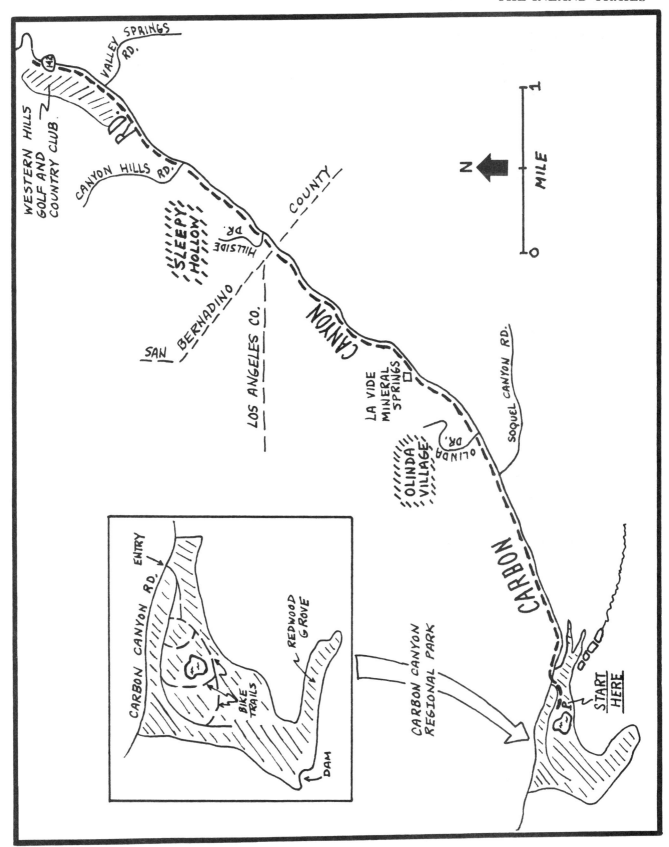

VALLEY SPRINGS RD.

WESTERN HILLS GOLF AND COUNTRY CLUB

CANYON HILLS RD.

SLEEPY HOLLOW

HILLSIDE DR.

SAN BERNADINO CO.

LOS ANGELES CO.

COUNTY

CANYON

LA VIDE MINERAL SPRINGS

OLINDA VILLAGE

OLINDA DR.

SOQUEL CANYON RD.

CARBON

N

MILE

1

0

CARBON CANYON RD.

ENTRY

REDWOOD GROVE

BIKE TRAILS

DAM

CARBON CANYON REGIONAL PARK

START HERE

TRIP #23 - CARBON CANYON WORKOUT

It is not recommended to proceed beyond the summit (i.e., the trip turnaround point). The descent on the north side is significantly steeper - a series of hairpin turns with no significant road shoulder for biking for the first 1/2 mile.

Bring a filled water bottle, particularly important for hot days.

TRIP DESCRIPTION: Before leaving the park, explore the general area by using the roughly two miles of bikepath/roadway within. There are also scenic hiking trails in the area, with the most lengtly trail exploring the redwood tree stand at the southwestern park edge.

Carbon Canyon Park to Olinda Village. Leave the park and turn left, immediately beginning on a workout upgrade. The route passes through a pleasant forrested area in this early segment. The roadway passes a large citrus grove and enters an area where the grade steepens (0.6). In 0.2 mile is an impressive canyon view looking north. The winding uphill road passes a horse grazing area and reaches a flat at 1.3 tough miles from the trip start. The vegetation transitions from lightly forrested to more of a high desert appearance as the road climbs and heads further back into the canyon. Just beyond is Olinda Village and a small market.

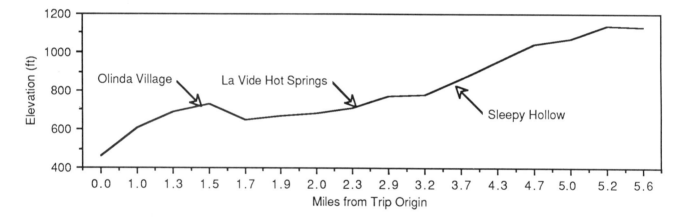

Olinda Village to Sleepy Hollow. Follow the steep downgrade which levels and passes the La Vide Mineral Springs (with resort). Pedal another winding upgrade through this short treed segment before reaching another flat (3.0). The route proceeds up again, crosses the San Bernardino County Line, and soon reaches Sleepy Hollow. At Hillside Dr. is the "Party House," with liquid refreshment and a shaded terrace (3.7).

Sleepy Hollow to the Summit. Continue on difficult uphill again (we didn't say that this was a picnic route!) on a 0.4 mile pull with scattered tree cover. Not far beyond the flat is Canyon Hills Rd. and Canyon Hills Stables (4.3). Bike alongside the Western Hills Golf Course, pass Valley Spring Rd. (5.0), and bike the quarter mile steep upgrade to the trip's summit. Pedal another 0.4 mile on the plateau to the horse pens which are alongside Carbon Canyon Rd. Enjoy the beautiful animals and then free-wheel the return downhill segment.

CONNECTING TRIPS: 1) Connection with the El Cajon Trail (Trip #22) - return to Valencia Rd., turn left (south) and continue 0.4 mile to Rose Dr. Turn left and follow that road 1-1/2 miles to the trip origin.

TRIP #24 - FULLERTON TOUR/CRAIG PARK

GENERAL LOCATION: Fullerton

LEVEL OF DIFFICULTY: Full loop - moderate to strenuous
Distance - 13.7 miles (loop)
Elevation gain - periodic moderate to steep grades

GENERAL DESCRIPTION: This trip tours the rural, hilly portions of Fullerton and takes in pleasant Craig Park as well. Craig Park could serve as a family bike outing on its own. This tour has everything from Class I to Class X bike routes, but is mostly on signed motor vehicle roadways (Class III). The general area is scenic and the interspersed hill climbs provide a little extra variety. Los Coyotes Park is an added bonus.

TRAILHEAD: From the Artesia Fwy. (Riverside Fwy.) take Harbor Blvd. north into Fullerton. Continue about three miles to Valencia Mesa Dr. and turn left (west). Find parking near the intersection, but be sure to comply with the local parking regulations.

Bring a moderate water supply. The primary watering holes are in the shopping area near the starting point and at Los Coyotes and Craig Regional Parks. The later points are at the westernmost and easternmost ends of the trip, respectively.

TRIP DESCRIPTION: Los Coyotes Park Loop. The trip starts southwest on Valencia Mesa Dr. travelling along a tree-lined route onto a moderate upgrade, then crossing over a small bridge near the crest (0.2). The route is Class III. For the next mile, the trip cruises through a peaceful, rural residential neighborhood. The route crosses Euclid Ave. (0.8) and later follows a steep downhill to Bastanchury Rd. (1.4). A hard right, 0.2 mile of pedaling, and a left turn on Parks Rd. leads the biker past Edward White Park (1.8) along an upgrade through a new residential area.

The upgrade continues to Rosecrans Ave. (2.2) where the tour heads left (west) and continues uphill. In this area, there is little biking room on the Class III roadway; an option is to use the narrow path along the fence that surrounds the neighborhood. The route crests at Gilbert St. (3.0), where there is a pleasant rest spot around the northeast corner at Coyote Hills Park.

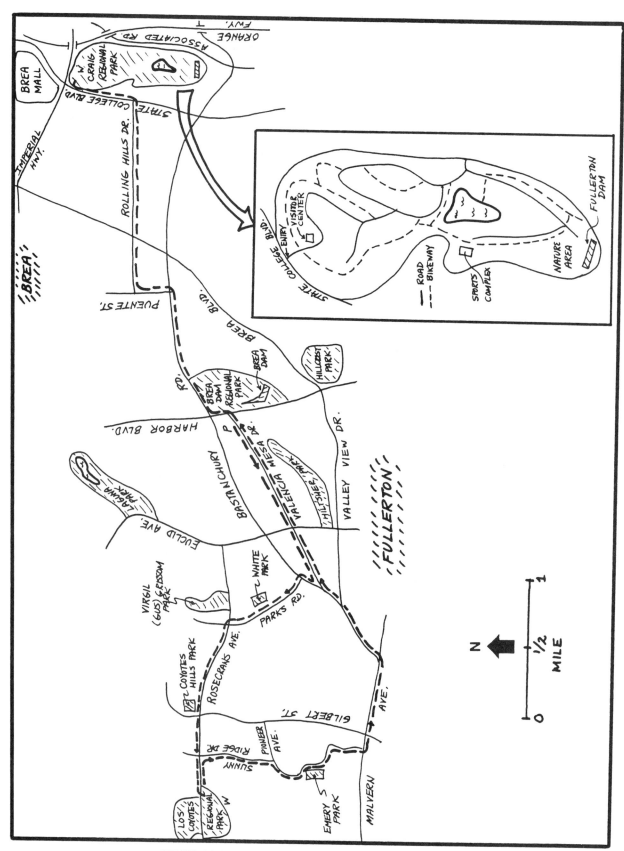

TRIP #24 - FULLERTON TOUR/ CRAIG PARK

Continue downhill another 1.2 miles to significantly larger Los Coyotes Regional Park. There are shade, water, and restrooms here. The park has picnic areas, a small lake, recreation fields, and playgrounds, all of which are under a sparsely-treed setting.

Return east on Rosecrans Ave. 0.5 mile to Sunny Ridge Dr. (4.7) and turn right (south). Follow a pleasant Class III path downhill through a residential neighborhood to Pioneer Ave. and turn right (5.2). Continue a short distance and follow the road as it turns left, passes little Emery Park (5.5), and suddenly recaptures its old name, Sunny Ridge Dr. The route winds its way downhill from this point to meet with Malvern Blvd. (6.0). Turn left (east) and continue 0.8 mile on a Class III roadway to Bastanchury Rd., then turn left again. Continue another 0.5 mile to Valencia Mesa Dr. (7.3). Head up the steep grade and return to the starting point (8.7). This loop, by itself, is a moderate trip on a 100% Class III route.

Craig Park Loop. One option is to pack up the bikes and drive to Craig Park. The other is to turn left (north) on Harbor Blvd., continue 0.2 mile and turn right on Bastanchury Rd. (8.9). Now comes a Class X route through some moderate-to-steep hills past the Fullerton Municipal Golf Course and an area with a view into the backside of Brea Dam. The dam drainage is virtually dry and is now Brea Dam Regional Park.

Just beyond the drainage area, turn left on Puente St. and continue 0.2 mile to Rolling Hills Dr. (9.9). Turn right and continue on a Class II roadway uphill through a residential area. At Woodline Ave. (10.2), the route heads downhill then back uphill to a crest 0.5 mile from that intersection. In a short distance, Rolling Hills Dr. ends at State College Blvd. (10.9). Head left and downhill and turn right at Rosalia Dr. to enter Craig Park (11.2). The return trip to the car from this point is 2.5 miles.

Craig Park. There are numerous ways to tour Craig Park. There are over two miles of Class I bike trails which make this an attractive family option. When the bike trails are hooked up with the slow-moving, lightly-travelled roads within the park, the number of potential bike routes is multiplied several times. The park also has picnic areas, shaded pavilions, hiking and equestrian trails, a natural amphitheater, lakes, and turfed play areas. This park rivals some of the other larger parks visited in our travels, e.g., Mile Square Park (Trip #5), Irvine Regional Park (Trip #26), and El Dorado Regional Park (L.A. County).

CONNECTING TRIPS: 1) Connection with the El Cajon Trail (Trip #22) - from Craig Park, bike south 0.9 mile to Bastanchury Rd. and turn left (east); continue 2.7 miles on mild Class X and Class II bikeways to the Anaheim Union Canal (about 0.5 mile east of Valencia Ave.; 2) connection with the Western Orange County Loop (Trip #33) - at Bastanchury Rd. and Malvern Ave., continue east on the latter road.

TRIP #25 - SANTA ANA CANYON ROAD

GENERAL LOCATION: Santa Ana Canyon, Anaheim Hills

LEVEL OF DIFFICULTY: One way - easy; up and back - moderate
Distance - 7.6 miles (one way)
Elevation gain - periodic moderate grades

GENERAL DESCRIPTION: This is a fine workout trip on a Class II bikeway that traverses one segment of Santa Ana Canyon. On clear days, there are excellent views north into the Chino Hills and east further into the canyon. The route traverses the base of the Anaheim Hills and parallels the Santa Ana River for most of the trip. The greater portion of the trip is unshaded and can be rather hot in the summer, particularly on the eastern segment.

TRAILHEAD: From the Costa Mesa Fwy., exit at Lincoln Ave./Nohl Ranch Rd. in the city of Orange. Follow Lincoln Ave. west a short distance and turn left on Tustin Ave. Turn right into the Park and Ride area just beyond.

Another option is to start the ride from Eisenhower Park. There is parking to the west (Lincoln Ave. to Ocean View Ave. and right on Main St.) and north (Lincoln Ave. to Ocean View Ave and right on Bixby Ave.). This is a pleasant, shaded little park with a small lake, picnic benches, play areas, a mini-barnyard and bikepath to boot! The park sits right next to The Brickyard, a shopping plaza. There is a fine restaurant in the plaza with a veranda area that looks out over the lake--a great place to end the trip.

Bikers should come prepared with a moderate water supply. The prime water sources are all off-route, specifically at shopping centers or at Featherly Park near the trip terminus.

TRIP DESCRIPTION: **Trailhead to Peralta Canyon Park.** Exit the Park and Ride area and head north a short distance to Lincoln Ave. Turn right (east) and continue under the Costa Mesa Fwy. Turn left on Santa Ana Canyon Rd. (0.2). Note that both streets change names at the intersection -- Lincoln Ave./Nohl Ranch Rd. and Santiago Blvd./Santa Ana Canyon Rd. The route starts with the hills to the right and the freeway to the left and passes through a eucalyptus-lined flat stretch.

At Lakeview Ave., the path pulls away from the Riverside Fwy. and starts a moderate upgrade (2.2). In 0.2 mile is the crest with a nice view into the Santa Ana River Canyon. Continuing through small rolling hills, the tour passes Pinney Dr. (north)/Royal Oak Rd. (south) (1.9). A short 0.1 mile detour on Pinney Dr. leads to Peralta Canyon Park, a sports and recreation paradise.

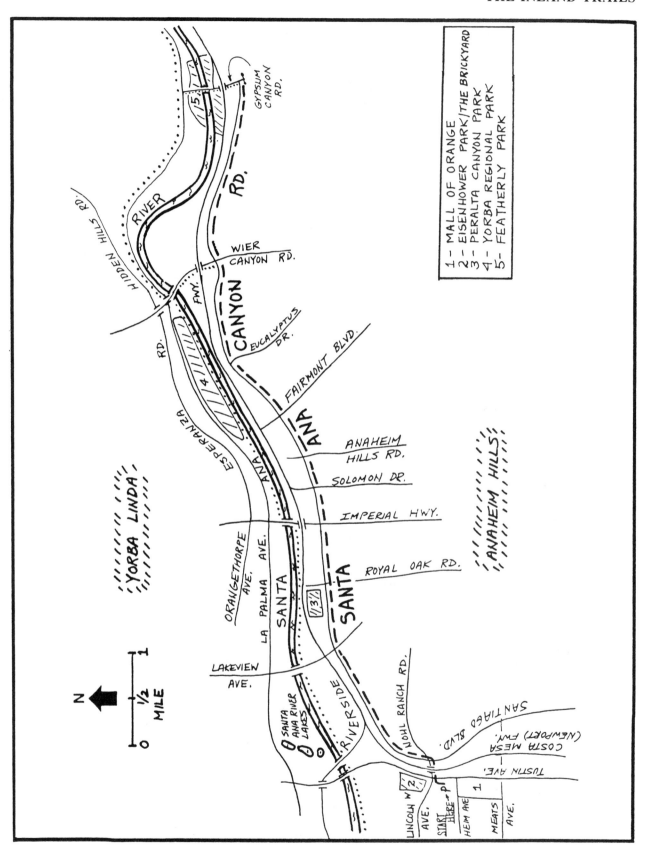

TRIP #25 - SANTA ANA CANYON ROAD

Anaheim Hills Proper. At Margarita Ave., there are shopping centers along both sides of the roadway (2.4). There are also nice views into the Peralta Hills (south) and across the canyon into the Chino Hills. The tour passes another tree-lined section of town with more small shopping centers at Imperial Hwy. (2.6). Beyond this intersection, the surroundings become significantly more rural.

The tour continues on a flat Class II bikeway past Anaheim Hills Rd. (3.2), Quintana Rd. and Eucalyptus Pk. (3.5), a small shopping center to the left (3.6), and reaches Fairmont Blvd. in another 0.1 mile. There are more excellent views across the canyon near this junction. The bikepath heads uphill in another 0.4 mile and crests in a short distance (4.3). The route returns near the freeway at this location; there is also a nice view further eastward into the canyon.

The Wide-Open Spaces. The remainder of the trip is more exposed and certainly more isolated. The bikeway heads up a 0.2-mile steep upgrade and crests near an area of large, open fields (4.7). The route then passes newer housing developments near Roosevelt Rd. (5.5), Weir Canyon Rd. (5.7), and in 0.2 mile reaches an area with an excellent view further into the Santa Ana Canyon. Shortly, the route narrows to one lane (6.1) and continues another 1.5 miles through dry, dusty brushland to Gypsum Canyon Rd.

CONNECTING TRIPS: 1) Continuation with the Santa Ana River Trail (Trip #17A) - at the terminus, continue west on Gypsum Canyon Rd. toward Featherly Regional Park. Turn right onto the Class I trail just before entering the park. (Note: also see Trip #17A for a loop connection with the Class I trail on the north bank of the Santa Ana River.); 2) connection with the Orange/Irvine Regional Park Loop (Trip #26) - near the trip origin, turn south on Santiago Blvd. from Lincoln Ave. and bike two miles on a Class II bikeway to Villa Park Rd.

TRIP #26 - ORANGE/IRVINE PARK LOOP

GENERAL LOCATION: Orange

LEVEL OF DIFFICULTY: Loop - moderate
Distance - 13.6 miles (loop)
Elevation gain - periodic moderate upgrades
(single moderate to steep grade)

GENERAL DESCRIPTION: A tour through a rural section of Orange County, this route works its way through some lightly trafficked, pleasant residential areas and terminates at Irvine Regional Park. The full trip starts and ends near Santiago Creek. The tour can be adjusted to various lengths, although any route planning should include the park, which is the highlight of the trip.

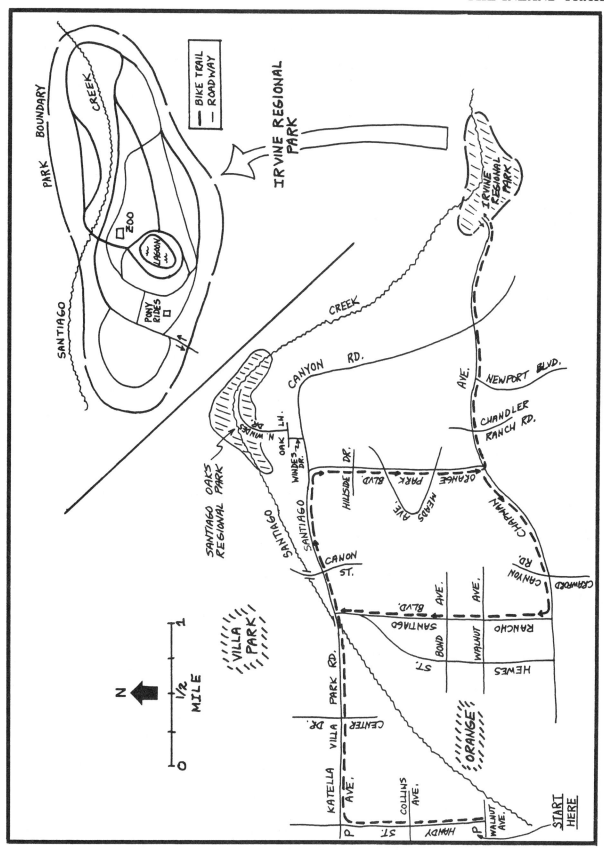

TRIP #26 - ORANGE/ IRVINE PARK

The general route is a Class II bikeway with a couple of tough upgrades. The park section is Class I and could serve as a family trip in itself. The park has several miles of bikeway, as well as picnic areas, pony rides, small zoo, lovely lagoon, and other attractions.

TRAILHEAD: From the Newport Fwy., exit at Katella Ave. and turn east. In less than one-half mile, turn right on Handy St. Proceed about one mile and park near the intersection of Handy St. and Walnut Ave.

Bring enough water (one or two filled water bottles) to travel to Irvine Regional Park. This is a relatively exposed trip and there are few, if any, water stops along this route. There is a concession stand at the park. However, this trip calls for carrying some of your own "munchies" as there are few convenient eateries or markets along the way.

TRIP DESCRIPTION: **Orange to Irvine Park.** The initial mile of the trip is through a quiet residential neighborhood on Handy St. The route heads right at Katella Ave./Villa Park Rd. and proceeds along this busy street past Wanda Rd. (1.3), slims down to a one-lane road in another 0.2 mile, and shortly passes Center St. (1.8). At Hewes St. (2.5), the roadway becomes Santiago Canyon Rd. and proceeds downhill with a view into Santiago Creek. There is a large quarry to the right and houses built high up on the hillside to the left. The bike route passes Canon St. (2.8) and in a short distance passes through a tree-lined portion of roadway (one of the few), passing a large gravel plant at the foot of the hills (3.2).

In a short distance, the tour reaches Orange Park Blvd. A diversion would be to continue on Santiago Canyon Rd. to Santiago Oaks Regional Park where there is water, shade, hiking, horse trails and limited biking areas. However, our reference trip turns right (south) and begins one of the most pleasant parts of the tour. This section passes through a lovely rural neighborhood with open fields and some tree cover on the biker's side of the road. The area is hilly and follows a downhill, then steep uphill near the first intersection with Meads Ave. (3.7). The trip continues through more moderate rolling hills past Meads Ave. again (4.5) and meets Chapman Ave 0.3 mile further.

The Class II and Class III route on Chapman Ave. has heavier traffic and is part of a steady, gritty upgrade that levels off at Equestrian Dr. (5.0). There is an outstanding view into the canyon and back into the residential areas at this point. A side trip up Equestrian Dr. provides a very steep spur up to the Orange Hill Restaurant and one of the most spectacular views of the Orange Country area. However, our trip continues on Chapman Ave. and follows a well-deserved downhill past Chandler Ranch Rd., Irvine Ranch Farmer's Market (5.6), and Newport Blvd. (5.8). The route breaks into a flat, open area and begins an upgrade that crosses Santiago Canyon Rd. (6.2). At 6.6 miles from the start, the biker reaches Irvine Regional Park.

Irvine Park. There is a multitude of ways to tour this park, which rivals Mile Square Park (Trip #5) and El Dorado Park (L.A. County) and which is certainly more in its natural state. Our tour started with a 1.9-mile ride around the bikepaths at the park boundaries and included a 2.0-mile interior tour.

The outside tour includes the route across (north of) Santiago Creek, a swingby of open expanses of the westernmost picnic and kite flying areas, and a pass-by tour of the William Harding Nature Area. The interior tour includes the Santiago Creek parallel path, middle park path through the playgrounds and group picnic areas, and a tour around the lagoon and zoo areas. In addition, there is an equal amount of roads through the area that are lightly travelled and serve as excellent bikepath options for all but the most inexperienced bikers. In short, the Irvine Park tour could, in itself, serve as part of an all-day family picnic and biking outing.

Irvine Park to Orange. The return trip requires a pedal on the Chapman Ave. upgrade beyond Newport Blvd. to the summit near Equestrian Dr. The route takes a long, steep downhill that passes Orange Park Blvd., Crawford Canyon Rd., and begins to level out before reaching Rancho Santiago Blvd. (9.6). The route heads right (north) at that roadway and passes through a level residential area on Class II bikepath, crosses Walnut Ave. (10.1), and meets Bond Ave. (10.3). In another 0.3 mile, the bikepath blends into the roadway and becomes a Class III route. The roadway ends/fuses into Hewes St. (10.8) and continues as Class III or Class X bikeway until the junction with Villa Park Rd. (11.1). Backtrack along the original route and return to the trip origin at 13.6 miles from the trip start.

CONNECTING TRIPS: 1) Connection with the Santiago Canyon Road route (Trip #27) - at the junction of Chapman Ave. and Santiago Canyon Rd., proceed southeast on the latter roadway; 2) Spur trip - continue on Santiago Canyon Rd. past Orange Park Blvd. about 1/4 mile and turn north on Windes Dr. Continue to Santiago Oaks Park.

TRIP #27 - SANTIAGO CANYON ROAD

GENERAL LOCATION: Santiago Canyon

LEVEL OF DIFFICULTY: One way - strenuous; up and back-very strenuous
Distance - 12.2 miles (one way)
Elevation gain - continuous moderate to steep
grades

GENERAL DESCRIPTION: This is an excellent workout trip through a scenic, but highly sun-exposed canyon. It is one of the most popular for serious bikers training against the clock. The tour is 12.2 Class II miles in rolling hills with numerous long, hard upgrades. On a hot day, this is a strenuous one-way trip. The route has several scenic points, passes near Irvine Lake, and ends near Cook's Corner at a rustic restaurant/bar. Just beyond this terminus is the stately structure of Saint Michael's Abbey. This trip also links up with three alternate canyon routes for the lion-hearted: Silverado Canyon Rd., Modjeska Canyon Rd., and Live Oak Canyon Rd.

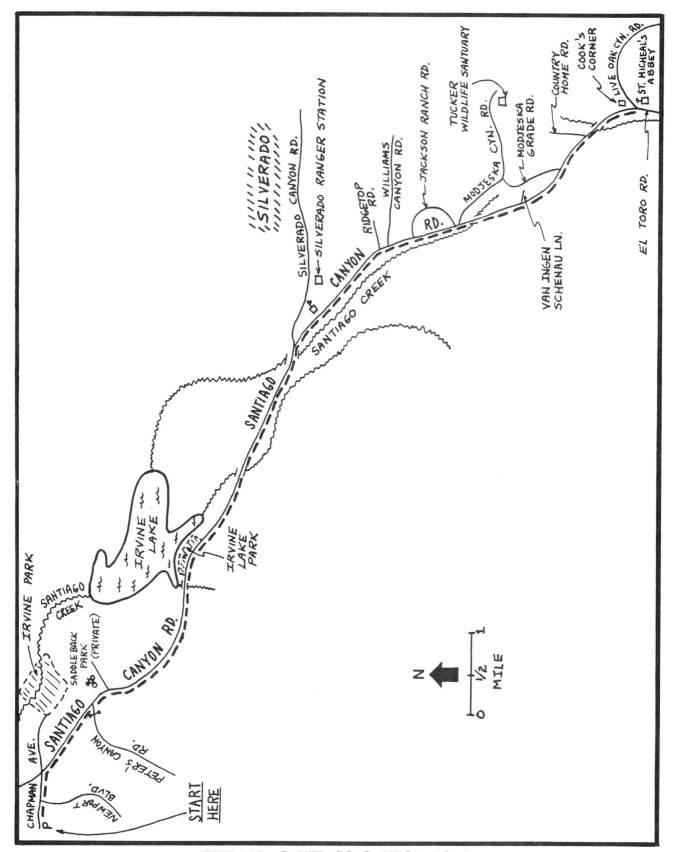

TRIP #27 - SANTIAGO CANYON ROAD

TRAILHEAD: From the Orange Fwy. or Costa Mesa (Newport) Fwy., take the Chapman Ave. turnoff east.   The distances to Santiago Canyon Rd. are 4-1/2 miles and 7-1/2 miles, respectively.   From the Santa Ana Fwy., turn north on the Costa Mesa Fwy. and take the Chapman Ave. turnoff as above.   Park along Chapman Ave.   An alternative is pay the entry fee and start at Irvine Regional Park.

Bring a conservative supply of water (two filled water bottles) and munchies.   There is water at Irvine Lake Park, although this is a tiring diversion off the main course.   The next convenient stop is at Cook's Corner at the trip's end.

TRIP DESCRIPTION: **Trailhead to Irvine Lake Park.** The tour begins in an open, flat area, proceeds along pastureland to the top of an upgrade (0.5), then continues on a rolling hill bikeway.   In another 0.5 mile, the route starts a long, tedious upgrade which continues for over a mile (2.2). Just beyond the summit is a fire station to the right (south) and a roadway into private Saddleback Park.

East Santiago Canyon Road

The road then heads down a long downgrade and flattens out near a viewpoint above the Irvine Lake area (3.1).   The roadway proceeds uphill again for about 0.4 mile, leveling out just before the Irvine Lake turnoff (3.6).   There are rental boats, swimming, shady picnic areas, and water at Irvine Lake Park.   Better yet, there is a little restaurant/bar here.   If you are tired, this is an fine spot to rest and also ponder turning back.

129

Irvine Lake Park to Silverado Canyon Road. Beyond the turnoff, the route proceeds moderately uphill and reaches the top of the grade where there is a lightly-treed area and a wide creek bed. The roadway continues through light rolling (mostly uphill) terrain along the creek and provides a superb view of Mt. Saddleback at the top of a couple of the rises (5.4). Continuing another half mile through this terrain, there is a downgrade with a view into Santiago Creek. Shortly thereafter, the bike route crosses a bridge over the creek (6.5). In another 0.1 mile is the Silverado Canyon turnoff. The Silverado Forest Station is about 3/4-mile further up that road.

Silverado Canyon Road to Cook's Corner. The bikeway stays near Santiago Creek and passes a small school (7.0). It then begins another mile-long upgrade which peaks at Ridgetop Rd. Shortly after, the flat route passes William's Canyon Rd. and Jackson Ranch Rd. (8.7), then proceeds uphill again to meet Modjeska Canyon Rd. at the crest (9.3). This road leads to the Tucker Wildlife (bird) Sanctuary and eventually to a long, tiring road route (on foot) to the Mt. Saddleback summit. Also, the tour leaves Santiago Creek at this juncture.

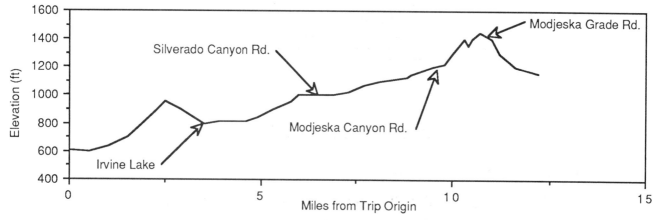

Again, the roadway winds upward with a steep grade just before the summit (9.9), flattens, and then starts uphill again. At the crest is a scenic turnout with a view of the surrounding canyonland and a "peek" southward into the city of Irvine (10.3). The path continues on the flat and then starts uphill, reaching the trip high point near Modjeska Grade Rd. (10.8).

Now all the hard uphill work pays off! The bikepath starts a long downhill, crossing Aliso Creek, Country Home Rd., then passing a newer housing tract to the right and a small established community to the left (11.6). The downhill continues all the way into the route terminus at the Live Oak Canyon Rd. junction at Cook's Corner (12.2). Stop and take a well deserved break at the rustic restaurant/bar.

Spur Trip Options. An option is to examine the architectually interesting St. Michael's Abbey a few hundred yards down the main highway (now named El Toro Rd.). There is also a scenic and <u>very challenging</u> 3-4 mile spur trip along Live Oak Canyon Rd. which visits pretty O'Neill Regional Park. There is plenty of greenery, water-filled creeks, and an improved campground within the park (see Trip #28).

CONNECTING TRIPS: 1) Continuation with the Aliso Creek Trail (Trip #29) - continue south on El Toro Rd. beyond the trip terminus; 2) connection with the Orange/Irvine Park Loop (Trip #26) - at the trip origin, continue east on Chapman Ave. to Irvine Park or west towards the city of Orange.

Bike Sweet Bike

TRIP # 28 - O'NEILL REGIONAL PARK

GENERAL LOCATION: Trabuco Canyon, Rancho Santa Marguerita

LEVEL OF DIFFICULTY: **O'Neill Regional Park.** Up and back - easy
Distance - 7.0 miles (up and back)
Elevation gain - moderate grades in Mesa
              Camping   area

Rancho Santa Marguerita to O'Neill Park.
Up and back - moderate to strenuous
Distance - 14.0 miles (up and back)
Elevation gain - periodic moderate grades;
              single steep upgrade east of
              O'Neill Regional Park

GENERAL DESCRIPTION: **O'Neill Regional Park.** The focus of this trip is O'Neill Regional Park with over four miles of bikeway on roads within an oak forest. The trip is a winner for families as it is contained within an enticing natural environment well removed from high traffic streets. The park roadway/bikeway visits the central picnic area and nature center, crosses Trabuco Creek, cruises the elevated Mesa Camping Area, then concludes with a countryside ride north, paralleling Live Oak Canyon Rd.

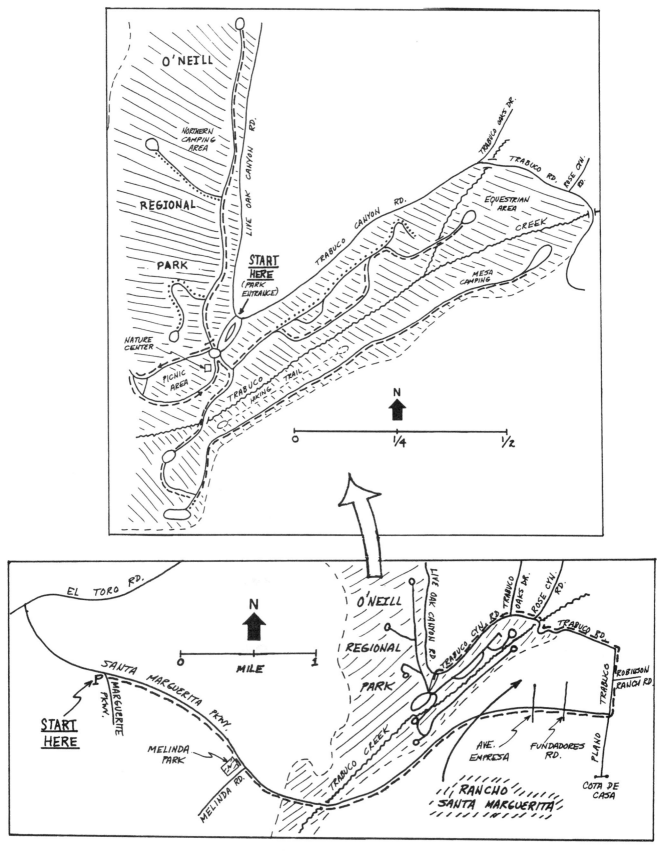

TRIP #28 - O'NEILL REGIONAL PARK

For bikers who tire of the park, try the roadway biking in the vicinity of the park entrance, which is reasonably flat . There are options to explore other roadways in the O'Neill Park area such as Trabuco Oaks Dr.

Rancho Santa Marguerita to O'Neill Regional Park. In contrast to the O'Neill Park tour, this is a tour for more experienced bikers, particularly "hillies," and bikers who enjoy exploring new territory. The route actually starts in northern Mission Viejo, cruises through the impressive and new city of Rancho Santa Marguerita on Santa Marguerita Pkwy., and enters O'Neill Park from the "back door." There is a steep 3/4-mile downgrade near the eastern park boundary which presents a healthy biking challenge on the return trip.

<u>TRAILHEAD</u>: **O'Neill Regional Park.** From the intersection of El Toro Rd. and Santiago Canyon Rd. at Cook's Corner, turn east onto Live Oak Canyon Rd. and drive about three scenic and hilly miles to the park.

Rancho Santa Marguerita to O'Neill Park. From El Toro Rd., turn east on Santa Marguerita Pkwy., drive one mile to Marguerite Pkwy., and park in the Portola Plaza.

Bring a filled water bottle for the Rancho Santa Marguerita to O'Neill Park ride. Refill at the park.

Family Tour, O'Neill Regional Park

BICYCLE RIDES: ORANGE COUNTY

<u>TRIP DESCRIPTION</u>: O'Neill Regional Park. Minors must accompany adults and a minimum travelling party of two is required -- there <u>are</u> limited inherent dangers such as mountain lions, rattlesnakes, poison oak, and rugged terrain in the park. This is particularly applicable for off-road hiking.

From the park entry area, cruise the half-mile day-use picnic loop. Pass the gate to the north camping area at the loop entrance and the nature center (spring and summer interpretive programs) near the loop exit. There are picnic facilities, turf play area, a softball diamond, playground, water and restrooms in the park.

Exit the loop (0.5) and stay to the right. Follow the road across Trabuco Creek, bike to the parking loop, and continue a hard left, pedaling on a workout upgrade. Note that there is a hiking trail below which parallels Trabuco Creek (2.2). Continue on a more modest incline along the eastern park boundary and the Plano Trabuco to the Mesa Camping area.

Return across Trabuco Creek and take the first right turn, following the flat roadway past the group camping areas. At the last junction, turn right and continue across a feeder creek to the Equestrian Camping area (we expected to see horses bedded down in sleeping bags!).

Bike back past the entrance, pass through the gate, and enter the road to the north picnic area (5.5). Follow that tree-covered road as it follows alongside (but remains fenced from) Live Oak Canyon Rd. There are two west-side spurs off the main route for those who want to explore every "nook and crannie" of this beautiful park. Return to the park entrance and plan the next park adventure (7.0)!

Rancho Santa Marguerita to O'Neill Park. Leave the shopping center parking lot, turning right (east) on Santa Marguerita Pkwy. Start one of several upgrades on Class II bikeway through exposed, semi-arid terrain. In 0.6 mile, bikers can look down into the new housing in the northern Mission Viejo area. The grade steepens, then reaches a crest in another 0.4 mile at Melinda Rd. near Melinda Park (playground, grass, water).

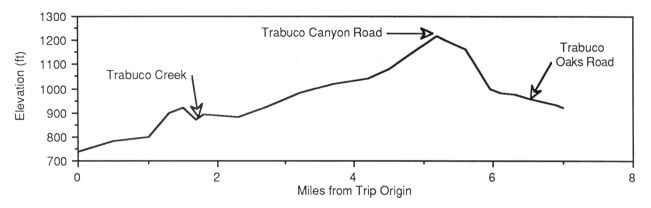

Follow the roller-coaster downhill-uphill and cross over Trabuco Creek (1.8). There are outstanding views into the local canyons in this area with Mt. Saddleback as an imposing backdrop.

Continue on an upgrade to Avd. Empresa; there is a direct view into Rancho Santa Marguerita from this point. Bike on the Class II flat route into the town, then follow a mild upgrade past Avd. de los Fundadores. There are Class I paths on the periphery of the development and a small lake to the left (north) (4.2).

Continue to road's end and turn left at Plano Trabuco (the private and exclusive Cota De Caza community is to the right). Bike 0.7 mile on the periphery of the developed community and turn left again at road's end at Trabuco Canyon Rd. (5.2). In 0.2 mile the road leaves the developed area and begins a steep, winding downhill (Class X, no bike shoulder), passes over Trabuco Creek, and meets Rose Canyon Rd. (6.1). In 0.2 mile is Trabuco Oaks Rd. and a more modest downhill which takes the biker through delightful, dense tree country. In 0.6 mile is the tiny Live Oak Shopping Center and a short distance further is the entrance to O'Neill Park (7.0).

NOTE: The three-mile west side outlet on Live Oak Canyon Rd. is on a winding road with a very steep upgrade-downgrade in the one-mile stretch before reaching Cook's Corner. This road is Class X with no shoulder. Although we did see a couple of hearty souls biking this segment, we decided that the most sensible return was to retrace the incoming route described above back to the trip origin.

CONNECTING TRIPS: 1) Connection with the Aliso Creek Trail/Bikeway (Ride #29A) - bike east one mile from the trip origin to El Toro Rd.;
2) connection with the Mission Viejo Bikeway (Trip #30) - from the trip origin, bike south on Marguerite Pkwy.

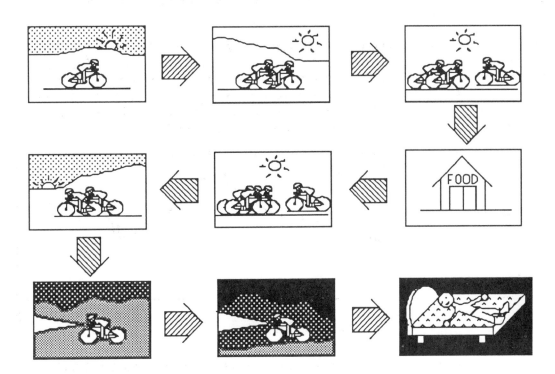

TRIPS #29A & #29B - ALISO CREEK TRAIL/BIKEWAY

The moderate-level Aliso Creek Trail/Bikeway from Cook's Corner to the terminus in Laguna Niguel (31.2 miles round trip) is broken up into two sections. The general area map for the entire trip is provided below. The trip is entirely Class I or Class II. The upper segment (Trip #29A) leaves from the foothills above El Toro, winds its way downhill and southward along Aliso Creek, visits El Toro Community Park, and ends at the Alicia Valencia Mall. The lower segment (Trip #29B) leaves the mall and follows several roadways south visiting Laguna Niguel Park/Sulfer Creek Reservoir, and ends at Crown Valley Community Park.

There are sections of the trail near El Toro Community Park where the trail may be flooded during winter storms. Plan ahead for route alternates if trips are planned under storm conditions.

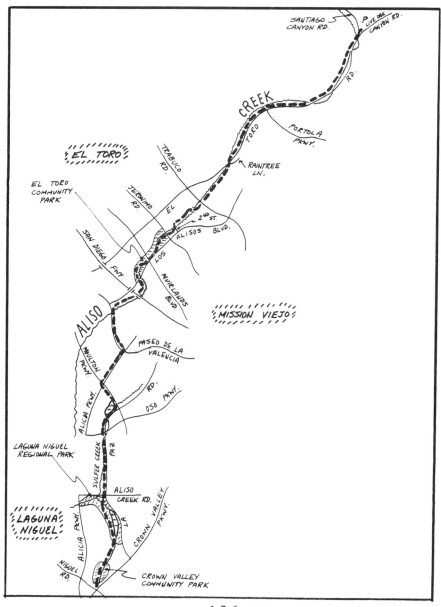

TRIP #29A - ALISO CREEK TRAIL/BIKEWAY
(NORTHERN SEGMENT)

GENERAL LOCATION: El Toro, Laguna Hills

LEVEL OF DIFFICULTY: One way - easy; up and back - moderate
Distance - 10.0 miles (one way)
Elevation gain - periodic moderate grades

GENERAL DESCRIPTION: This primarily Class I trip segment starts in the foothills above El Toro, winds its way downhill and southward along Aliso Creek and terminates near the intersection of Paseo De Valencia and Alicia Pkwy. at the Alicia Valencia Plaza. One of the most pleasant rides in Orange County, this route explores significant stretches of relatively unspoiled bottomland in the middle of high-density residential areas. The upper portion of the trip segment takes the biker through undeveloped, open, high-desert terrain, while the lower portion winds through the developed city of El Toro below. There is a fine rest stop at pretty, shaded El Toro Community Park at about 7.5 miles into the trip. Portions of this route may be flooded during storms.

TRAILHEAD: From the San Diego Fwy., exit north at El Toro Rd. and continue about eight miles north to the road junction at Oak Canyon Rd. Park in the lot at the junction at Cook's Corner.

From the Newport/Costa Mesa Fwy., exit east at Katella Ave./Villa Park Rd. Follow that roadway, which becomes Santiago Canyon Rd., roughly eight miles to Cook's Corner. This option is presented since the route is scenic.

Bring at least one filled bottle of water. There are few reliable and available water stops directly along the path. The single public water stop that we found (near the trip midpoint) is just northwest of the El Toro Community Park tennis courts at the elementary school (Arrowood St.).

TRIP DESCRIPTION: **Cactus Country.** From Cook's Corner, pedal south about 1/4 mile on El Toro Rd. and follow a small asphalt path leading diagonally away from the main roadway (on the right hand or west side). This path leads down to an old two-lane road which is blocked off to auto traffic. (Note that there is also an entry on the east side of the road just south of St. Micheal's Abbey.) The route stays parallel to and below El Toro Rd. passing through a high-desert terrain with an abundance of cactus (1.5).

In another 0.5 mile is the first alternate entry to the trail. In a short distance, the route passes alongside a eucalyptus grove that is next to El Toro Rd.; the first highly-developed area to be seen from the bikeway is just across the road (2.2). The path crosses two more bike entries and exits the eucalyptus-lined portion of the route (3.1), although it remains just next to El Toro Rd. At Normandale Dr., cross over to the east side of El Toro Rd. and bike on the sidewalk/bikeway.

137

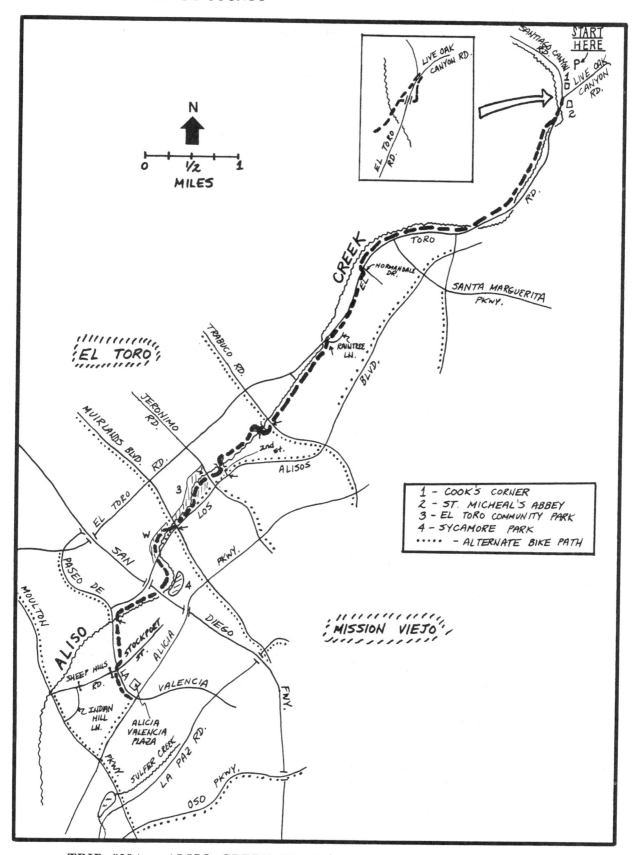

START HERE

SANTIAGO CANYON RD.

LIVE OAK CANYON RD.

P

1

2

LIVE OAK CANYON RD.

EL TORO RD.

N

0   1/2   1
MILES

CREEK

EL TORO RD.

NORMANDALE DR.

SANTA MARGUERITA PKWY.

TRABUCO RD.

EL TORO

RAINTREE LN.

BLVD.

JERONIMO RD.

MUIRLANDS BLVD.

2nd ST.

ALISOS

EL TORO RD.

3

LOS

SAN

W

PKWY.

DIEGO

1 - COOK'S CORNER
2 - ST. MICHEAL'S ABBEY
3 - EL TORO COMMUNITY PARK
4 - SYCAMORE PARK
•••• - ALTERNATE BIKE PATH

PASEO DE

4

MOULTON

MISSION VIEJO

ALISO

STOCKPORT ST.

ALICIA

SHEEP HILLS RD.

LA

VALENCIA

FWY.

INDIAN HILL LN.

ALICIA VALENCIA PLAZA

SULFER CREEK

LA PAZ RD.

PKWY.

OSO PKWY.

TRIP #29A - ALISO CREEK TRAIL/BIKEWAY (NORTHERN SEGMENT)

Raintree Lane to El Toro Community Park. Continue 0.9 mile further through this higher-density residential area to Raintree Ln. (4.2). At the southeast corner of that intersection, follow the Class I path beyond the trail sign. Just beyond Raintree Ln., Aliso Creek shifts to the southeast side of El Toro Rd. The bikepath passes through a pleasant treed, rural setting alongside the creek through a residential community for the next two miles.

In 0.5 mile, the bikeway follows a moderate downhill past Creekside, then spends the next 0.7 mile alongside a mini forest. The route passes under Trabuco Rd. (5.9), follows alongside a beautiful stand of eucalyptus, and crosses over the creek on a bikeway/walkway (6.6). In this section the creek is concreted and there are residences on both sides. The path crosses down near creek level (this may flood during storms as may the undercrossings at Muirlands Blvd. and Los Aliso Blvd.), crosses under Jeronimo Rd., then passes under a railroad tressel (7.0).

The trail takes a wide turn to the south and parallels Los Alisos Blvd. at the road level (7.4), then ducks back down below creek level at Muirlands Blvd., coming up on the opposite side into the most popular and scenic part of El Toro Community Park (7.6). This is a nice place to stop and rest. There is water just northwest of the park tennis courts at an elementary school (Arrowood St.).

El Toro Community Park to Aliso Creek Exit to Alicia Valencia Plaza. Follow the bikepath nearest Los Alisos Blvd. In 0.2 mile, the path dips down into the creek bottom and crosses the creek over a metal plate. Just beyond, the route passes under Los Alisos Blvd. and turns east. The creekbed opens up 0.3 mile further in the vicinity of Sycamore Park which is across the creek (8.2). In another 0.2 mile is a cross-over trail leading to that park followed by a passage under the San Diego Fwy. (also note that this may be flooded during or after storms). There is a trail junction here. Snacks are available near the Alicia Pkwy. turnoff from the San Diego Fwy.--the "snackaterias" can be reached by following the left (southeast) junction.

Our route heads right and proceeds up a short grade, then back down into a more open canyon area. In 0.3 mile, there is a three-way junction. Two legs travel a short distance and die out at local roadways. Take the middle route which has a trail marker for bikers coming from the opposite direction (8.9). In a short distance, the route reaches Paseo De Valencia and the bike trail leaves the creek. Turn left (southeast) on Paseo De Valancia (stay on the north side of the street) and follow the signed trail uphill past Kennington Dr. (9.3) and Beckenham St. (9.5) to a crest near Stockport St. (9.7). Continue downhill another 0.3 mile to Alicia Pkwy. and do some "R & R" at Alicia Valencia Plaza.

CONNECTING TRIPS: 1) Continuation with the lower Aliso Creek segment (Trip #29B) - turn south at Alicia Pkwy.; 2) connection with the Mission Viejo Bikeway (Trip #30) - at Los Alisos Blvd. and Jeronimo St., turn north onto Los Alisos Blvd. There are numerous other connection points (refer to Trip #30 map); 3) continuation with the Santiago Canyon Rd. trip (Trip #27) - bike north from the trip origin on Santiago Canyon Rd.; 4) connection with the O'Neill Regional Park tour (Trip #28) - at Santa Maguerita Pkwy., turn east.

TRIP #29B - ALISO CREEK TRAIL/BIKEWAY
(SOUTHERN SEGMENT)

GENERAL LOCATION: Laguna Hills, Laguna Niguel

LEVEL OF DIFFICULTY: Up and back - easy
Distance - 5.6 miles (one way)
Elevation gain - periodic light grades

GENERAL DESCRIPTION: This Class I/II trip segment is the southern connector for the Aliso Creek Trail/Bikeway. The route starts at the Alicia Valencia Plaza, proceeds several miles on several connecting roadways, then enters Laguna Niguel Regional Park. The route from this park to the trip terminus at Crown Valley Community Park is on a scenic and interesting Class I bikeway. The highlight of the trip is Laguna Niguel Park where there are several interesting family mini-tours and a lake to explore. The terminus is located in an area surrounded by eateries (hint, hint!). More serious bikers can continue the route on Crown Valley Pkwy. 3.2 more miles to Pacific Coast Hwy., and further beyond to the Pacific Ocean.

TRAILHEAD: From the San Diego Fwy., exit south on Alicia Pkwy. and drive about one mile to the Alicia Valencia Plaza at Paseo De Valencia.

Bring a light water supply. This is a short trip with strategically placed water supplies.

TRIP DESCRIPTION: **Alicia Valencia Plaza to Laguna Niguel Park.** Leave the plaza and cross Paseo De Valencia. Continue a short distance on Alicia Pkwy. and take the Class I path down into the drainage of an alternate branch of Aliso Creek. Follow this wide trail downhill in the open canyon area 0.7 mile to Moulton Pkwy. Cross at the intersection and follow that street southeast. The Class II roadway heads uphill through open fields and newer housing areas. In 0.6 mile, turn right on La Paz Rd. and continue through hot, dry territory past new housing in the hills, a segment of Oso Pkwy (2.0), and Avila Rd. (2.4). After an additional 0.6 mile of riding through this exposed, hill-surrounded route, there is an "oasis" in the form of a shopping center at Aliso Creek Blvd. (3.0).

Laguna Niguel Park. In another 0.1 mile, there is a small bikeway/walkway entry into Laguna Niguel Park that follows alongside Sulfer Creek. In a short distance is the spur path to the main park entrance where there are restrooms and a water fountain. Stay to the right on the park periphery (do not take the right turn to the tennis courts, however). Continue up a short steep roadway which crests near the north end of the Sulfer Creek Reservoir (3.6).

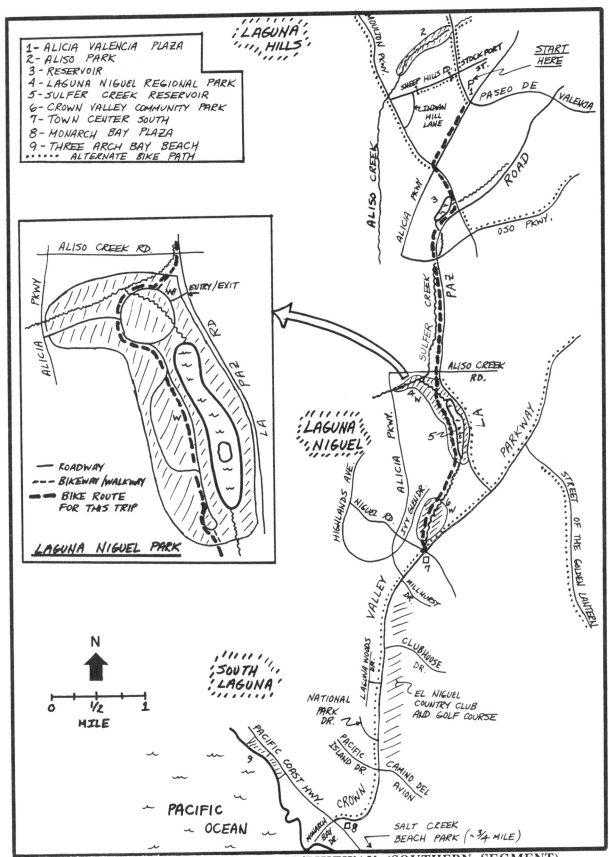

1- ALICIA VALENCIA PLAZA
2- ALISO PARK
3- RESERVOIR
4- LAGUNA NIGUEL REGIONAL PARK
5- SULFER CREEK RESERVOIR
6- CROWN VALLEY COMMUNITY PARK
7- TOWN CENTER SOUTH
8- MONARCH BAY PLAZA
9- THREE ARCH BAY BEACH
...... ALTERNATE BIKE PATH

—— ROADWAY
- - - BIKEWAY/WALKWAY
━ ━ BIKE ROUTE
FOR THIS TRIP

LAGUNA NIGUEL PARK

N

0   1/2   1
MILE

TRIP #29B - ALISO CREEK TRAIL/BIKEWAY (SOUTHERN SEGMENT)

Bring a fishing pole; this reservoir is a pleasant spot for a short biking diversion. There are small fenced-in fishing "piers" spread along the edge of the reservoir. The road passes the Laguna Niguel Lake concession and boat rental (4.1) and runs near the tree-lined southern end of the reservoir in 0.3 mile. That area is reached by crossing a small bridge over the outlet creek.

Laguna Niguel Park to Crown Community Park. The bike route reaches a parking lot cul-de-sac; just beyond is a small trail heading south. That trail parallels the outlet creek, passes a small water treatment plant (4.7), then enters a wide-open canyon. There is a direct view of hillside residences and the first glances at Crown Valley Pkwy. At (5.3), the trail passes between the Crown Valley Community Park and a gymnasium/pool. There is a small footbridge over to the park, a putting green, and restrooms.

Continue along the path across a road access to the park's parking lot. There are small picnic/barbecue spots in this area. The bikeway passes through a shaded corridor along the creek and ends in a short distance near Niguel Rd. and Crown Valley Pkwy. (5.6).

Alternate Return Route. From this point, there are options to stop at one of the many eateries in this area, return to the park, continue south on Crown Valley Pkwy. about four miles to Salt Creek Beach Park, or take an alternate return route. In the latter case, the route is completely Class II, but in a section of high-speed traffic. From Niguel Rd. bike northeast on Crown Valley Pkwy. The bikeway heads uphill 0.5 mile through the local hills, then flattens out before reaching La Paz Rd. in another 0.4 mile. La Paz Rd. is a hilly road that passes above Sulfer Creek Reservoir. There are several nice viewpoints down into the park beginning at about 0.3 mile from the intersection. The road passes Yosemite Rd. in another 0.5 mile and heads downhill to Aliso Creek Rd., returning to the original route.

CONNECTING TRIPS: 1) Continuation with the upper Aliso Creek segment (Trip #29A) - from the trip origin, bike northwest on Paseo De Valencia; 2) connection with the Laguna Niguel Bikeway (Trip #11) - at the trip terminus at Niguel Rd., proceed in either direction on Crown Valley Pkwy.

TRIP #30 - MISSION VIEJO BIKEWAY

GENERAL LOCATION: Mission Viejo, El Toro, Laguna Hills

LEVEL OF DIFFICULTY: Loop - moderate to strenuous
Distance - 16.6 miles (loop)
Elevation gain - continuous moderate grades

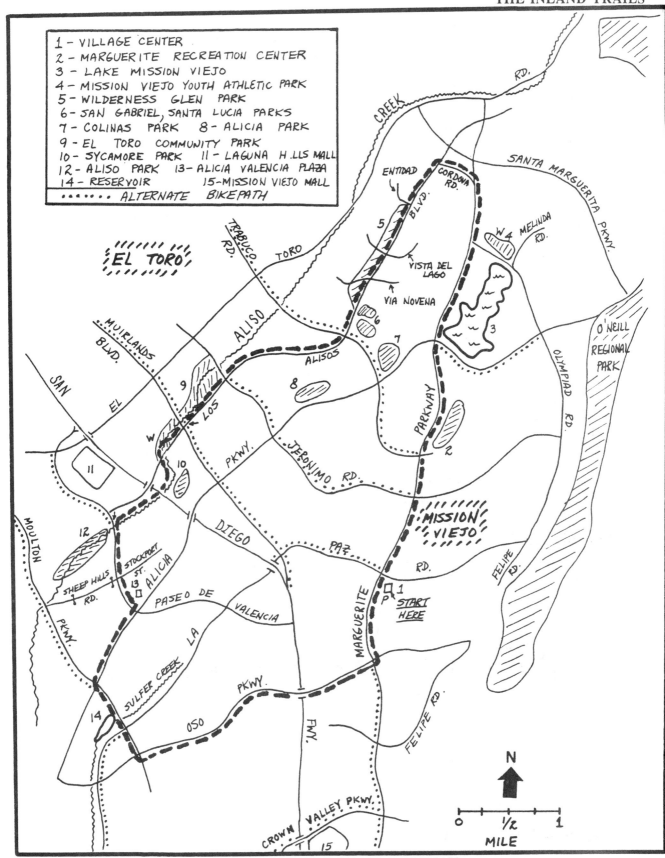

1 – VILLAGE CENTER
2 – MARGUERITE RECREATION CENTER
3 – LAKE MISSION VIEJO
4 – MISSION VIEJO YOUTH ATHLETIC PARK
5 – WILDERNESS GLEN PARK
6 – SAN GABRIEL, SANTA LUCIA PARKS
7 – COLINAS PARK 8 – ALICIA PARK
9 – EL TORO COMMUNITY PARK
10 – SYCAMORE PARK 11 – LAGUNA HILLS MALL
12 – ALISO PARK 13 – ALICIA VALENCIA PLAZA
14 – RESERVOIR   15 – MISSION VIEJO MALL
• • • • • • • ALTERNATE BIKEPATH

TRIP #30 - MISSION VIEJO BIKEWAY

GENERAL DESCRIPTION: A loop trip that tours a part of the Mission Viejo Bikeway System, this trip is primarily a mixed Class I/II adventure that hits several of the local highlights. The trip is hilly with moderate mileage, providing a wide variety of natural and man-made scenery.

The route leaves the Village Center and passes near the Marguerite Recreation Center, Lake Mission Viejo, Mission Viejo Youth Center, cruises through Wilderness Glen Park, and picks up the segment of the Aliso Creek Trail/Bikeway that passes through El Toro Community Park. The northern and middle portions of the route are in developed residential areas, while the most southern portion is in a sparsely-developed region of open and exposed hills.

TRAILHEAD: From the San Diego Fwy., exit east at La Paz Rd., continue about 1-1/4 miles to Marguerite Pkwy. Cross that street, turn right, and find parking under a tree in the Village Center parking area.

Bring plenty of water (two filled bottles on hot days) unless you plan to divert off the main route or stop at one of the shopping plazas along the way. There is water at the baseball diamonds just north of El Toro Community Park. The southern trip section between the Alicia Valencia Plaza and the Village Center is essentially waterless.

TRIP DESCRIPTION: **Village Center to Marguerite Recreation Center.** Exit the Village Center and bike north on Class II Marguerite Pkwy. The area is residential with some tree cover and a hillside above the roadway to the left (west). Much of the northern segment of the trip is on hillside-surrounded roadways. The route passes Via Florecer (0.3) and heads into a steady, light upgrade past Jeronimo Rd. (0.7) to a crest near Trabuco Rd. (1.1). Just across the intersection is a shopping center to the west and the Marguerite Recreation Center to the east (tennis courts, pools, and playgrounds).

Lake Mission Viejo. Just beyond, the primary route transitions into a Class I bikepath on the sidewalk. In another 0.5 mile the path tours alongside the Casta Del Sol Golf Course. There is a view of the hills to the west from this point into what we labeled "Condo Canyon" (1.6). The bike route begins another steady upgrade and reaches Alicia Pkwy. in 0.6 mile and the uphill crest 0.1 mile further. There is a magnificent view into the local mountains from this area. Continue to Vista Del Lago, turn right (east), and bike 0.2 mile to a great overlook of Lake Mission Viejo; there is also a market alongside the lake.

Cordova Road. Return to Marguerite Pkwy. (3.1) and continue the hilly route 0.3 mile further to Olympiad Rd. The route transitions to Class X and continues another mile to Cordova Rd. Turn left and bike 0.3 mile further to Los Alisos Blvd. (4.7). There is a new shopping center at this intersection.

Wilderness Glen Park. Turn left again and start south and downhill on a Class I path. Bike through this residential area with a high hillside and homes to the left (east). The route passes a school and recreation field and reaches Entidad (5.3). There is a maze of trails below this street along English Creek, none of which connect up with a southern route extension. The "through route" is achieved by staying along Los Alisos Blvd. and crossing Entidad (the same is true at Vista Del Lago and Via Novena).

144

Continue on the Class I sidewalk/bikeway alongside the north edge of Wilderness Glen Park (5.6). There are trees and a forrested creek bed with some canyon-like areas for the next mile. There are also some off-road bicycle paths scattered through the park. Continue downhill past Vista Del Lago to Via Noveno (6.5); stop and look back at the line of condos that look like a castle on a hill. In 0.4 mile, the path heads steeply downhill and passes a particularly well-forrested section of the park. The roadway levels and passes Via Santa Lucia and Santa Lucia Park across the street (7.0). In a short distance, the park ends, and just beyond the path meets Trabuco Rd. (7.2). There is a small shopping center and some eateries at this intersection.

Lake Mission Viejo

El Toro Community Park. Cross the intersection and continue through a residential area passing Vallejo (7.7) and Madero (8.2). Next is Jeronimo Rd. (8.5). There is a shopping center at this intersection. Continue 0.5 mile further and just before Muirlands Blvd., leave the roadway and join the Class I Aliso Creek Trail. The bikepath crosses under Muirlands Blvd. near creek level (see the discussion on flood warnings from Trip #29A) and comes back up on the opposite side into the most popular and scenic part of El Toro Community Park (9.1). There is water just northwest of the park tennis courts at an elementary school (Arrowood St.).

El Toro Community Park to The Aliso Creek Exit. Follow the bikeway nearest Los Alisos Blvd. In 0.2 mile, the path dips down into the creek bottom and crosses the creek over a metal plate. Just beyond, the route passes under Los Alisos Blvd. and turns east. The creek bed opens up 0.3 mile further in the vicinity of Sycamore Park, which is on the opposite bank (9.6).

In 0.2 mile is a cross-over trail leading to the park, followed by a passage under the San Diego Fwy. There is a trail junction here. Snacks are available near the Alicia Pkwy. turnoff from the San Diego Fwy.--these eating spots can be reached by following the left (southeast) junction.

Our route heads right and proceeds up a short grade, then back down into a more open canyon area. In 0.3 mile, there is a three-way junction. Two legs travel a short distance and end at local roadways. Take the middle route which has a trail marker for bikers coming from the opposite direction. In a short distance, the route reaches Paseo De Valencia and the bike trail leaves the creek.

Alicia Valencia Plaza. Turn left (southeast) on Paseo De Valencia (stay on the north side of the street) and follow the signed Class I trail uphill past Kennington Dr. (10.7) and Beckenham St. (10.9) to a crest at Stockport St. (11.1). Continue 0.3 mile downhill to Alicia Pkwy.; there is a shopping plaza at this intersection. Note that there are no identified water sources from this point to the trip's end.

The Southern ("Dry Hills") Section. Turn right (southeast) on Alicia Pkwy. and take the Class I path down into the drainage of an alternate Aliso Creek branch. Follow this wide trail downhill in the open canyon area 0.7 mile to Moulton Pkwy. Cross at the intersection and follow that street southeast. The Class II roadway heads uphill through open fields and areas of newer housing construction. In 0.6 more mile is La Paz Rd. and just beyond is Oso Pkwy. (13.0).

Turn left (west) on Oso Pkwy. and join up with the Class I trail on the north side of the highway. The territory consists of low, dry hills with scattered residences and very limited tree cover near the path. The trail crosses Nellie Gail Rd. (13.6) and proceeds through a small canyon. The route heads uphill and crests at (14.4); at this point Oso Pkwy. heads downhill with the bikeway parallel to and above the roadway. In another 0.2 mile, the bikeway crosses Cabot Rd. where there are indications of a return to the "big city."

The "Home Stretch." The path returns to Class II and crosses a bridge over Oso Creek and the San Diego Fwy. In 0.3 mile the route cuts through the center of a golf course, then heads downhill past Montanoso Dr. (15.4). The bikepath then proceeds uphill to a crest at Marguerite Pkwy. (15.6). Turn left (north) and bike past the Mission Viejo Fire Station. There is a fine view of Mt. Saddleback from this area (16.0). Begin a moderate upgrade which passes Estanciero Dr. (16.3) and reaches the top of the grade at the trip origin at La Paz Rd. and Village Center (16.6).

<u>CONNECTING TRIPS</u>: 1) Connection with Aliso Creek Trail/Bikeway (Trip #29) - multiple connections by riding west from Los Alisos Blvd. (for example, Cordova Rd., Trabuco Rd., or Jeronimo Rd.) or by turning south onto La Paz at the Moulton Pkwy. intersection; 2) connection with Laguna Niguel Bikeway (Trip #11) - from the Oso Pkwy. intersection, continue 1-1/2 miles south on Marguerite Pkwy. to Crown Valley Pkwy. Turn right (west); 3) connection with the O'Neill Regional Park tour (Trip #30) - at Marguerite Pkwy. and Cordova Rd., continue north on the former street.

TRIP #31 - LOWER EL TORO ROAD

GENERAL LOCATION: Laguna Hills

LEVEL OF DIFFICULTY: One way - moderate to strenuous; up and back - strenuous
Distance - 5.8 miles (up and back)
Elevation gain - continuous steep grades

GENERAL DESCRIPTION: This is another Class II Orange County canyon venture. It is presented separately since it provides some tough elevation gain over a short distance. The workout involves biking to the route crest just beyond Calle Sonora and then generally coasting from there. The route is semi-exposed (read that as hot in the summer). There is some moderately interesting canyon scenery, but little, if any, formal rest areas along the way. For the heartier biker, this path can be hooked up to Moulton Parkway and, ultimately, the Mission Viejo Bikeway System.

TRAILHEAD: From the San Diego Fwy., exit at El Toro Rd. and drive southwest. Continue about one mile and park on El Toro Rd. near the southern edge of the Laguna Hills Golf Course. Check the signs for compliance with local parking laws.

Bring water and snacks. The single source of "goodies" is at the trip origin.

TRIP DESCRIPTION: **The Upgrade.** Before starting, look northeast on Moulton Pkwy. for a fine view of Mt. Saddleback. Now put your head down, bottom up and start a short, tough, uphill pedal for 0.4 mile. The roadway rounds a single sweeping curve and heads directly up to a flat at Calle Sonora. To the right is a residential neighborhood and to the left a newer condominium group high on an adjacent hill. The bikepath heads steadily uphill again and reaches the crest in 0.2 mile. Stop and take in the view of El Toro, Irvine, Mt. Saddleback, and the canyon area ahead.

The Downgrade. The downhill stretch is relatively open and generally undeveloped. The route continues down the canyon past Calle Corta and the largest developed area (1.5). In 0.3 mile is Canyon Hills Dr. and a short, level grade. The remaining 1.1 miles is downhill through a series of winding turns past The Club Dr. (and a lot of newer residences) to the El Toro Rd. junction (2.9). Now the real fun is doing the trip in reverse!

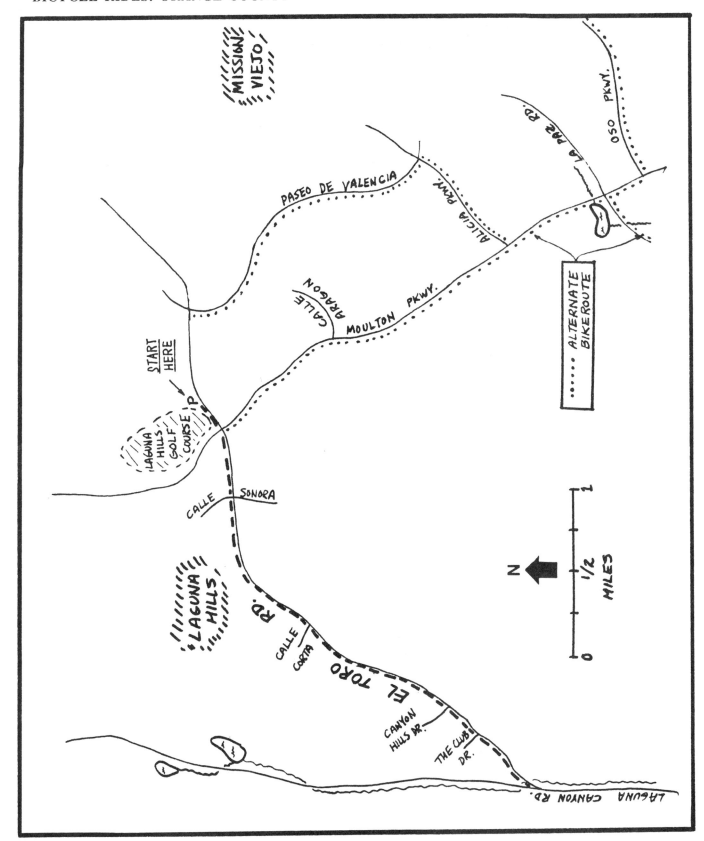

TRIP #31 - LOWER EL TORO ROAD

CONNECTING TRIPS: 1) Continuation with the Laguna Canyon Rd. tour (Trip #9) - at the end of El Toro Rd., take the route right (north) to Irvine or left to Laguna Beach; 2) spur trip - at the trip origin, take Moulton Pkwy. east 2-3 miles on Class I bikeway.

TRIP #32 - LAKE FOREST TOUR

GENERAL LOCATION: Lake Forest

LEVEL OF DIFFICULTY: Loop - easy
Distance - 5.3 miles (loop)
Elevation gain - periodic light grades

GENERAL DESCRIPTION: The Lake Forest loop trip is entirely on a Class I/II bikeway within this very pleasant community. The trip includes a tour along residential streets, as well as a romp through Serrano Creek Community Park. The street route includes a passby of a lovely man-made lake community along Toledo Way. The park ride meanders through a major loop with several minor spurs and provides a very pleasant tree-sheltered environment. This is a fine family bike trip, but still only for experienced riders on the roadways.

TRAILHEAD: From the San Diego Fwy., exit north on Lake Forest Dr. and travel about two miles to Toledo Way. Turn left (northwest) and find parking within the local residential area. Check local parking signs and carefully avoid parking on any private streets, specifically those along Toledo Way.

Bring a moderate supply of water. The trip is short, but we didn't find any obvious water stops along the way.

TRIP DESCRIPTION: **Serrano Creek Community Park.** From the parking area, proceed in the direction away from Lake Forest Dr. (northwest) on a Class II bikepath. Turn right at Serrano Rd. (0.3) and continue along the north sidewalk to a downramp that leads to the Class I trail within Serrano Creek Community Park. Proceed along the park trail through lush, tree-shaded surroundings to the picnic/playground area at the east end of the park (0.8).

The trail passes through a tight turn, crosses the creek, and continues to parallel the creek. There are several small trail spurs off this section of path and a horse trail as well. There are also a few short "ups and downs" on the route to give it some variety. The path reaches the west end of the loop, recrosses the creek and returns to the park starting point (1.1). Turn around and head back across the creek, but turn left at the next junction and proceed 0.2 mile to the trail exit near Serrano Dr. and Lake Vista.

149

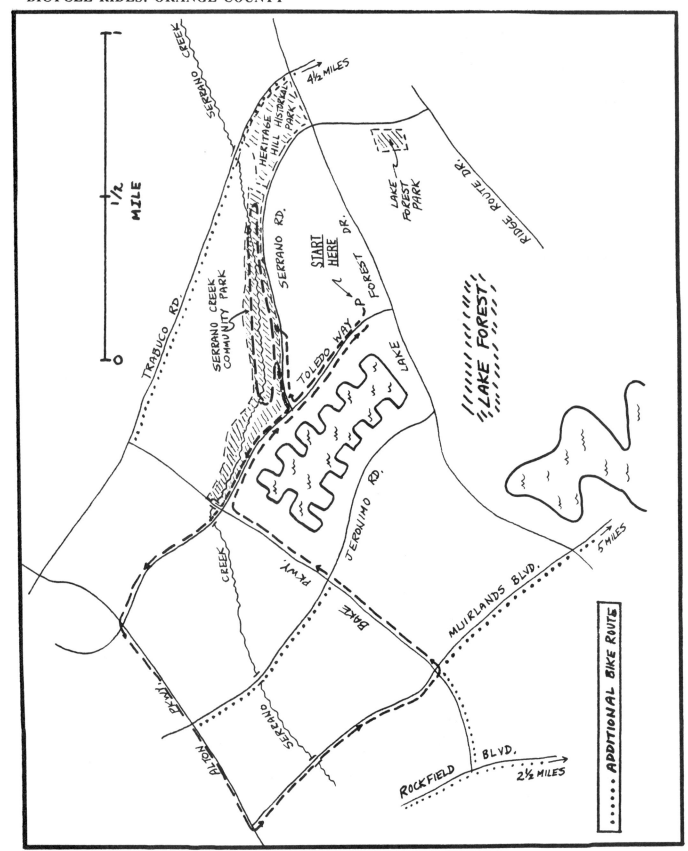

TRIP #32 - LAKE FOREST TOUR

Toledo Way and the Industrial Loop. Turn right on Serrano Rd. and return to Toledo Way, admiring the view of the residential areas surrounding the local man-made lake. Turn right (northwest) on Toledo Way and proceed on the Class II bikeway across Bake Pkwy. (1.7). This begins a 2.9-mile loop through a modern, light industrial area on a Class II bikeway. The route proceeds 0.5 mile to Alton Pkwy., turns left and proceeds 0.6 mile to a bridge over a railroad. There is a fine view into the foothills to the southwest from this point (and a long-distance view of the Lion Country Safari marker).

Continue 0.2 mile to Muirlands Blvd. and turn left. The tour proceeds another 0.8 mile to Bake Pkwy. and follows that roadway another 0.8 mile to complete the industrial loop. Continue 0.7 mile along Toledo Way admiring the waterfront Lake Forest community and return to the starting point.

CONNECTING TRIPS: 1) Connection with Aliso Creek Trail/Bikeway (Trip #29A) - take Bake Pkwy. northeast to Trabuco Rd. Turn right and proceed across Lake Forest Dr., Ridge Route and El Toro Rd. about 2-1/2 miles to the Aliso Creek Trail. Turn left to head northeast toward Santiago Canyon and right to head southwest toward El Toro.

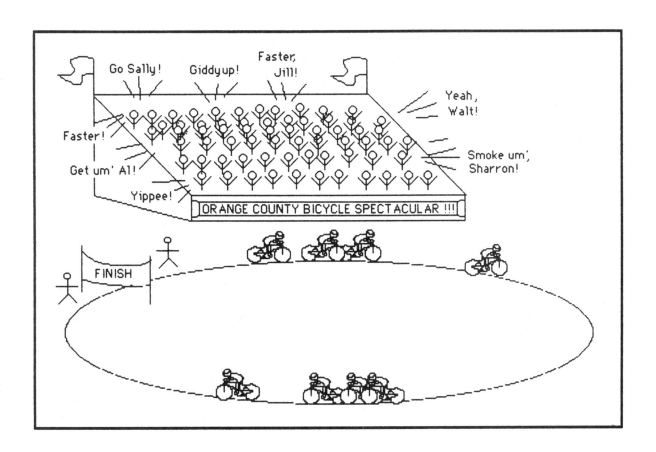

THE "BIG GUYS"

Santa Ana River Near the Pacific Ocean

TRIP #33 - WESTERN ORANGE COUNTY LOOP

GENERAL LOCATION: Strand Bike Trail - San Gabriel River - Coyote Creek - Fullerton - El Cajon Trail - Santa Ana River

LEVEL OF DIFFICULTY: Loop - strenuous
Distance - 63.2 miles (loop)
Elevation gain - periodic moderate grades

GENERAL DESCRIPTION: This grand "looper" provides a testy mileage workout combined with a wide variety of bikeways and scenery. Well over half of the trip is on Class I bike trails. The tour begins at Huntington Beach State Park near the Santa Ana River outlet, proceeds along the coastal strand bikepath, then follows the San Gabriel River and Coyote Creek inland. The route meanders through Buena Park and Fullerton, joins up with the El Cajon Trail in Yorba Linda, and follows a 21-mile runout down the Santa Ana River to the trip origin. The scenery along the coastline, the lower San Gabriel River, the El Cajon Trail, and selected Santa Ana River segments is exceptional. There are numerous top-of-the-line parks on or near this tour, including El Dorado Regional Park, Craig Park, Yorba Regional Park, Centennial Regional Park, and both Huntington Beach and Bolsa Chica Beach State Parks.

TRAILHEAD: From the San Diego Fwy., exit south at Brookhurst St. Continue about five miles to the road's end, turn right, and drive 3/4 mile to Magnolia St. to the Huntington Beach State Park entrance. There is also free parking off of the inland residential streets.

From Pacific Coast Hwy. (PCH) southbound, continue four miles past the Huntington Beach Pier and turn right at Magnolia St. For northbound traffic, drive 1-1/4 mile beyond the Santa Ana River and turn left at Magnolia St.

Bring a couple of filled water bottles in order to minimize water stops. There are scattered water sources at the parks on the route. The biker may have to buck the on-shore late afternoon winds on the last leg of the Santa Ana River segment. If this is of concern, select an alternate starting point.

TRIP DESCRIPTION: **Huntington Beach State Park to the San Gabriel River.** This trip description details only new or potentially confusing portions of the ride. The tour starts at Huntington Beach State Park and continues northwest on the coastal strand trail to the northern end of Sunset Beach (see Trip #4, Middle and Northern Segment Maps). Follow the Seal Beach/Sunset Beach Tour (Trip #1) through Seal Beach to the San Gabriel River (10.0).

San Gabriel River and Coyote Creek. Follow the Coyote Creek Trail (Trip #20), exiting at La Palma Ave. (19.0).

The Inland Jigsaw (Buena Park to Fullerton). Turn right and bike 3.2 miles west on La Palma Ave. on mixed Class II and Class X path. At Western Ave., directly under the Knott's Berry Farm parachute ride, turn left (north) and proceed 1.9 miles on Class III bikeway. Pass under the Artesia and Santa Ana Fwys., turn right at Artesia Blvd., and left in 0.5 mile at Dale St. (25.2).

153

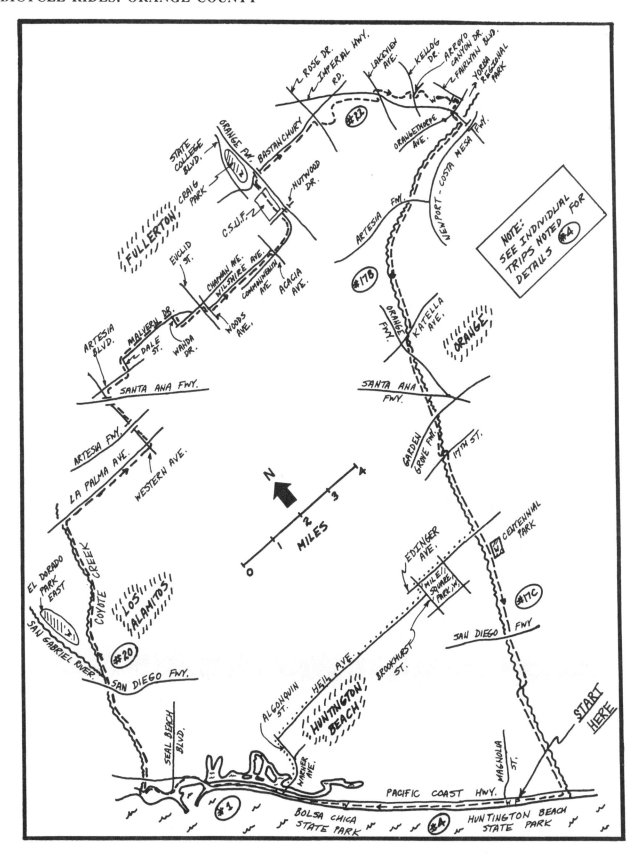

TRIP #33 - WESTERN ORANGE COUNTY LOOP

Bike 1/4 mile to Malvern Ave. and turn right just before reaching the intersection. This is a Class I route that transitions into Class III just beyond Sunnyridge Dr. Continue past Gilbert St. and Bastanchury Rd. In another 1/4 mile (two miles from Dale St.), turn right onto tiny Wanda Dr. and left again at Chapman Ave. This is the beginning of a 4-1/2 mile Fullerton residential tour. Follow Chapman Ave. 3/4 mile until it reaches Woods Ave., turn right and bike to Wilshire Ave., then turn left.

Follow Wilshire Ave. 2.3 miles to Acacia Ave. Turn right and then left again at Commonwealth Ave. until this roadway takes a long 90-degree curve northward and meets Nutwood St. (31.5).

Calfornia State University, Fullerton to Yorba Linda. Cross Nutwood St. on the west side of the intersection. At the "can't miss" CSUF sign, turn right and bike on Class I trail through the campus to Associated Rd. at the north end. Follow this Class II road 0.3 mile to Bastanchury Rd. and turn right, pedaling uphill on Class III street under the Orange Freeway. The route peaks in 0.3 mile and the ride flattens for the 2.0 miles to Rose Dr. (35.0).

California State College, Fullerton

El Cajon Trail. Turn right on Rose Dr. and in 0.2 mile cross the street to the east side at the Class I path entrance. Follow the El Cajon Trail (Trip #22) for 5.6 miles to the intersection of Fairlynn Blvd. and Esperanza Rd. Turn right (this departs from the Trip #22 route) and bike 0.3 mile to Imperial Blvd. Turn left and continue 0.7 mile to the bridge across the Santa Ana River (41.8).

Santa Ana River. Follow the Class I Santa Ana River Trail (Trips #17B and #17C) 21.4 miles to the trip origin. The total trip mileage is 63.5.

155

Trip Alternate. Note that the loop can be altered by using the Heil Ave. segment in Huntington Beach. The Heil Ave./Santa Ana River coastal loop is a nice 25-mile ride in itself.

CONNECTING TRIPS: 1) Connection with the Carbon Canyon Workout (Trip #23) - at Rose Dr. and Bastanchury Rd., bike north on Rose Dr.; 2) connection with the Fullerton Tour/Craig Park ride (Trip #24) - at Malvern Ave. and Bastanchury Rd., turn north onto the latter road. Also see individual trip writeups.

TRIP #34 - EASTERN ORANGE COUNTY LOOP
(THE "GRANDADDY")

GENERAL LOCATION: Santiago Canyon - El Toro - Laguna Niguel - Laguna Beach - Newport Beach - Santa Ana River - Villa Park

LEVEL OF DIFFICULTY: Loop - very strenuous
Distance - 77.9 miles (loop)
Elevation gain - periodic moderate grades;
          frequent steep grades in Santiago
          Canyon area

GENERAL DESCRIPTION: The grandaddy of Orange County trips, this super 78-mile loop trip covers the southeastern half of the county and has the Santa Ana River as a common boundary with Trip #23 The variety in biking territory is mind boggling! The itinerary includes the rolling hills of Santiago Canyon, the mountains-to-sea ride down the Aliso Creek corridor, a fifteen mile grand tour of the southern Orange County coastline, a pedal up the Santa Ana River, and a short return segment through the cities of Orange and Villa Park. Most of the trip is on Class I or Class II routes.

With a modest Santa Ana River/Santa Ana Canyon Rd. extension, this trip can be turned into a "Century" tour.

TRAILHEAD: From the Orange Fwy. or Costa Mesa (Newport) Fwy., take the Chapman Ave. turnoff east. The distances to Santiago Canyon Rd. are 4-1/2 miles and 7-1/2 miles, respectively. Continue on Chapman Ave. across that road about one mile to the road's end at Irvine Park. From the Santa Ana Fwy., turn north on the Costa Mesa Fwy. and take the Chapman Ave. turnoff as above.

Bring two filled water bottles in order to minimize water stops. There are scattered water sources along the route as noted in the individual trip writeups. The hilly and exposed 12.2-mile Santiago Canyon segment is essentially waterless.

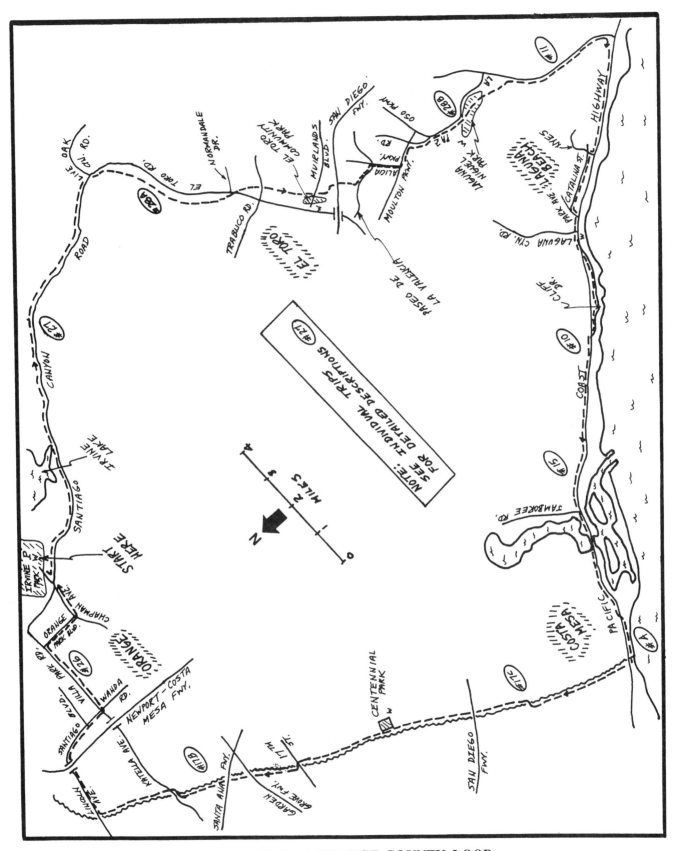

TRIP #34 - EASTERN ORANGE COUNTY LOOP

TRIP DESCRIPTION: **Santiago Canyon and Aliso Creek Corridor.** Bike back to Santiago Canyon Rd., turn left, and follow the Santiago Canyon Rd. tour (Trip #27) (12.0). From the road's end at Cook's Corner, pedal about 1/4 mile south on El Toro Rd. and pick up the origin of the Aliso Creek Trail/Bikeway (Trip #28). Follow that route to Crown Valley Community Park in Laguna Niguel (27.6).

Laguna Niguel Bikeway. Follow the southern segment of the Laguna Niguel Bikeway (Trip #11) from the Crown Valley Community Park to the trip's end at PCH (30.8).

Coastal Segment. Turn right at PCH and bike 2.3 miles on Class X roadway through rolling coastal hills to Aliso Beach County Park. From this point, bike the Laguna Beach Tour (Trip #10) in reverse to Seaward Rd. in Newport Beach (42.2). Bike PCH to Tustin Ave. or follow one of the paths shown for the Newport Beach/Corona Del Mar Tour (Trip #15). The former option is more direct, but is on some narrow and heavily trafficked roads (47.2).

Bike one mile further on PCH to Balboa Blvd. and turn right. Turn right again at 46th St. and pedal 0.2 mile to Seashore Dr. Follow the Sunset Beach to Newport Beach Strand (Trip #4) back to the Santa Ana River (49.4). Note that there is a faster pace option to stay on PCH in this stretch on good biking road.

Santa Ana River. Follow the Santa Ana River Rides #17C and #17B in the northernly direction. Exit the river east at Lincoln Ave. (67.8).

The Return Segment. Follow Class X Lincoln Ave. 1.5 miles on a steady workout upgrade to Tustin Ave.; Eisenhower Park is just north of the intersection. Continue under the Orange Fwy., turn right onto Class II Santiago Blvd. and follow that road 2.0 miles. Continue straight ahead on Wanda Rd. at the point where Santiago Blvd. veers sharply eastward; in 0.3 mile turn left at Villa Park Rd. (71.6). Follow the eastbound segment of the Orange/Irvine Park Loop (Trip #26) to the trip origin at Irvine Park (76.9).

"Century Trip." A modest trip extension can easily turn this into a hundred-miler. A recommended option is to continue north on the Santa Ana River to Green River Road (Trips #17A and #17B). For variety on the return leg of this extention, continue south on Santa Ana Canyon Rd. beyond Wier Canyon Rd. and return to Lincoln Ave. via that roadway (Trip #25).

CONNECTING TRIPS: Certainly you are kidding! See the individual trip writeups.

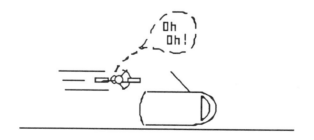

TRIP #35 - ORANGE COUNTY "CENTURY"

GENERAL LOCATION: Santiago Canyon - Laguna Niguel - Laguna Beach - Huntington Beach - Coyote Creek - Fullerton - Villa Park

LEVEL OF DIFFICULTY: Loop- very strenuous
Distance - 105.3 miles
Elevation gain - frequent moderate to steep grades, Santiago Canyon, South Laguna Beach and Laguna Beach

GENERAL DESCRIPTION: Yes Martha, you can build a "century" trip by riding the periphery of the Eastern and Western County Loops (Trips #34 and #33, respectively). This morning-to-evening adventure provides a bike tour of the best that Orange County has to offer: Santiago Canyon, the Aliso Creek Corridor, nearly 20 miles of scenic coastline, the San Gabriel River and Coyote Creek, and the El Cajon Trail. Go for it!! However, if this is your first "century," bring some phone change.

TRAILHEAD: Start at Irvine Park (see Trip #34) in order to complete most of the toughest trip segments in the first 40 miles. The 3.4 mile segment from Orange Park Blvd. and the park is also a hilly workout. If your persuasion is to end the trip on an easier, more laid-back note, start the trip at Eisenhower Park near Lincoln Ave. and Tustin Ave. (see Trip #25).

TRIP DESCRIPTION: The route starts from Irvine Park and follows the Eastern Orange County Loop for the 49.4 miles to the Santa Ana River. Cross the river and bike along the coast, following the Western Orange County Loop. Bike the latter loop 46.8 miles to the Santa Ana River exit at Lincoln Ave. From this intersection, follow " **The Return Segment**" described in Trip #34 an additional 9.1 miles back to Irvine Park.

TRIP MAP: See the Trip #33 and #34 maps.

OTHER BICYCLING INFORMATION SOURCES

Our experience has been that new bike route options can be found using a variety of sources. Our condensed recommendation list for information sources for Orange County is as follows:

1. **CALTRANS: District 07 - L.A., Orange, Ventura Counties**
   Address: State of California
   Department of Transportation
   P.O. Box 2304
   Terminal Annex
   L.A., CA. 90051
   or
   California Department of Transportation
   120 S. Spring St.
   L.A., CA. 90012

CALTRANS provides a fine "starter kit" publication which includes bicycling laws and safety tips, sources of additional information, Park and Ride locations, bike facilities at beaches and coastal parks, and selected bike routes.

2. **County Government**
   Address: Orange County Environmental Management Agency
   1020 N. Broadway: Suite 100
   Santa Ana, CA. 92701
   (Bike Trails: 714 834-3111)

EMA publishes an Orange County map which details existing bikeways and color codes those bikeways by class. Write EMA for current cost.

3. **City Government**
   Address: Write to individual City Hall, Public Works, or Park and Recreation Departments for the city of interest.

4. **National Forests, State and Local Parks**
   Addresses: U.S. Department of Agriculture
   U.S. Forest Service: Angeles National Forest
   150 S. Los Robles
   Pasadena, CA. 91101

   Department of Parks and Recreation
   Orange County Area Office
   128 Paseo De La Plaza
   Los Angeles, CA. 90012

5. **Bicycle Touring Organizations** (examples)
   Addresses: California Association of Bicycle Organizations
   P.O. Box 2684
   Dublin, CA. 94566

Bicycle Club of Irvine
c/o Turtle Park Comm. Park
1 Sunnyhill
Irvine, CA. 92715

Cerritos Cyclepaths
21313 Norwalk. Blvd. (#133)
Hawaiian Gardens, CA. 90716

Ciclistas Capistrano
31762 Camino Capistrano
San Juan Capistrano CA. 92675

Fullerton Freewheelers
1639 W. Walnut
Fullerton CA. 92633

Golden West Cyclers
19771 Coventry Ln.
Huntington Beach, CA. 92646

Los Angeles Sherrif's Cycling Club
5871 National Place
Chino, CA. 91710

Orange County Wheelmen
Box 219
Tustin, CA. 92681

6. **American Automobile Club** (membership required)
   Address: Bicycling Tour Counselor/L.A. District Office
   Automobile Club of Southern California
   2601 S. Figueroa St.
   L.A., CA. 90007

7. **Human Powered Transit Authority**
   Address: Human Powered Transit Authority
   P. O. Box 1552
   Reseda, CA. 91335

HPTA concentrates on bicycle commuting to work and to other general destinations. HPTA also has an abundance of material on the California Vehicle Code, bicycle repair/maintenance, and cues for riding in traffic

8. **Other Sources**
   Addresses: Bicycling and sports shops, bicycle
   magazines available free at bicycle shops
   (e.g. *California Bicyclist, City Sports, Competitor,*
   and *Southwest Cycling*), fellow bikers, and (God
   forbid) other bicycling books. A dandy reference
   for mountain bike tours and other rural adventures
   is Centra Publications' *Cycling Orange County* by
   Jerry Schad.

161

INDEX: ORANGE COUNTY

INDEX: LOS ANGELES COUNTY

ODDS N' ENDS

Orange County has a master plan for the longer term development of Class I-III bikeways criss-crossing the county. The plan was originally adopted in 1971 and a detailed map titled "Master Plan of Countywide Bikeways" (containing almost 100 existing and proposed trails) was approved in 1988. An update to that plan is currently under review. On the opposite page is a map, drawn from the current Master Plan, showing the most lengthy Class I trails. In that figure, both existing and proposed routes are identified. The status of proposed routes can be checked by contacting the Environmental Management Agency (EMA) (see "Other Information Sources" in this book).

Further information about the Class I trips which are highlighted in the opposite map is provided below (the relevant Trip Number in this book is noted in brackets):

o *Coyote Creek Trail* - the current terminus is at Foster Rd.; the route would be extended to Meyer Rd. in Santa Fe Springs {#20}.

o *Santa Ana River Trail* - this existing bikeway travels from the ocean to the county border {#17}. Recent construction has resulted in detours onto county roadways. Contact EMA at (714) 567-6222 for trail status.

o *San Diego Creek* - the trail follows the creek from Upper Newport Bay to Jeffrey Rd. in Irvine {#18}.

o *Huntington State Beach Park Trail* - the route can currently be extended along the *Boardwalk* {#4} or along Pacific Coast Hwy. through various class routes to just below Harbor Blvd. The proposed plan is to develop a Class I extension to just beyond Crystal Cove State Park.

o *Wier Canyon & Gypsum Canyon Trails* - both trails would originate near Santa Ana Canyon Rd., merge, and follow Peters Canyon Wash to a fusion with the San Diego Creek Trail. As with other completely new trails, they are generally being built in segments, starting with areas of new residential development.

o The *Santiago Creek Trail* - this bikeway would follow that creek channel from the city of Orange past Irvine Park and Irvine Lake, terminating near Santiago Canyon Rd. Limited segments between Collins Ave./Prospect St.-Walnut Ave. in the City of Orange and in Irvine Park exist.

o *Aliso Creek Trail* - the route would be extended south from Laguna Niguel Regional Park to the beach at South Laguna {#29}.

o *San Juan Creek Trail* - the path would be extended roughly parallel to the Ortega Hwy. to Caspers Wilderness Regional Park {#13}.

o *Trabuco Creek Trail* - the bikeway would extend from the National Forest boundary, pass in proximity of O'Neill Regional Park, and connect with the existing Oso Creek Trail {#12}.

166

ORANGE COUNTY MAJOR CLASS I BIKE TRAILS

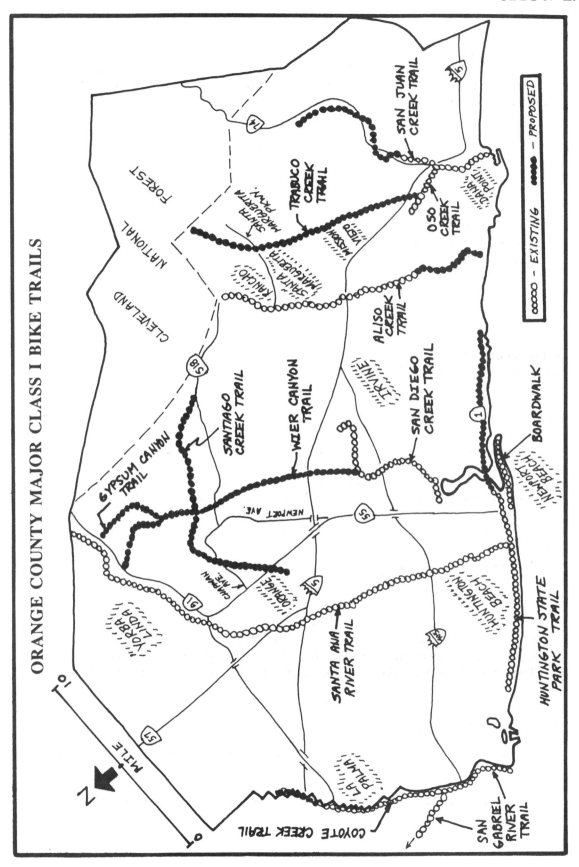

167

BICYCLE RIDES: SANTA BARBARA AND VENTURA COUNTIES

Published: 9/94
68 Trips including 15 Best Mountain Bike Rides
ISBN 0-9619151-6-1
Library of Congress Catalogue Number 94-094025
- **City of Santa Barbara** (Santa Barbara City, Hope Ranch, UCSB Campus Tour, Mountain Drive)
- **East County** (Gibralter Rd., Upper Santa Ynez River, West Camino Cielo, Santa Barbara-Solvang)
- **West County** (Jalama Beach, Solomon Hills, Los Coches Mtn. Loop, Point Sal State Beach)
- **Ventura Coast** (Point Hueneme, Ventura to Ojai, Ventura to Santa Barbara, Coastal Century)
- **Inland/Urban** (Agoura Hills, Westlake Village, Simi Valley, Rocky Peak, Potrero Rd.)
- **Mountains/Backcountry** (Sycamore Canyon, Ojai-Santa Paula, Casitas Pass, Pine Mtn., Mt. Pinos)

BICYCLE RIDES
Santa Barbara & Ventura Counties

BY DON AND SHARRON BRUNDIGE

MOUNTAIN BIKING L.A. COUNTY (SOUTHERN SECTION)

Published: 9/96
66 Trips and 100 Individual Mountain Bike Rides
ISBN 0-9619151-7-X
Library of Congress Catalogue Number 95-094085
- **Santa Monica Mountains (SMM)-East** (Franklin Cyn., Dirt Mulholland, Sullivan Canyon, Trippet Ranch/Eagle Rock Loop, Will Rogers/ Backbone Trail)
- **SMM-Central** (Redrock Canyon/Calabasa Peak, Crags Road/Malibu Creek, Bulldog Loop, Paramount Ranch, Castro Peak, Zuma Ridge, The Edison Road, Charmlee Park, Los Robles Trail)
- **SMM-West** (Sandstone Peak, Sycamore Canyon, Guadalasco Trail, Rancho Sierra Vista/Satwiwa)
- **Mountclef Ridge/Simi Hills** (Mountclef Ridge, Wildwood Park, Cheeseboro & Palo Camado Canyons)
- **Santa Susana Mountains** (Rocky Peak, Limekiln/ Aliso Canyons, Mission Peak/Bee Canyon)
- **Verdugo Mountains** (Brand Mtwy., Beaudry Loop, Summit Ride, Hosteller/Whiting Woods Mtwys.)
- **Puente Hills** (East and West Skyline Trails)
- **Potpourri** (Walnut Canyon, Bonelli Park, Palos Verdes Peninsula, Santa Catalina Island)

MOUNTAIN BIKING L.A. COUNTY
(Southern Section)

BY DON AND SHARRON BRUNDIGE

SANTA MONICA MOUNTAINS
SANTA SUSANA MOUNTAINS   SIMI HILLS
VERDUGO MOUNTAINS/SAN RAFAEL HILLS   PUENTE HILLS
PALOS VERDES PENINSULA   SANTA CATALINA ISLAND